Scarecrow Professional I.
Series Editor: Jan Goldman

In this post–September 11, 2001 era, there has been rapid growth in the number of professional intelligence training and educational programs across the United States and abroad. Colleges and universities, as well as high schools, are developing programs and courses in homeland security, intelligence analysis, and law enforcement, in support of national security.

The Scarecrow Professional Intelligence Education Series (SPIES) was first designed for individuals studying for careers in intelligence and to help improve the skills of those already in the profession, however, it was also developed to educate the public in how intelligence work is conducted and should be conducted in this important and vital profession.

1. *Communicating with Intelligence: Writing and Briefing in the Intelligence and National Security Communities* by James S. Major. 2008.
2. *A Spy's Résumé: Confessions of a Maverick Intelligence Professional and Misadventure Capitalist* by Marc Anthony Viola. 2008.
3. *An Introduction to Intelligence Research and Analysis* by Jerome Clauser, revised and edited by Jan Goldman. 2008.
4. *Writing Classified and Unclassified Papers for National Security: A Scarecrow Professional Intelligence Educational Series Manual* by James S. Major. 2009.
5. *Strategic Intelligence: A Handbook for Practitioners, Managers, and Users*, Revised Edition by Don McDowell. 2009.

If you know the enemy and know yourself, you need not fear the results of a hundred battles. If you know yourself, but not the enemy, for every victory you will suffer a defeat. If you know neither yourself nor the enemy, you are a fool and will meet defeat in every battle.

—Sun Tzu

An Introduction to Intelligence Research and Analysis

Jerome Clauser

Revised and Edited by
Jan Goldman

*Scarecrow Professional Intelligence
Education Series, No. 3*

THE SCARECROW PRESS, INC.
Lanham, Maryland • Toronto • Plymouth, UK
2008

SCARECROW PRESS, INC.

Published in the United States of America
by Scarecrow Press, Inc.
A wholly owned subsidiary of
The Rowman & Littlefield Publishing Group, Inc.
4501 Forbes Boulevard, Suite 200, Lanham, Maryland 20706
www.scarecrowpress.com

Estover Road
Plymouth PL6 7PY
United Kingdom

British Library Cataloguing in Publication Information Available

Library of Congress Cataloging-in-Publication Data

Clauser, Jerome.
  An introduction to intelligence research and analysis / Jerome Clauser ;
revised and edited by Jan Goldman.
    p. cm. — (Scarecrow professional intelligence education ; 3)
  Includes bibliographical references and index.
  ISBN-13: 978-0-8108-6181-7 (pbk. : alk. paper)
  ISBN-10: 0-8108-6181-X (pbk. : alk. paper)
  ISBN-13: 978-0-8108-6273-9 (ebook)
  ISBN-10: 0-8108-6273-5 (ebook)
  1. Intelligence service—History. 2. Intelligence service—Methodology. I.
Goldman, Jan. II. Title.
  HV7961.C53 2008
  327.12—dc22   2008022473

∞™ The paper used in this publication meets the minimum requirements of
American National Standard for Information Sciences—Permanence of Paper
for Printed Library Materials, ANSI/NISO Z39.48-1992.
Manufactured in the United States of America.

Contents

Introduction

Jan Goldman

For any intelligence community to operate effectively in support of national security policy, it needs analysts who can analyze information and turn it into intelligence. Additionally, intelligence research and analysis is used at the operational and tactical level in directing or initiating action that supports those policies. Since the September 11, 2001, terrorist attacks on American soil, the organizational structure of the U.S. intelligence community, which had existed since 1947, was changed. New agencies and departments were developed, and reportedly, since that fateful day, almost 60 percent of the current intelligence-community workforce was hired. There are no exact figures of how many of those individuals were hired to do intelligence analysis, since there are other jobs that need to be done in the intelligence community. Conducting research and analysis is only one portion of the intelligence cycle, which also includes tasking, collecting, processing, and dissemination.

Nevertheless, as things change, the more they stay the same. In the mid-1970s, as the United States began to pull out of the Vietnam conflict, the intelligence community sought to standardize and codify analytical techniques. In 1976, a small 382-page unclassified red hardback book appeared on the desks and in training centers in the intelligence community. The book, *Intelligence Research Methodology: An Introduction to Techniques and Procedures for Conducting Research in Defense Intelligence,* was written by Jerome K. Clauser with assistance from Sandra M. Weir.[1]

It was known as the "little red book" since it easily fit in the back pocket of the reader; however, it was probably meant more to be a sarcastic twist on another book that was published at the time: Communist

Chairman Mao Zedong's collection of quotations and speeches, also known as "The Little Red Book," of which almost a billion copies were printed and which was required reading by everyone in China.

In the book's original introduction, it states:

> This book should not be construed as a text for training intelligence analysts, even though analytic processes and problems are described. The purpose of the text is to provide guidance to the inexperienced researcher who must thread his way through a tortuous maze of procedures and steps as he defines his research problem, collects his information, analyzes it, and prepares his report. . . . Numerous books have been written on research methodologies appropriate for various disciplines—history, education, psychology, anthropology, and so on. This book was prepared to fill a gap, namely, to describe research procedures and representative techniques specifically related to intelligence . . . . Obviously, not all of the content will be highly relevant to all of the readers, nor will all of the content be comprehended easily by all of the students. Therefore, it is suggested that the reader use the text selectively. Although the sequence of research phases is fairly rigidly established and pertinent to all kinds of research activities, the methodologies described in the later chapters should be examined primarily with an eye to possible application to the researcher's problem. The intent of the sections dealing with methodologies is not to train professional "methodologists." Instead, the intent is to familiarize the researcher with techniques that have been and are being used in intelligence research and analysis.

A lot of the chapters discuss how to conduct research and analysis using specific methodologies. The authors go on to state,

> An attempt has been made to describe the various methodologies, and to show where and how they might be applied in intelligence research. However, since many of the methodologies would require volumes to describe in detail, this book cannot be considered a how-to-do-it manual for these methods . . . . Obviously, not every methodology used in intelligence analysis or research has been described in this book. Many techniques are highly specialized and would require months of training before the researcher could apply them. Examples of these techniques would be photo and image interpretation and signal analysis. Psycho-analytic techniques referred to in the methodology sections would also require years of training.
>
> Security considerations prevented the relating of certain techniques to specific situations. Here the imagination of the reader will be required to see exactly where and how a technique could have been used in a specific context. For example, one of the more universal analytic

approaches involves the use of analogies. In instances in which the researcher is denied access to certain real-world data, he may have no other recourse than to fall back on analogous situations and infer from these. The potential fallacies of the approach are numerous . . . . intelligence researchers are required to arrive at conclusions despite the unavailability of reliable data. Where analogies are used in addressing current intelligence problems is not indicated in this text, but the reader can assume that the practice is universal.

Many examples cited in the text are genuine. However, for purposes of security, contexts may have been changed, and the perennial "other country" may have been substituted for a real name. Any work attempting to encompass a topic as large as intelligence research methodology must, by necessity, exclude certain content.

An Introduction to Intelligence Research and Analysis is an abridged version of that book. Several years ago, I worked on another book, which was originally classified and used as a manual to develop analytical capabilities for intelligence analysts. The book, *Anticipating Surprise* by Cynthia Grabo, focused on the process of strategic warning and analysis.[2] Currently, many schools and institutions are using that book to teach how indicators for threat scenarios are developed and the internal and external problems facing the production of intelligence analysis for forecasting threats. Although that book and this publication were both written over thirty years ago, the subject matter remains as relevant today as when it was written.

This book is intended to help develop the skills and traits needed to develop good work habits in doing research and intelligence analysis. This book is abridged from the original twenty chapters. The chapters that were removed dealt with how to collect basic information during the initial phase of research. The chapters describe in detail where to find and how to utilize a card catalog in the library and how to develop specific punch-card procedures to help extract information from referenced work.[3] It is doubtful the authors could have envisioned the resources currently available, such as the Internet as a tool to collect data and information. Overall, these chapters are outdated, making this information irrelevant in today's saturated information society and in the intelligence community. Today, it is not that intelligence analysts do not have enough information to analyze, but rather that they have too much.

I tried to keep the focus of the book on the qualities necessary to be a good intelligence analyst while providing the author's original intent: how to think, write, and produce useful intelligence. According to the original introduction, "Numerous books have been written on research methodologies appropriate for various disciplines—history, education, psychology, anthropology, and so on. This book was prepared to fill a gap, namely, to describe research procedures and representative techniques specifically related to intelligence."

This book is one of the earliest attempts to professionalize intelligence work and an essential addition to the field of knowledge in basic intelligence education. This book represents an early attempt to develop an awareness as to "what it takes to become an intelligence analyst." This book is also a window into history. Numerous references are made to the Communist threat; or, specifically, North Korea's intentions to its neighbor in the south. Although some threats may no longer exist (e.g., Communism and the Soviet Union), some of these threats continue to hold the world's attention. This book gives the reader an insider's view of how the threats were perceived at the time and how the intelligence community tried to make sense of it all. In many ways, things haven't changed.

NOTES

1. Although both names appear on the cover of the original publication, Ms. Weir was responsible for one chapter in the book. That chapter, "Characteristics of an Analyst," has been folded into chapter 2. As was proper during the time this book was first published, "he" and "his" were used throughout the book, rather than using a more politically correct, non-gendered subject. Additionally, this reference reflected the overwhelming dominance of male analysts in the intelligence community at the time.

2. The book, classified in 1972 and remaining classified until it was publicly released in 2002, is *Anticipating Surprise: Analysis for Strategic Warning* by Cynthia Grabo (Lanham, MD: University Press of America).

3. A card catalogue was the location where index cards were kept for each book in the library's holdings and punch cards were perforated cards that would be turned into data when fed into a very large computer.

The Evolution and Definition of Strategic Intelligence

Intelligence research is an activity most commonly associated with strategic intelligence production. Strategic intelligence, in the sense that it is known today, is a fairly recent innovation that evolved from its predecessor, tactical (or "combat," or "military") intelligence. This section traces briefly the evolution of strategic intelligence, which shows that as methods of resolving conflict became more complex, so did strategic intelligence production become more complex.

ORGANIZED WARFARE AND THE NEED FOR STRATEGIC INTELLIGENCE

When conflict had to be resolved on a man-to-man basis there was little need for intelligence. The principals knew each other and the field of battle was familiar to both combatants. When conflicts involved tribes and, later, when conflicts involved armies, conditions changed. Although combatants may have known who their adversaries were, they needed additional information. The necessity of moving large groups of soldiers quickly and efficiently made certain types of knowledge imperative—knowledge of the terrain, location of the enemy, his strength, and his deployment. Apparently, it was recognized very early that the average soldier was not a suitable agent for procuring this information. Skillful, perhaps, in handling his weapon and formidable in endurance, the average soldier was not able to insinuate himself into the enemy ranks, was not able to estimate well, probably was not able to read nor record, and was hardly able to process mentally all of the needed information relating to the ability of an opposing force to do battle. Therefore, it is not surprising that early intelligence "systems" were built around spies and agents—those specialists who, either by training or by inclination, understood what kinds of information were significant and were sufficiently cunning or deceitful to obtain it.

Agents and spies have always been a part of any covert intelligence system and will probably continue to be so. For example, prior to his campaign against Rome in the third century BC, Hannibal infiltrated his agents into northern Italy, and, undoubtedly, one of their more essential elements of information related to passes through which Hannibal could move his cavalry and elephants.[1] Similarly, Genghis Khan in the thirteenth century used scouts for ground reconnaissance, but he also used well-placed agents for spreading rumors of his terror and intrepidity. Obviously, the Khan's systematic employment of rumor as a terror weapon exploited someone else's intelligence system, as unstructured as it may have been.

But it is significant to note that even as early as the Middle Kingdom of Egypt (1580–1150 BC), the necessity of obtaining intelligence on a regular and systematic basis was perceived, and units were specially trained and employed to collect it. The Hyksos in Egypt, according to Field Marshal Bernard Montgomery, had an unusually effective intelligence organization that utilized a variety of communication media, from torches to runners, and employed special reconnaissance units to scout terrain and capture prisoners for interrogation. Interestingly, reports sent by officers to their superiors at headquarters had to indicate the source of their information, a practice that, with variations, is still practiced today by the U.S. intelligence community. This is one of the earliest indications of systematic procedures for obtaining intelligence, but according to the Old Testament, there were procedures that even predated the Hyksos.

SUN TZU: FIRST AMONG FEW WRITERS OF A VERY OLD PROFESSION

Aside from biblical references, the first writer to document the importance of evaluated information about a real or potential enemy was Sun Tzu in 500 BC. What enabled the wise sovereign and the good general to achieve things beyond the reach of ordinary men, according to Sun Tzu, was foreknowledge. Clearly, today's technology has changed the nature of the process of developing this foreknowledge, and the assertion by Sun Tzu that knowledge of the enemy's disposition can be obtained only from other men (spies) is indeed quaint in an era in which major powers employ satellites, where few secrets are held for long in the "ether," and where practically every emanation of the "other side"—heat, light, RF energy, seismic waves, and so on—is a potential source of information. What is significant about Sun Tzu is not that he recognized the importance of intelligence, but that he recorded his maxims on the collection and evaluation of intelligence information. Sun Tzu's *Art of War* influenced Chinese and Japanese military thinking for over 2400 years, and, even in recent times, this classic was required reading for all of Mao Zedong's lieutenants.[2]

From the time of Sun Tzu to the Middle Ages, there is increasing evidence of intelligence as a necessary concomitant of warfare. Alexander's empire could not have survived as long as it did without Alexander's lieutenants possessing a knowledge and understanding of the customs of the conquered people. Mithradates, a one-man intelligence staff and an intellectual genius who mastered twenty-two languages, collected his basic intelligence firsthand by wandering on foot throughout Asia Minor. During the first century BC, his army constituted the gravest threat to Roman hegemony in the Mediterranean. Mithradates's knowledge of the external enemy was superior to his knowledge of the internal enemy, however, because he was unable to anticipate a mutiny in his own ranks.

* * *

Hannibal's employment of agents as part of his campaign against Rome was mentioned earlier, and Scipio, the nemesis of Hannibal, was equally adept at using information about the enemy's disposition to his own advantage. The Roman general Suetonius Paulinus, who with 10,000 men defeated 230,000 Britons in 62 AD, had been a former intelligence officer in Africa in 47 AD. His descriptions of the intelligence terrain and habitants—presumably intelligence studies—still survive.[3] Other than recorded instances of success or failure due to surprise (the very thing intelligence is intended to avert), very little has been recorded about early intelligence doctrine, methods, or procedures. One of the earliest examples of intelligence doctrine, however, is found in Vegetius's *Military Institutions of the Romans* (circa 400 AD), and the tenets set forth about the importance of information of terrain, avenues of approach, and routes of march are still relevant today.

From the Middle Ages to the Renaissance, little was recorded about the production or utilization of intelligence. This is strange because significant and decisive events occurred during the period, for example, the battles of Tours and Hastings, the Crusades, the intercontinental campaigns of Genghis Khan and later Kublai Khan, and the battle of Crécy. From what details exist of the conflicts, it would appear that intelligence played a very small role in determining the outcomes of these events. With the exception of Genghis Khan, commanders apparently paid little attention to collecting or utilizing intelligence in any systematic way. Edward III, for example, had so little information about the terrain prior to the battle of Crécy that he had to bribe a local French peasant to guide his army to a ford in the Somme.

In the East, internal security was the dominant focus of all intelligence activities. During the Edo period in Japan, for example, the *metsuke* (spies, censors, and agents provocateurs) monitored activities of dissident elements;[4] and earlier, the ninja—perhaps the most versatile agents of all time—were trained and utilized in the martial arts of scouting and reconnaissance and in the covert arts of political assassination.[5] Although the exploits of the ninja have been depicted in numerous Japanese motion pictures and television productions, the extent to which these tales are apocryphal is unknown. What is known, however, is that the evolution of the art of ninjutsu was influenced by the writings of Sun Tzu. Likewise, in the West, at least until the seventeenth century, more effort seemed to be devoted to internal security than to a systematic analysis of another country's capabilities and vulnerabilities. In part, this was a function of the spirit of the times, in which court intrigue constituted perhaps more of a threat to a reigning monarch than did some foreign power; hence, Elizabeth had her Walsingham and Cromwell his Thurloe.

SYSTEMATIC STRATEGIC INTELLIGENCE PRODUCTION IGNORED: SOME HYPOTHESES

Several hypotheses might be postulated to account for why relatively little emphasis was placed upon the systematic production of strategic intelligence. First, the element of surprise was difficult to maintain. Once a decision had been made to engage in an act of war, the signs were fairly obvious. For example, in 1587 it was common knowledge (at least to those to whom the information was important) that an armada would be dispatched from Spain. Admittedly, exactly when and from which ports an armada would sail were unknown initially. As a matter of interest, the timely raid on Cádiz by Drake set back the departure of the Spanish Armada by at least a year, and even Philip II did not know exactly when the armada would be ready. When the armada did set forth (after a series of storms that further delayed the departure), picket boats quickly alerted the English, who had prepared for months for this engagement.

Another reason for the relatively little emphasis placed upon the production of strategic intelligence was the manner in which warfare was conducted. Military campaigns usually involved one or a series of set-piece battles in which the personalities of the leaders—their audacity, tactics, and modes of employing infantry, cavalry, and artillery—were known to the key participants. Not only were personalities known to the opposing combatants, but also the tactics employed by all combatants were generally the same. Interestingly, when innovations were introduced, the results were indeed disastrous for the opposing side. For example, the Spanish intended to employ the armada against the English in the same manner as they engaged the Turks in the Battle of Lepanto. Warships would make physical contact and the infantry would board the English ships, clear the decks, and capture the ships.

However, the English engaged the enemy by cannon and refused to close with the Spanish men-of-war. Thus, the tactic that worked so well in the past was useless against an innovative opponent. Gustavus Adolphus of Sweden was an outstanding military innovator. He drilled his cannoneers to such a degree of perfection that his artillery could fire three rounds to the enemy's one. The high rate of fire, combined with mobility, made his artillery a terror weapon in the Thirty Years' War. Gustavus was innovative in the field of intelligence as well. His addition of a "chief of scouts" to his staff predated by nearly a hundred years similar intelligence staffs in the French and German armies.

Still another reason why relatively little emphasis was placed on the production of strategic intelligence was that in the period between the Middle Ages and the mid Renaissance conflicts were not global; hence, the necessity for large amounts of detailed information about terrain (other than routes of march), customs of the people, and so on was not perceived to be essential to the success of a campaign. One notable exception to "global conflicts," of course, was the Crusades, and today one cannot but be amazed at the audacity (or arrogance) of the first crusaders, who, with little knowledge of the enemy's strength, terrain, routes of march, or logistics, nevertheless undertook a campaign that crossed a continent.

It should be stated that there may have been instances in which strategic intclligence was produced systematically on a global scale prior to the sixteenth century. Such systems, if they existed, were certainly not publicized, and the extent and nature of their operations are unknown.

But one would not necessarily expect to find the details of the intelligence production activities publicized. Battlefield innovations became common knowledge after their introduction, but intelligence innovations, if they did exist, probably succeeded because little was known of them by the opposing side. Elizabeth, for example, would have been eager to have her court chroniclers document the successes of her reign—the New World explorations, the exploits of the privateers (after she broke with Spain), and the defeat of the Armada—but it is unlikely that she would have permitted anyone to document her agents' penetration of the court of Tuscany.

PRECURSORS TO THE "MODERN ERA" IN STRATEGIC INTELLIGENCE PRODUCTION

The latter part of the fifteenth century marks what might be called the beginning of the modern era in strategic and military intelligence production. This was the beginning of the era of global exploration and the beginning of the decline of dynastic rule, although dynastic rule would continue for another five centuries. This was also the beginning of the period in which the technology and techniques of warfare began to evolve rapidly. Gustavus Adolphus, mentioned earlier, was one of the first modern innovators, and others followed, such as Frederick the Great and later Marlborough and Napoleon.

Like Vegetius more than a thousand years earlier, tacticians and strategists again began to formulate doctrine, and, significantly, military intelligence was an important element of this doctrine. Admittedly dated and perhaps quaint, the early precepts are nevertheless still timely. For example, writing primarily for Prussian officers, Frederick the Great fully appreciated the importance of information relating to the enemy's country, and his exhortation that "knowledge of the country is to a general what a rifle is to an infantryman and the rules of arithmetic are to the geometrician," is as pertinent today as it was in the mid eighteenth century.

Maurice de Saxe, who gained firsthand experience under Marlborough and Eugene of Savoy, stated in his *Reveries* some general rules for the interpretation of "signs"—those physical manifestations of battle that, if interpreted correctly, give some indication of the opposing army's intent. Although the interpretations of specific signs may no longer be pertinent, the act of drawing reliable inferences from commonplace signs is a procedure that is very relevant today to intelligence analysts and researchers.[6]

Despite the paucity of information relating to governments' systematic production of strategic intelligence prior to the seventeenth century, there is documentation attesting to other institutions' use of (and production of) strategic intelligence. For example, one of the earlier instances of a nongovernmental agency's strategic intelligence activities was the one carried out by the various banking houses in Europe in the mid sixteenth century. But even prior to the activities of the large banking houses were the "strategic intelligence" activities carried out by western traders and merchants in the Middle Ages. To these vendors, economic information, customs and practices, routes of communications, and political information relating to "target" eastern countries and populations were critical to the success or failure of their enterprises. The extent to which merchants shared this information about their customers is unknown. But it is known that very little systematic use of this information was made by governments—a monumental blunder at a time when the East constituted the major strategic threat to all of Western Europe.

U.S. INTELLIGENCE ORGANIZATIONS: NEWCOMERS TO AN OLD CLUB

Compared with England, France, Spain, and Portugal, the United States is a relative newcomer to the international arena of power and politics; therefore, it is not surprising that the U.S. history of strategic intelligence production is a short one. Although scouts and agents (and even detectives[7]) had been used to gather and evaluate intelligence about the opposing sides during the earlier conflicts in America, it was not until World War I that the necessity for producing strategic intelligence on a global scale became evident.

Having only a skeletal intelligence organization at the outbreak of World War I, the United States was forced to rely heavily upon the intelligence produced by the British and French. Although lessons were learned quickly and a cadre of intelligence personnel was trained, little remained of this cadre during the interim between World War I and World War II other than the organizational structure.

In World War II, the United States again had to create a large-scale strategic intelligence production capability, and again the Americans learned much from their British counterparts. By the time America entered the war, the British, with the participation of scholars, had developed massive amounts of global strategic intelligence.

It is significant that since the time of Elizabeth, scholars have played an important role in strategic intelligence production. Elizabeth recruited her agents from Cambridge and Oxford. Scholars from these same institutions became the analysts and researchers who contributed so much to British expertise in World War II. In his introduction to J. C. Masterman's *The Double-Cross System in the War of 1939 to 1945*, Norman Holmes Pearson points out that

> another contribution of British intelligence was that of so-called overt intelligence, by which scholarly sources, when studied by scholars, revealed information which had long since been gathered but already been covered by dust. Timetables for tides involved in invasion landings, the location of bombing targets within metropolitan areas, amounts of precipitation to provide against, and rainy seasons to avoid: these not-at-all trivial data emerged from otherwise ignored pages of books rather than from the impossibly delayed reports of agents. American intelligence services learned much from the British example of research and analysis carried on at the universities.[8]

Likewise in the United States, General William Donovan, director of the Office of Strategic Services (OSS), "assembled the best academic and analytical brains that he could beg, borrow, or steal from the universities, laboratories, and museums."[9] The Research and Analysis Branch of OSS, according to R. Harris Smith,

> resembled a star-studded college faculty. A peek into the R&A offices might reveal a heated discussion between historian Sherman Kent and political scientist Evron Kirkpatrick. A committee meeting of the Economics Division might find Charles Hitch, Emile Despres, Charles Kindelberger, and Richard Ruggles sitting side by side. In other rooms, classicist Norman O. Brown could be writing a report on Greek politics, historian John King Fairbank studying an aspect of Chinese foreign policy, philosopher Herbert Marcuse analyzing German social structure, or anthropologist Cora DuBoise pondering the problem of European colonialism in Asia.[10]

World War II marks the real beginning of the United States's strategic intelligence production capabilities. Although the names of intelligence organizations have changed and their missions have been modified, major intelligence organizations that exist today had their progenitors in World War II. In recent years, the introduction of new weaponry has made the development of countermeasures imperative. Again, a change in the manner of resolving conflict has changed the nature of strategic intelligence production. Available time to react to new threats has been reduced drastically, and this reduction in response time makes adequate intelligence (foreknowledge) all the more important. The need for adequate intelligence has given rise to new intelligence collection devices which, in turn, require new technologies to handle the voluminous amounts of raw data collected daily. Yet, despite sophisticated collection devices and techniques, the man in the system is as important as ever. Automated data storage and retrieval systems make it possible to manipulate large quantities of data, but only the trained intelligence analyst or researcher can make judgments, draw conclusions, or derive meaning from data.

PROBLEMATIC INFORMATION AND THE NEED
FOR INTELLIGENCE

The winter of 1943–1944 was especially severe for the U.S. Fifth Army and the British Eighth Army in Italy. The northward advance of the Allied forces was halted by a stubborn force of Axis defenders at the Gustave Line, a line of fortifications built on the commanding terrain overlooking the Rapido River and the Liri Valley and anchored on the left flank by a monastery on Monte Cassino. This monastery, it was felt, was the key defensive position of the entire line. According to best opinions at the time, the monastery provided excellent cover for German artillery observers, who had an unobstructed view of Allied forces dug in on the valley floor. Destroying the monastery became more than a military objective: it soon became an obsession with every Allied commander whose casualties mounted daily as a result of enemy action and weather.

Conventional methods failed to destroy what was perceived to be the key enemy stronghold. Artillery had little apparent effect on the massive stone masonry, and tactical bombing was equally ineffectual. The key to destroying the bastion was information—information about the construction details of the monastery—because only on the basis of this information could the optimum size and nature of the destructive devices to be used against the monastery be determined. But who had this information? Where was it located? How could it be obtained?

Exhausting all intelligence staff resources available at division and corps, Major General F. I. S. Tuker, commanding officer of the 4th Indian Division, took matters into his own hands. He drove to Naples, combed bookstores until he found an old book relating to the monastery, and located precisely the information he needed. On the basis of this information, appropriate weaponry was designed, and the monastery was destroyed.[11] The key to the destruction of this military objective was intelligence—collected, evaluated, and interpreted information significant to military planning and operations.

Numerous lessons could be derived from the incident related above; for example, the necessity of an intelligence staff to perform its assigned functions, or the importance of basic intelligence in military operational planning. But the feature of the incident that is most relevant to this text is the activity that General Tuker performed, namely, intelligence research. General Tuker perceived an operational situation in terms of a problem to solve, delineated his research objectives, considered likely sources of information, located the information, evaluated it, and made it available to ultimate users. This chapter discusses the purpose for which intelligence is produced, the conventional forms and components of strategic intelligence, and the organizations whose intelligence research activities address the various components of strategic intelligence.

PURPOSE OF INTELLIGENCE

Intelligence is evaluated information. It is produced to help policy makers and planners make effective decisions. For the greater part, strategic intelligence—that intelligence required for use at the national and international level—is used for strategic *planning*. Strategic planning involves establishing courses of action, usually long-range courses of action. A course of action could relate to a military activity, but it could also relate to a political or economic activity or to a combination of military and political activities, such as the recognition of a new head of state or an embargo, boycott, or blockade. Strategic planning may address existing problems or conditions, or anticipated or hypothetical problems and conditions. In the latter cases, the strategic planning would be called contingency planning.

Strategic planning, like all planning, must be based on information. However, information required for strategic planning is often inaccessible because other countries' military or political groups realize the importance that certain types of information may have for others who may be real or potential enemies. Consequently, these countries take extensive measures to deny, limit, or falsify certain types of information and data. Thus, in addition to the methodological problems of obtaining and utilizing information commonly encountered by most planners, strategic planners encounter the very significant problem of obtaining information that others wish to deny to outsiders.

This act of denying certain information to others is what has given rise to intelligence organizations. Without the denial or inaccessibility of certain types of information, intelligence organizations would be unnecessary since information required for strategic planning would be available from other governmental agencies or from the countries or foreign groups directly.

Not only has the denial of information to others given rise to large intelligence organizations and activities, but it has also determined the nature of the operations performed by intelligence organizations. For example, intelligence organizations must employ an array of data collection procedures and devices ranging from sophisticated sensors to human observers. In addition to the necessity of using an extensive array of collection systems, intelligence organizations must spend much time and effort assessing the quality of their data. No estimate or projection is any more reliable than the input upon which it is based; consequently, establishing the reliability of data is one of the main functions of any intelligence organization.

Another characteristic function of intelligence organizations that evolved because certain types of information are denied is the necessity to use inferences when facts are unavailable. Major intelligence analyses or research projects are devoted to the systematic establishment of strong inferences, to the testing of these inferences, and to the gradual substitution of strong inferences (and, ideally, facts) for initial tenuous inferences and guesses. It is this last characteristic that sets intelligence apart from many other types of information-gathering activities, and it is the topic that this text addresses throughout.

FORMS AND COMPONENTS OF STRATEGIC INTELLIGENCE

Strategic intelligence encompasses eight major subject matter areas and requires the application of knowledge and skills of dozens of academic disciplines ranging from information science and data processing to anthropology and political science. There are many ways of classifying intelligence and its related activities. However, for the purpose of this text, intelligence—the product resulting from the collection, evaluation, analysis, integration, and interpretation of information concerning a foreign nation or an area of operations—will be classified according to two criteria: (1) the basic purpose for which it is produced, i.e., its form; and (2) the subject matter addressed. These basic forms and subject areas of strategic intelligence are described briefly below in order to emphasize the range of potential types of research that may be required to support strategic intelligence production.

On the basis of the first criterion, intelligence may be produced to enhance the existing body of knowledge about a country. This type of intelligence is encyclopedic in nature. It is produced partly in anticipation of kinds of information that would be required should a conflict break out involving a given country. It is also produced in order to permit better interpretations of current activities to be made. This kind of intelligence is referred to as basic intelligence. The name is most appropriate. Basic intelligence invariably constitutes the bases for deriving meaning from other types of intelligence.

Basic intelligence—its collection and analysis activities—is the least spectacular of all types of intelligence operations, but nevertheless, this type of intelligence is most essential. It is difficult to imagine how the Normandy landings in World War II could have been conducted without knowledge of the landing beaches—their gradients, load-carrying capabilities, tides, and natural and man-made obstacles. Basic intelligence is oriented around past and present conditions and events. Intelligence is also produced to keep track of events occurring in various parts of the world that would impact U.S. policies and national interests. This type of intelligence is called current intelligence. It is characterized by change—aptly enough—and requires the constant updating of earlier conclusions, analyses, and judgments. When events occur rapidly, this type of intelligence gives rise to intense activity.

Surprises are anathema to any intelligence organization, and one of the fundamental reasons for having intelligence organizations is to reduce the likelihood that any foreign power could commit an act, develop a capability, or establish a relationship that was unanticipated. Thus, in a further attempt to reduce surprise, a third type of intelligence has evolved: estimative/predictive intelligence. This type of intelligence addresses the likelihood of a country engaging in a certain type of activity in the immediate or foreseeable future. Ideally, this type of intelligence attempts to establish the intent of decision makers in foreign countries. More realistically, estimative/predictive intelligence attempts to anticipate future actions based on current capabilities. Although it is concerned with prognostication, estimative/predictive intelligence is founded on descriptions of current realities.

Evaluation is addressed in all three types of intelligence. Quite literally, evaluation is involved in the determination of the actual costs of the other side's war-making machinery, a task that is normally the purview of basic intelligence.[12] Evaluation might also relate to estimative/predictive functions. An example of evaluation used for predictive purposes would be determining the enemy's cost/benefit ratios for alternative methods for addressing a scientific or technical problem and then predicting the likely course of action on the basis of the approach that would provide the greatest payoff for the minimum risk. Implicit in this evaluation would be the assumption (or the prediction) that the other side would elect to follow the more "rational" approach.[13] With respect to tenuousness of conclusions and obsolescence of products, estimative/predictive intelligence ranks highest in the potential for mistakes. Estimative/predictive intelligence is oriented around present and future conditions, activities, and events. In addition to being classified by function and time orientation, intelligence can also be classified according to subject matter addressed. Some categories of intelligence subject matter are also known as the "components of strategic intelligence." The components include the following:

- Biographic intelligence is about collecting and evaluating information relating to key personalities.
- Economic intelligence is about collecting and evaluating information relating to resources and capabilities for production, economic vulnerabilities, and the availability of strategic commodities.
- Sociological intelligence is about collecting and evaluating information relating to social stratification, value systems, traditions, beliefs, and other social characteristics of selected populations.
- Military intelligence is about collecting and evaluating information relating to orders of battle, equipment, doctrine, logistic capabilities, personnel, and so on.
- Geographic intelligence is about collecting and evaluating information relating to understanding terrain, weather and climate, coasts, and landing beaches.
- Political intelligence examines governmental structures, national policy, and political dynamics.

As any student of intelligence will point out quickly, the classification of types or categories of intelligence is arbitrary and incomplete. For example, indications and warning intelligence is subsumed under current intelligence and combat, tactical, and operational intelligence are excluded entirely in this classification. The various "INTs" of intelligence—SIGINT (signals intelligence), ELINT (electronics intelligence), IMINT (imagery intelligence), HUMINT (human intelligence), and so on—are not addressed specifically in this breakdown of types of intelligence, but obviously, their outputs contribute to all components and to all forms of intelligence.[14] It should be noted that each component of strategic intelligence is concerned with each of the three forms of intelligence. In biographic intelligence, for example, an individual who shows promise of rising to positions of authority would be a subject pertinent to estimative/predictive intelligence analysis and research. Individuals currently in power or currently occupying leadership positions would be addressed by current intelligence analysts. And individuals who formerly held high positions but who were replaced, abdicated, resigned, or died become the subjects of basic intelligence research or analysis. In short, even "static" subject matter becomes seemingly "dynamic" in strategic intelligence production.

Within the total framework of forms and components of strategic intelligence, two basic functions of intelligence are evident: (1) to explain, account for, or describe a phenomenon; and (2) to predict, forecast, or estimate.[15] These two functions will be recurring themes throughout the rest of this text.

SUMMARY

- Although the importance of strategic intelligence was recognized and documented as early as 500 BC, little is known about the manner in which this intelligence was produced.
- Strategic intelligence activities by governments became apparent in Europe in the sixteenth century. Initially, these activities were directed toward specific target groups such as political dissidents, a specific country, or a religious group.
- In the seventeenth and eighteenth centuries, strategic intelligence activities by governments began addressing global issues in a systematic manner.
- In World War I and in the beginning of World War II, U.S. intelligence organizations had to rely heavily upon the intelligence produced by the Allied nations.
- Scholars and academicians were an important part of intelligence organizations at least as early as the sixteenth century.
- Precursors of all major intelligence organizations were the activities carried on by merchants, vendors, and lending houses.
- Modern technology has revolutionized intelligence data collection and processing, however, the man in the system is as critical as ever because only he can derive meaning from the data.

- Intelligence, collected and evaluated information about a foreign country or an area of operations, is essential for strategic planning.
- That many countries deny certain information to outsiders makes intelligence organizations and activities necessary.
- The denial of information determines both the nature of the activities conducted by intelligence organizations and the nature of the products these organizations produce.
- Strategic intelligence can be classified on the basis of the various forms of intelligence as well as by the subject matter addressed in the various forms.
- Forms of intelligence include basic intelligence, current intelligence, and estimative/predictive intelligence.
- Components of strategic intelligence, that is, the subject matter areas addressed, include biographic, economic, sociological, geographic, military, political, and scientific and technical intelligence.

NOTES

1. For the researcher with a bent for "historical" intelligence analysis, determining the source of Hannibal's elephants might provide a stimulating diversion. Did the elephants come from India or from Africa? If they came from India, how did they make the trek westward? If they came from Africa, where were the herds located?

2. Allen Dunes, *The Craft of Intelligence* (New York: Harper and Row, 1963), 13.

3. It is interesting to note how many prominent military leaders spent at least a part of their careers in intelligence. Aside from Mithradates and Suetonius Paulinus, of course, there are Gordon of Khartoum, T. E. Lawrence, Orde Wingate, and Joseph W. Stilwell (as a military attaché in Peking). All of these officers ultimately distinguished themselves as military leaders in those countries where they had served in some intelligence capacity.

4. Edwin O. Reischauer and John K. Fairbank, *East Asia: The Great Tradition* (Boston: Houghton Mifflin, 1960), 607.

5. Donn F. Draeger and Robert W. Smith, *Asian Fighting Arts* (Tokyo: Kodansha International, 1969), 120 ff.

6. Saxe wrote that when you hear much ruing from the enemy camp, you may expect an engagement the day following because the men are discharging and cleaning their weapons (Marshal Maurice de Saxe, *My Reveries Upon the Art of War*, in Major Thomas R. Phillips, *Roots of Strategy*, 292).Military Service Publishing Company, 1955. This is reminiscent of the World War II practice of Allied aircraft test firing their weapons shortly after takeoff and the

standing operating procedure for U.S. forces in Vietnam to discharge the weapons in a perimeter defense shortly after daybreak.

7. President Lincoln employed the Pinkerton Detective Agency to conduct the Union's intelligence operations during the Civil War.

8. J. C. Masterman, *The Double-Cross System in the War of 1939 to 1945* (New Haven: Yale University Press, 1972), vii–viii.

9. Allen Dulles, quoted in R. Harris Smith, *OSS: The Secret History of America's First Central Intelligence Agency* (Berkeley: University of California Press, 1972), 13.

10. Ibid.

11. Fred Majdalany, *Cassino: Portrait of a Battle* (London: Longmans, Green and Co., 1957), 114. Ironically, after the Gustave Line had fallen, it was learned that the Germans had not used the monastery as an observation post.

12. *Appraise* would be a more precise term to use since it connotes the fixing of monetary worth.

13. Many predictions in intelligence are based on the assumption that the other side is "rational," and rationality is usually defined in terms of the value system of the person making the judgment. This gives rise to problems when it fails to consider that value systems may differ considerably. The assumption of a rational enemy also fails to account for behaviors such as Hitler's "emotional" and fatal decision to bomb urban areas during the Battle for Britain rather than to continue to eliminate the British early warning systems or Hitler's decision to sacrifice Paulus's Sixth Army at Stalingrad rather than yield any conquered territory. Surprise in warfare is often possible because it seemingly violates the canons of rationality. "Irrational" risks are undertaken when the potential payoff is high; hence, the Japanese attack on Pearl Harbor and the Soviet Union's placement of missiles in Cuba. Given no knowledge to the contrary, the hypothesis that the "other side" is rational by one's own values is nevertheless a plausible and practical starting point.

14. To confuse matters further, some intelligence organizations are organized on a geographical basis, for example, China Asia Division, Western Area Division; or on an analytical function versus an operational function basis; or on a foreign intelligence, domestic counterintelligence basis, and so on.

15. Estimation addresses two types of problems. For example, an analyst might be assigned the task of estimating the size of an enemy garrison. In this case, the enemy garrison comprises a finite number of personnel at any specific time, which, theoretically, could be counted. On the other hand, an agricultural economist might be assigned the task of estimating the size of the Soviet Union's wheat crop—a crop that would not be ready for harvest for months to come. This type of estimation involves more than counting. It requires the analysis of those variables that would affect the crop (precipitation, temperature) and the determination of the effects of these variables; hence, it involves prognostication. The first type of estimation is essentially description. The second type of estimation involves an element of prediction.

2

Research: A Description of the Activity and the Analyst

ORIGINAL MEANING AND MODERN PERMUTATIONS

Many activities referred to as research do not satisfy the requirements of the term. This chapter describes briefly the various interpretations of the term and sets forth three criteria that must be satisfied in order for an activity to qualify as research.

Research (or re-search) evolved from the French verb *recherché*, which, strictly speaking, means to search again, or to explore something that has already been explored. The activities of Copernicus and Tycho Brahe would qualify well as examples of research in the original sense of the word. Both astronomers examined their recorded observations of the movements of heavenly bodies time and time again. Their contributions to the science of astronomy were significant not so much for the addition of new facts but for their better interpretations of the then-existing information.

Today, the generally accepted meaning of the word *research* is diligent and systematic inquiry into a subject to discover new information or principles. Admittedly, if the formulation of principles were the only criterion, very few "diligent and systematic inquiries" would qualify as research. More commonly, research involves the formulation and testing of hypotheses, those precursors of the more elusive theories, principles, or natural laws.

From the standpoint of semantics, the word *research* should be defined rigorously and its use restricted, or it should be stricken from the English vocabulary. Denotatively, the meaning of the original term is quite explicit: namely, to search again, to explore something that has already been explored. Connotatively, however, *research* means much more. A cursory examination of the titles of theses submitted by candidates for advanced degrees reveals that activities involving experimentation, surveys, examination of historical documents, development of techniques and algorithms, unusual applications of established methodologies, testing of materials, and the creation of artistic works have all qualified as research in the sense of satisfying the requirements for an advanced degree.

On a typical university campus, one can expect to find as many different interpretations of what constitutes research as there are academic disciplines represented in the sample of respondents. And the person performing research in intelligence is very likely to encounter researchers to whom any investigation outside of their own particular specialties would not warrant the title of research. For example, the physical scientist (and many behavioral scientists) would perceive research as an activity involving some sort of an experiment; a historian might perceive research as an activity involving an intensive examination of records of events; an analytical philosopher might perceive research in terms of a critical examination of the meaning of terminology used in philosophic discourse; and an engineer could perceive research in terms of submitting various materials or structures to tests.

Not only is the term *research* used to encompass a wide range of activities pertaining to an even wider range of subject matter areas, but it is sometimes also used to add a degree of respectability to activities that otherwise would be considered trite and mundane. Numerous attempts have been made to dictate the desired use of terminology, but generally these attempts fail. The Queen of Heart's disclaimer to Alice in the book *Alice in Wonderland* that "words mean whatever I want them to mean" is an apt description of most users of modern languages.

But with the use of words that mean different things to different people, meanings are obscured, concepts cannot be shared, and misunderstandings result. Therefore, for those investigators or students who will be faced with the requirement to perform research, an understanding of the term is most important. From a very practical standpoint, an understanding of the more precise meaning of the term will help eliminate time lost in planning and conducting an activity that would not qualify as research. This understanding will also broaden one's perspective of the wide range of activities (and products) that do qualify as research.

For example, the author recalls an incident in which a paper that traced the creation and evolution of a military unit was shown to a psychologist. The psychologist read the paper and commented that the paper qualified as a "piece of journalism" but hardly as an example of "research." The report, which corrected a number of misstatements that had been promulgated for years, was compiled after a lengthy and painstaking examination of hundreds of documents contained in repositories in three countries. The psychologist's comment is pertinent for two reasons. First, it revealed a bias that any type of inquiry not cast in a certain framework—in this case, an experiment, the research model with which the psychologist was most familiar—was not acceptable as legitimate research. Second, by implication, the comment denigrated journalistic or reportorial research, an activity that when done well involves extensive "systematic inquiry" and requires the same amount of attention to detail, concern about sources, objectivity, and thoroughness that should characterize all research.

It should be apparent that an activity does not qualify as research merely because certain subject matter is addressed or because certain methodologies are employed. However, an activity may qualify as research provided three criteria are met:

1. The activity is *purposeful*, that is, it is conducted with a specific objective in mind;
2. The activity is *performed systematically*; and
3. The activity *contributes new knowledge* (or new interpretations of old knowledge).

RESEARCH AS A PURPOSEFUL ACTIVITY

In research, purposefulness implies the existence of an objective—a clearly identifiable, specifiable, and meaningful end in its own right, which, if achieved, could be recognized not only by the researcher, but also by independent observers as well. For example, an intelligence analyst who constantly updates an order of battle (OB) is *not* performing research by this criterion since orders of battle always require updating. The updated order of battle is tentative and is only a means to some other end. A technician performing quality control tests on materials is not performing research because, again, no specific identifiable end is addressed. Testing is merely a set of procedures for maintaining a level of quality; it is not an end in itself.

On the other hand, an OB specialist *would* be performing research if he formulated hypotheses relating to a command hierarchy or the location of an unnamed unit and systematically tapped his sources to confirm or refute his hypotheses. And a quality control technician *could* be said to be performing research if he devised and tested a procedure for sampling. In both examples, the criterion of addressing a specific, finite objective was satisfied and a clearly identifiable end product resulted.

Aims, objectives, and *goals* are three terms commonly associated with purpose. As it is used in this text, *aims* refers to the general intents of the investigator. Aims are manifested in the direction that an investigator's endeavors might take. *Objectives,* on the other hand, refers to clearly specifiable and identifiable ends of an investigation. Objectives are often stated in terms of some finite time period. *Goals* refers to those ultimate ends that, for most practical purposes, are never achieved. Thus, the aim of military planners might be to sever the enemy's lines of communication. The aim could be cast in terms of specific objectives, for example, destroying a railroad marshalling yard, a bridge, or a critical stretch of highway within a specified period of time. The ultimate goal of these endeavors might be to bring about a lasting peace, or "to make the world safe for democracy."

In the context of intelligence research, the aim of the researcher might be to study North Korean propaganda and North Korean political or military behavior. His specific objective might be to determine whether or not any correlation existed between North Korean public announcements relating to unification, and incidents along the DMZ during the period January 1, 1972, to July 4, 1972. The overall goal of the researcher might be to formulate generalizations about the words and deeds of North Korean policy makers that might be used as a basis for anticipating future behavior.

RESEARCH AS A SYSTEMATIC ACTIVITY

In order to qualify as research, the act of inquiry must be conducted in a systematic manner. The exact nature of the system employed, of course, would be a function of the subject matter addressed. Systematic implies that an investigation adheres to an organized and methodical order of procedures—a plan, for example. The main reason for emphasizing a systematic and orderly approach to an investigation is to ensure that significant elements are not excluded. For example, there are certain critical steps in experiments that, if they were not addressed initially, would render later findings worthless.

Another reason for emphasizing a systematic approach is to make explicit the manner in which conclusions were reached. Systematic procedures make it possible for other researchers to replicate a study in order to determine if the findings necessarily derived from the data and not from some spurious element accidentally (or intentionally) introduced by the investigator. One of the most devastating things that can befall a graduate student is to be informed at the time he is defending his thesis that he overlooked a significant work. Equally frightening, and potentially far more serious for the intelligence researcher, is to be in a situation of defending an estimate that overlooked significant data held by another agency. Attention to detail and an organized and orderly manner of progression throughout the research phases are ways of precluding these nightmares.

RESEARCH AS AN ACTIVITY THAT CONTRIBUTES NEW KNOWLEDGE

The final criterion of research is that it contributes new knowledge. Ultimately, this is the most significant criterion and the end toward which the other two criteria contribute. At the outset it should be made clear that new knowledge is not necessarily synonymous with new information. For example, new interpretations of old information would qualify as new knowledge in those instances in which the investigator could make a plausible case for his new assertions. (Copernicus, for example, in disproving the geocentric theory in favor of the heliocentric theory, did precisely that.) Much historical research utilizes essentially no new information but instead reexamines existing information in order to formulate and test new hypotheses. Obviously, obtaining new information for generating new knowledge plays a significant part in many research programs, and it is highly likely that in most intelligence research, new information or data would have to be obtained.

INTELLIGENCE RESEARCH/ACADEMIC RESEARCH: SIMILARITIES AND DIFFERENCES

Some people typically associate research with universities. But obviously, research is conducted in many nonuniversity settings as well, for example, in industry, in private institutions, and of course, in numerous governmental agencies. Despite the variety of activities performed under the rubric of research, despite the subject matter addressed, and despite the organization sponsoring the activity, the basic concept of research that persists is the academic model—academic in the sense that the activity conforms to certain scholastic traditions or rules. Academic research must be purposeful and systematic, and must contribute new knowledge. But in addition, the activity or the product should exemplify reasoning ability, judgment, intellectual honesty, and objectivity on the part of the individual performing the activities. Although the canons of academic research still constitute the underlying model for intelligence research, often the canons cannot be satisfied. Thus, in many respects, intelligence research may be the antithesis of academic research.

TIME CONSTRAINTS

With the possible exception of journalists, no professionals work under the constant press of time constraints as much as intelligence analysts or researchers.[1] Admittedly, the graduate student anticipating a June graduation works under a kind of time constraint, and a researcher who wants to capture a Nobel Prize works under a competitive time constraint, but these constraints are artificial in the sense that survival is seldom at stake. With respect to urgency, perhaps the closest analogy to intelligence research would be medical research directed toward developing an immunization for a particularly virulent disease that was decimating a population.

Time constraints ultimately affect other characteristics of intelligence research as well, for example, the intelligence researcher may not have enough time to collect all of the information that he felt was essential to arrive at a conclusion, or he may not have the time to corroborate or establish the validity of his input and, consequently, must qualify his conclusions. It should be noted that the individual with a penchant for an unhurried and exhaustive analysis of his research problem may find that he is exceedingly unhappy and frustrated by the necessity of producing estimates long before he is satisfied with his input or with his analysis. As the nature of conflict changes, the intelligence researcher may find that the tempo of his activities changes accordingly. Time constraints may induce an intolerable level of stress. Admittedly, some individuals not only adapt to the necessity of producing under stress, but also seem to thrive in this kind of environment. Other individuals, whose perceptions of research are limited to the "academic" model, may never learn to adapt and eventually drop out of (or are dropped from) the profession.

CONTROL OF VARIABLES

Much academic research involves experimentation. An experiment is essentially a set of procedures used to test a hypothesis. The experimental ideal is a situation in which the independent variables can be manipulated and controlled in such a manner that the dependent variable follows unambiguously and irrefutably. The outcome of the experiment is determined by the design and by the controls imposed by the design. These conditions can be created and controlled fairly well in the laboratory. In the field, however, experimental controls are rarely possible. Many social scientists (and inexperienced intelligence researchers) are dismayed when they discover that the experimental ideal they addressed so effectively in the university setting is so elusive in the field that it tends to be nearly irrelevant in application. Again, many researchers learn to adapt, to be pragmatic, and to alter and modify their approaches to accommodate the constraints imposed on their research activities. Other researchers feel that adaptation is tantamount to compromising standards and consequently refuse to work in this type of environment regardless of the fact that decisions must still be made and the decisions will be made with or without the knowledge that even a "compromised" experimental design might yield.

In intelligence research, the researcher has virtually no control of the variables other than the methods he employs himself. The enemy, or the "other side," is notably uncooperative. The enemy may refuse to respond to a "stimulus" (for example, a propaganda message), he may deliberately alter his mode of behavior to avoid any indication of a pattern, and he may change his response modes constantly in order to preclude anticipation of a future action. In short, and in the language of the social scientist, the other side is a notoriously poor subject; yet he is the subject of inquiry to the intelligence researcher.

Adequacy of Data versus the Necessity of Reporting

Incompleteness is a feature that characterizes nearly every intelligence product. Sometimes an assessment or a prediction is incomplete because no data exist. Data may not exist because the other side may not have manifested any observables.[2] More often, an intelligence product is incomplete because the enemy does a good job of denying certain kinds of information to outsiders. It is this type of situation that the intelligence researcher is most likely to encounter. In both instances, however, the intelligence researcher is required to arrive at conclusions: conclusions that may have profound implications for national security, but that are founded on theories, assumptions, and sometimes simply guesses when data or information are not available.

Unlike academic research, in which the researcher may delay publishing his findings until he or his advisers are satisfied that the findings are adequate to justify his conclusions, the intelligence researcher may not have time to collect additional data, or the political or military situation may have changed so much that additional data could not be collected even if time were available. Again, this condition induces much frustration in those to whom the academic model of research is inviolable.

Unknown Quality of Data

The academic researcher attempts to use data of the highest quality. He checks sources, corroborates information, excludes information from notably unreliable sources, and withholds publication until he is satisfied that his conclusions are founded upon irrefutable evidence. The intelligence researcher attempts to emulate his academic counterpart but often encounters situations in which the only data available are from sources whose reliability has not been established. Furthermore, the intelligence researcher sometimes encounters data that have been prepared deliberately to deceive or to mislead.

Emphasis on Prediction

Of all the intellectual activities performed by man, none is so fraught with potential for error as prediction. Yet prediction (in its various forms) constitutes a major part of the activities in intelligence and is, in fact, the purpose for which even basic intelligence is produced (foreknowledge). The greater part of prediction is based upon observed regularities. For example, a certain combination of meteorological phenomena invariably results in another predictable type of phenomenon. Natural laws are essentially predictive statements that take into account the interaction of regularly occurring phenomena.[3]

The problem of prediction in intelligence is exacerbated by two conditions. First, unlike most naturally occurring phenomena, humans have the ability to alter and control certain conditions and interactions. A cautious enemy, for example, will avoid repetitive acts that would permit his opponent to anticipate his future behavior, or the enemy may deliberately maintain one pattern in order to conceal another type of behavior. Thus, the intelligence researcher may be uncertain as to how much credibility he can assign to an observed behavior.

The second condition that gives rise to difficulties in prediction is unique events—events that have no precedent. Examples of such events might be the appearance of a new RF signal in an area in which all signals had been accounted for or the enemy's construction of a peculiar type of structure whose purpose cannot be determined from its shape or size. Although procedures exist for dealing with unique events, such as the generation of alternative scenarios and gaming, for example, none of the procedures has the predictive power for a researcher to state unequivocally that, given conditions x and y, z will result invariably. Yet this is the kind of assertion that policy makers seek from intelligence organizations. Much has been said about the weighty responsibility of the decision maker, but little attention has been paid to the person who makes the predictions upon which decisions are made. How many people, for example, recall the name of the meteorologist who predicted clearing weather prior to the Normandy invasion?[4]

Lest the picture of intelligence research be painted too bleakly, it should be noted that an increasing amount of "academic" research is also addressing predictive problems, for example, predicting volumes of vehicular traffic in urban planning, predicting mineral yields, predicting the effects of population on groundwater quality and consumption, predicting the economic impact of new industry in a region, and so on. In addition, courses on futurology are becoming increasingly common on campuses throughout the country. Futurology, as the name implies, is the study of future conditions based on current and anticipated trends.

Emphasis on Security

To a real or potential enemy, the awareness that the other side is attending to certain conditions or events within his country provides a tactical advantage. Consequently, intelligence organizations avoid advertising what they are examining and how they are going about it. This security is essential for safeguarding human and other sources of information as well as for avoiding embarrassment at diplomatic levels. To the analyst or researcher, the result of this emphasis on security is anonymity. This usually means that the analyst may not discuss his activities with his academic counterparts and that the product of his efforts will not be attributed to him personally. Many researchers whose psychic rewards come in the form of papers published in professional journals find that the enforced anonymity is intolerable. Other researchers, of course, learn to accept this condition. Again, the picture is not all bleak for those who desire to perform both academic and intelligence research, because there are many types of intelligence research activities that need not be classified and probably will not be classified in the future.

Secrecy in intelligence will always exist. But changes are occurring rapidly, and activities that were formerly classified (or not acknowledged) are now openly admitted. It would take an extremely naive individual, for example, to assume that the Soviet Union or the People's Republic of China were not primary concerns of U.S. intelligence organizations.

Utility

To the question, "Why do you climb mountains?" George Leigh Mallory responded, "Because it is there." Poetic, perhaps, and provocative, this response would not suffice should an intelligence researcher be asked why he was researching a certain topic. Although all research is purposeful in the sense that it attempts to provide new knowledge, intelligence research must address a utility goal as well. In other words, it must assist in solving a problem—most likely, a decision-making or policy-planning problem.

The fact that intelligence research serves utilitarian purposes does not mean that "scholarly" research has no place in intelligence. The criterion of utility says nothing about the subject matter of the research nor anything about the research methodology. The utility criterion simply means that the product of the research must address either an existing need or a plausible potential need: in short, intelligence research must yield more than "truth for truth's sake." At times the precise manner in which a research product will be (or could be) used may be difficult to predict. For example, in 1965, an anthropologist and three other investigators prepared a report dealing with indigenous tribes of the Republic of Vietnam. Although the overall relevancy of such a work was apparent even in 1965, little did the authors realize that the sections of the report relating to burial habits would be extremely useful nine years later when attempts would be made to ascertain the fate of downed U.S. airmen.

A seemingly academic research project such as determining precedents (if any) for the Russians' use of massed artillery (as in World War II) may well provide a basis for anticipating Soviet artillery doctrine in future conflicts. And an exhaustive examination of France's employment of static defenses, such as the Maginot Line and the fortresses of Dien Bien Phu, might reveal subtleties in French military doctrine that would not be apparent at a superficial level.[5] Conflicts between the Soviet Union and the People's Republic of China in the 1960s had precedents as early as the thirteenth century, when the Mongol hordes sacked Russian settlements in the Donetz Basin. An analysis of these early conflicts may throw some light on the present Sino-Soviet conflict.

Research topics evolve from perceived needs of the operational situation, and many times topics for investigation will be assigned to the researcher rather than chosen by him, as will be discussed later. But the intelligence researcher who is thoroughly familiar with a body of subject matter is in an excellent position to anticipate research requirements, and in these instances the researcher can often define and select his own research topics.

Briefly, then, because a research topic does not have any immediate utility should not necessarily discourage an intelligence researcher from pursuing it. It is the potential usefulness as well as the immediate usefulness of the product that establish its worthiness as a suitable topic for research in intelligence, as evidenced by the large amounts of basic information contained in the old National Intelligence Estimates.

CHARACTERISTICS OF THE INTELLIGENCE RESEARCHER

Ask any authority to identify those human traits that are absolutely essential for anyone proposing to carry out research and four traits are mentioned invariably: reasoning ability, accuracy, intellectual honesty, and open-mindedness. Other traits that are mentioned very often include judgment, diligence, thoroughness, originality, and so on. There is no question that the possession of these traits is a necessary condition for producing an acceptable research product, but the possession of these traits alone is not a sufficient condition to guarantee that a research product will be acceptable. Furthermore, because of the uniqueness of intelligence research, certain additional human traits are required as well. Finally, even the more familiar traits have special implications for the intelligence researcher. These necessary (but not sufficient) traits of the intelligence researcher are discussed below.

Reasoning Ability

Invariably, any individual thinks he reasons well and that the inabilities of others to accept his conclusions are reflections of their inadequacies, not his. Little, Wilson, and Moore point out that

> it is not easy to see the errors in our own thinking. Many of us are confident that our thinking is above error. But confidence is no guarantee. In fact, those who seem most confident in their thinking are usually the ones who fall into the most serious errors. Fanatics are far more confident in their conclusions than are normal people. . . . We may believe we have thought matters over thoroughly when, as a matter of fact, we have merely unconsciously accepted beliefs or conclusions from someone else and then done a bit of window dressing to convince ourselves and others that the conclusion resulted from logical procedures.[6]

Examples of the inability to reason well abound. It is not uncommon to find analysts failing to distinguish between facts and inferences or operating on the assumption that an inference was a fact. It is not unusual to hear an analyst announce that his conclusions followed "logically" from the evidence, even though generalizations arrived at inductively are not subject to logical proof. That different types of inquiry are subject to different types of "proof" is an alien concept to many researchers. And the common misuse of *infer* and *imply* reflects not only a lack of knowledge of terminology but also an unfamiliarity with underlying concepts of logic as well.

The seemingly simplistic solution of requiring the researcher to "take a course in logic" will not necessarily guarantee an improvement in his reasoning ability. But an exposure to logical fallacies, a familiarity with deductive and inductive processes, and an exposure to those subjective factors that influence thinking should at least heighten the researcher's sensitivity to the potential for error. An exposure to logical fallacies, for example, may reveal to the researcher fallacies in his own thinking of which he was unaware. The researcher will also discover that, despite the vigor of the approach, conclusions reached deductively are only as good as the assumptions upon which they were made, and that in intelligence research many decisions must be made, problems must be solved, and conclusions must be drawn without the benefit of validated assumptions. Finally, the researcher will discover (if he doesn't know it already) that the most difficult type of reasoning he will have to perform is induction—a type of reasoning for which hard and fast rules do not exist.

Accuracy

Accuracy has two meanings. In one sense, it means preciseness or exactitude. Thus, the identification of a geographic location by use of an eight-digit grid coordinate could be said to be more accurate than the same location identified by the description "about ten miles northeast of _____." Accuracy also means freedom from error, or "conformity to truth." Both interpretations are relevant to intelligence research. For example, at one time during the Korean War much confusion existed among U.S. military planners because of the failure to distinguish between the place-names Pyongyang, Pyonggang, and Pyongan. The assignment of a target the size of a county (Pyonggang) provided little guidance for U.S. air strikes, when in fact the intended target was Pyongyang, the capital of North Korea.

Potential for error is high in intelligence research, particularly in those numerous instances in which the researcher does not work with raw data but instead works with data that have been preprocessed by others. For example, an analyst working with someone else's interpretation of a foreign-language input is subject not only to errors that he may commit but also to errors made by the original translator. Even when working with raw data, for example, with a foreign-language newspaper, the researcher may find that there are no direct English-language equivalents for a word or a concept addressed and that the best he can do is to approximate the original meaning of the work; hence, the potential for error exists.

Aerial reconnaissance is highly touted as a producer of "accurate" raw data. But any intelligence researcher who has observed two photo interpreters nearly coming to blows over the issue of whether an object was a truck or a tank comes away with an uneasy sensation that the potential for error exists even when the best data collection techniques are used. Sensors do not lie, of course, but humans may lie unintentionally when preconceived notions, biases, and strong convictions interfere with perception. Unless the researcher is at least aware that he may be adding error to what is already unclear, the impact may be serious. Again, the necessity for developing an awareness of subjective factors that influence behavior becomes apparent.

Necessity for accuracy exists at every stage in the intelligence cycle from collection to dissemination. An ambiguously prepared intelligence information report (IIR) sets the stage for equivocal interpretations, and these in turn yield products of dubious quality. The inadvertent deletion of a zero transposes 40,000 to 4,000, perhaps with disastrous consequences. Obviously, the potential for drawing erroneous conclusions is the most serious effect of inaccuracy in either data collection or data analysis. But the intelligence researcher who is working under severe time constraints should also recognize that correcting errors, should they be detected, is also a costly and time-consuming operation. The fact that much of the input with which the intelligence researcher must work is of dubious quality and the fact that even presumably "hard" data may have been cunningly altered by the other side to mislead are sufficient reasons for the researcher to be all the more accurate in the operations he performs on the data—operations such as recording, counting, citing, interpreting, or quoting.

Intellectual Honesty

In the context of academic research, intellectual honesty usually relates to such things as attributing information to appropriate sources and giving recognition to others who may have contributed significantly to an effort—in short, giving credit where credit is due. In the context of intelligence research, however, these forms of intellectual honesty may be largely irrelevant, except, of course, in those instances when a research product is submitted in fulfillment of academic requirements.

But the other sense of intellectual honesty—accepting information that runs contrary to prevailing opinion—is critical in intelligence research despite the fact that the analyst may be under pressure to support a particular position. Furthermore, although it is easy to pay lip service to intellectual honesty, the researcher is tested severely in those instances in which his entire research effort is jeopardized by the last-minute discovery of a bit of information that would tend to refute his main thesis. It is an unusual man, indeed, who would not entertain even momentarily the idea of conveniently "losing" the unpropitious discovery. But in intelligence research, more than egos or reputations are at stake; consequently, intellectual honesty is imperative even if it means that an entire project has to be scrapped and started anew. As Barzun and Graff so aptly put it, "Elsewhere honesty may be the best policy, but in research it is the only one."[7]

Open-Mindedness

Open-mindedness relates to one's receptivity to the arguments of others. It has been stated that whereas several geese constitute a gaggle and several cows constitute a herd, several intelligence analysts or researchers constitute an argument. Bright people often have strong egos, and researchers deeply immersed in their subject matter think (often justifiably so) that they have better insights into their problem areas than others. But this deep immersion is often the very thing that precludes the researcher from seeing the real issues. Anthropologists have discovered, for example, that it is very useful to have a "naive" observer accompany a field researcher to ensure that the trained specialist does not overlook the obvious in his concentration on the more subtle manifestations of culture.

Open-mindedness implies that one is receptive to others' opinions and interpretations—for example, alternative hypotheses that could account for a certain condition or event even though these interpretations may run contrary to one's own position. It should be noted that receptivity does not mean an abject acceptance of every countervailing opinion. At a certain point in every research effort, decisiveness is essential and a position must be taken if the effort is to be completed. But as a safeguard against committing oneself prematurely to a position that may later become untenable, it behooves the researcher to be receptive to alternatives when there is still time to take appropriate action.

Skepticism

Skepticism is absolutely essential in intelligence research. Most countries withhold certain types of information, making the information that is released all the more suspect. Experience is the best guide for the researcher in attributing credibility to a source. Certain countries' "public announcements" are so systematically misleading that a researcher can nearly always assume the opposite of what is reported. Certain types of informants believe their worth as sources of information is directly proportional to the significance of the information they provide. Consequently, their input is exaggerated and distorted. Many would-be sources are notoriously poor observers, particularly when they purport to observe an object or an activity with which they have no familiarity.

But skepticism may work to the detriment of the researcher, and a distinction should be drawn between "healthy" skepticism and (for lack of a better term) "unhealthy" skepticism. The former type of skepticism is applied situationally; the latter type is applied universally. Thus, a hardheaded skeptic would discount categorically any statement from a provincial radio broadcasting station in Hsi-ning that described problems between the People's Liberation Army and the Chinese Communist Party simply because it is uncharacteristic of Communist countries to admit publicly the existence of internal problems. In academic research, one normally assumes that one's information is reliable until one finds evidence to the contrary. In intelligence research, the opposite is true, and this generalization holds as much for input from controlled sources as it does for input from uncontrolled sources.

Detachment

The intelligence researcher who becomes involved emotionally with the subject of his investigation soon loses objectivity. One of the authors noted this lack of detachment in a number of young military analysts who were examining North Korean, North Vietnamese, and Communist Chinese propaganda that was directed against the United States. Despite admonitions to the contrary, many of the young analysts were not viewing their daily "take" dispassionately but were, in fact, reacting emotionally. For example, their first impulse in reading a particularly vitriolic attack against "U.S. imperialism" was to come up with counterarguments to refute the charges. Whatever emotionalism is generated by the researcher should take the form of enthusiasm in attacking a particularly vexing problem. Intelligence researchers should attempt to perceive their activity as a game—a serious game in which two opposing sides strive for complementary goals.

One side tries to conceal, hide, deceive, or mislead, whereas the other side attempts to penetrate the screen of ruses and stratagems in order to perceive reality. Emotionalism requires energy that should be directed elsewhere for more positive ends. In the case of the propaganda analysis just described, what was significant was not the contents of the anti-U.S. diatribes (which tended to be highly repetitive), but rather that the diatribes were being uttered in the first place and with a high degree of regularity. These facts tended to be overlooked in the analysts' emotional reaction to only the content. It would be unrealistic to expect anyone engaged in an activity as serious as intelligence to love his enemy, but a rabid hatred of the other side interferes with one's perception and invariably destroys objectivity.

Patience, Diligence, and Perseverance

Intelligence analysts and researchers who anticipate quick solutions to difficult problems are in for a rude awakening. Rarely do reports that contain succinct summaries or brilliant deductions give any indication of the amount of sheer drudgery their production entailed. Yet drudgery is more the common rule than the exception in intelligence research. Dramatic solutions to intelligence problems are fairly rare events, and the researcher who requires this type of positive reinforcement may soon become discouraged when he finds that solutions elude him, when he discovers that he has been proceeding up blind alleys, and when he is forced to reexamine for the hundredth time the same material he had been working with for months.

Tycho Brahe, Johannes Kepler, and Copernicus made thousands of observations for many years before they were in a position to publish their discoveries. Darwin pondered, reflected, and reexamined his findings for years, and, if another biologist had not been ready to announce findings similar to his, Darwin probably would have procrastinated even longer in publishing his theories on evolution.[8] Admittedly, these examples provide little solace to the intelligence researcher working under severe time constraints. But the urgency of the problems requiring solutions makes patience, diligence, and perseverance all the more important.

Imagination

The trait that distinguishes best between the very adequate researcher and the outstanding researcher is imagination. And unlike other traits, which can be acquired by training, this trait is indeed difficult for many researchers to develop. Imagination in the context of research does not refer to flights of fanciful musing, daydreams, and the like (although serendipitous spin-offs sometimes occur in this manner). Imagination in the context of research relates to releasing a kind of creative energy that provides unorthodox (but effective) approaches to problems that seemingly defy solution. Sometimes this creativity manifests itself in an ingenious approach for data collection. In other instances, this creativity takes the form of assembling data in such a manner that new implications become apparent.

Margaret Mead, in discussing the problem of studying cultures at a distance (cultures to which the researcher is denied access or cultures that no longer exist), describes the importance of imagination in anthropological research.

> For the study of culture at a distance, however, additional capacities are needed, because in every case the research worker who uses a particular kind of material—interviews, films, art forms, games, slang, and so on— is required to go beyond his or her source material, to delineate in terms of a larger whole, the culture, that is, the total shared, learned behavior of the members of the group or society or period being studied. In historical studies this has been called the historical imagination—the ability to reconstruct from a set of parchments, epitaphs on gravestones,

lists of purchases by a steward for a manor, or of expenditures for the costumes worn in a morality play, the life of a long-past period as a whole. For such reconstruction, the student must be able to move from one set of clues to another, so that if he has a painting that shows the costumes worn in a period, a list of expenditures for stuffs, a list of the foods that were sold in the shops, a few bars of religious music, a knowledge of the climate, a calendar, he will be able to *see, hear, and smell* a thronged medieval street down which a Whitsunday procession passed. Only so, by fitting together separate sets of clues or traces into a reconstructed living whole, can the parts be made meaningful.[9]

Obviously, the admonition to go beyond one's source material must be heeded with discretion, and certainly no researcher is justified in making assertions that are not supported by facts. But facts alone do not constitute intelligence research. The critical question in all research is "What do the facts mean?" And this is where imagination plays its important role. For example, intelligence problems that cannot be solved directly are often "solved" by analogy. Yet, selecting or constructing an appropriate analogy requires imagination. One of the techniques employed by futurologists and by war gamers is to construct "alternative futures." Constructing alternative futures is a creative act involving speculation in the form of "What would happen if . . . ?"

An outstanding example of the role that imagination can play in the practical problems of data collection in the social sciences are the "unobtrusive measures" described by Eugene J. Webb et al. For example, unable to measure directly the interest shown by spectators to various displays at a convention, one ingenious social scientist counted the number of nose prints on the various glass display cases. In similar applications, the researchers measured the amount of wear on floor tiles in front of various displays to determine which displays attracted the greatest number of viewers.[10] Admittedly, some of the techniques produce only "squishy" data (as opposed to "hard" data), but in many cases even "squishy" data are sufficient to permit decisions to be made.[11]

Imagination sometimes takes the form of a hunch, that humble precursor of the more eloquent hypothesis. Washington Platt, no stranger to intelligence research, defines a hunch as follows:

A scientific hunch is a unifying or clarifying idea which springs into consciousness suddenly as a solution to a problem in which we are intensely interested. In typical cases, it follows a long study but comes into consciousness at a time when we are not consciously working on the problem. A hunch springs from a wide knowledge of facts but is essentially a leap of the imagination, in that it goes beyond a mere necessary conclusion which any reasonable man must draw from the data at hand. It is a process of creative thought.[12]

Hunches, insights, intuition, alternative solutions, alternative approaches, and the ability to envision an ideal (e.g., a source of data or an end product) are all manifestations of imagination that have very practical applications in intelligence research.

The intelligence researcher "cannot lay in stock" of imagination, but, as Barzun and Graff point out, he can learn techniques for releasing whatever imaginative powers he has. Constraints to imagination and creativity appear to be largely self-induced. Because of fear of error, fear of ridicule for suggesting unorthodox approaches or conclusions, and excessive concentration on a problem, many researchers consciously or unconsciously limit their own creativity.

Platt discovered that many successful researchers had their most creative insights just before falling asleep, or when they were engaged in some activity unrelated to their investigation: when they were listening to music or when they were just plain relaxing. There may be some truth to the story of Archimedes formulating his theories of buoyancy while in the bath. But before the naive researcher sets out to create those conditions most conducive to creativity, it is important to note that, as Platt points out, "Most [researchers] reported that hunches came during periods of apparent idleness—following, however, long periods of intensive work."[13]

SUMMARY

- In order to qualify as research, an activity of inquiry must satisfy three criteria.
  - The activity must be purposeful in the sense that it addresses an identifiable end or objective; for example, that it attempts to answer a specific question or set of questions.
  - The activity must be performed systematically: it must conform to a plan or a design.
  - The activity must contribute new knowledge or new interpretations of existing knowledge.
- Intelligence research attempts to emulate the academic model of research in the sense that it is (or should be) purposeful and systematic and it should provide new knowledge.
- Unlike academic research, intelligence research is constrained

by limited time, little or no control over experimental variables, insufficient data, and the necessity of using data of unknown quality at times.

- Apart from constraints, intelligence research differs from academic research in four other respects as well:
  - ○ Much emphasis is placed upon prediction in intelligence research, whereas description and interpretation predominate in academic research.
  - ○ Intelligence research uses means of collecting data that eclipse the capabilities of any university or private institution.
  - ○ Unlike academic research findings, intelligence research findings are usually classified.
  - ○ The product of intelligence research must address an actual or potential problem; it must yield more than truth for truth's sake.
- Because the academic model of research can be approximated by intelligence research only at times does not imply that intelligence research is a less rigorous or degraded form of research. It is, however, a more pragmatic form of research than its academic counterpart.
- Certain human traits are essential for anyone attempting to perform acceptable research: reasoning ability, accuracy, intellectual honesty, and open-mindedness. These are necessary (but not sufficient) traits for any researcher.
- For the intelligence researcher, additional traits are required. These additional traits include skepticism, a sense of detachment, patience, diligence, perseverance, and imagination.
- Imagination is especially necessary in intelligence research in order to develop innovative techniques for collecting and analyzing data that the other side wishes to deny to outsiders. Imagination is also necessary for generating various alternative hypotheses or theories to account for conditions or events; hypotheses that could be tested at a later date.

NOTES

1. Significantly, journalism is an excellent model for intelligence researchers. The time constraints under which reporters typically operate and the consequences of publishing incorrect or incomplete information are most analogous to the intelligence researcher's constraints.

2. To put it another way, the other side may take a "wait and see" stance and, thus, not react to a situation in any overt manner.

3. Interestingly, the science of astronomy evolved from the necessity of priests to be able to predict movements of heavenly bodies. The ability to predict enabled the priests to exercise power, and today the relationship of predictive ability and power still holds.

4. RAF Group Captain J. N. Stagg gave the final meteorological report and prediction to General Eisenhower and his staff prior to D-day.

5. Ironically, the fall of Dien Bien Phu and the subsequent decline of French influence in Indochina were brought about largely by the Viet Minh's employment of massed artillery. The French defenders of Dien Bien Phu ruled out the likelihood that the Viet Minh would or could use artillery because of the mountainous terrain and the absence of roads, a classic example of an intelligence failure.

6. Winston W. Little, W. Harold Wilson, and W. Edgar Moore, *Applied Logic* (Boston: Houghton Mifflin, 1955), 1.

7. Jacques Barzun and Henry F. Graff, *The Modern Researcher* (New York: Harcourt, Brace and World, 1970), 60.

8. Data collection for Darwin's epochal work *On the Origin of Species by Means of Natural Selection* began twenty-eight years before the book was published. (*Origin of Species* also included the results of later observations, of course.) This is a classic example of an instance in which the data collection phase occurred before the problem definition phase of a research project. It is interesting to speculate whether Darwin could have published his results many years earlier had his data collection efforts on the voyage of the Beagle been guided by formal hypotheses.

9. Margaret Mead and Rhoda Metraux, eds., *The Study of Culture at a Distance* (Chicago: The University of Chicago Press, 1953), 11.

10. Eugene J. Webb et al., *Unobtrusive Measures: Nonreactive Research in the Social Sciences* (Chicago: Rand McNally, 1966).

11. Lest the reader take affront at the use of slang, "squishy" has been defined as "without any well defined mathematical formulation that unambiguously captures the substantive problem." Ralph E. Strauch in his report *A Critical Assessment of Quantitative Methodology as a Policy Analysis Tool* (Santa Monica, CA: The Rand Corporation, 1974) has given a new respectability to a term that has been used by social scientists for years.

12. Washington Platt and Ross A. Baker, "The Relation of the Scientific 'Hunch' to Research," *Journal of Chemical Education* 8 (1931): October.

13. Ibid.

3

Types of Inquiry and the Nature of Proof

Under a cover of low, thick clouds, a carrier strike force in the North Pacific launched an air strike consisting of bombers, torpedo planes, and fighters. The destination was Pearl Harbor; the objective, units of the U.S. Pacific Fleet. The approach to Oahu was completely undetected, and the result of the air strike was the theoretical destruction of the whole Pacific Fleet. The destruction was theoretical because the air strike was part of a U.S. naval war game conducted (ironically) on Sunday, February 7, 1932. The activity was a simulation. It was a representation, or a model, of a genuine attack that could occur in the future. Some years after the exercise, General Billy Mitchell, one of the observers of the game and a man noted for his outspokenness, said,

> If the President [Roosevelt] can be made to see that the trouble will start with Japan, perhaps we'll have more planes in the Philippines and Hawaii. For years he's had the idea that a war in the Far East would be impracticable and that an attack upon us by Japan is inconceivable. That's Navy thinking. The Japanese will not politely declare war. Hawaii, for instance, is vulnerable from the sky. It is wide open to Japan . . . and Hawaii is swarming with Japanese spies. As I have said before, that's where the blow will be struck—on a fine, quiet Sunday morning.[1]

The prediction (or better, *prophecy*) made by General Mitchell was founded on inspiration, judgment, and imagination. His prophecy was not a prediction in the scientific sense of the term because it was not based on observations of recurring phenomena. Many "predictions" in intelligence, of necessity, cannot be made on the basis of recurring phenomena simply because the phenomena of greatest concern are those that have not yet occurred or, if they did occur, would not be repeated. The most obvious example, of course, would be a nuclear attack by one of the major powers against the other.

This chapter is about descriptive and predictive research because these two kinds of activities constitute the major portion of intelligence research and analysis activities. This chapter will discuss how the nature of proof differs between descriptive and predictive research. It will be shown, for example, that much of the research which purports to be predictive is really a variation of descriptive research. This chapter will also discuss models—of which the naval war game conducted in 1932 was an example—and will show the relevancy of model validation to intelligence research, particularly to predictive research.

At the outset, it should be noted that the distinction between predictive research and descriptive research is a nebulous one. For example, most valid predictions are based on descriptions of past activities or observations of recurring phenomena. As the term will be used throughout this work, *predictive research* will refer primarily to the activities involved in developing and testing models that foretell what the outcomes will be, given the interaction of certain variables.

DESCRIPTIVE RESEARCH

As its name implies, descriptive research relates to activities that attempt to reconstruct, explain, interpret, account for, or describe a phenomenon.[2] This type of inquiry may be used when unique phenomena or recurring phenomena are examined. An example of a unique phenomenon would be a one-of-a-kind event, object, or individual. Recurring phenomena, of course, are activities or events that occur many times; for example, missile firings, communications, and tactical maneuvers.

Like all research, descriptive research attempts to provide new information—information that might support earlier conclusions or cause entirely new conclusions to be formulated. In intelligence research, new information may require that new estimates be prepared. In scientific research, new information may require that new principles be formulated when existing principles no longer adequately account for facts.[3]

Predictions evolving from only descriptive research, if any, tend to be "squishy" in the sense that they do not lend themselves to any well-defined mathematical formulation that unambiguously captures the substantive problem. An example of a squishy prediction evolving from descriptive research is the statement, "By the year____, the Soviet Union's missile arsenal will consist of ____ ICBMs and MRBMs." Clearly, this type of prediction is a far cry from the prediction of solar eclipses, from the prediction of movements of subatomic particles, and from the prediction of meteorological phenomena.

NATURE OF PROOF IN DESCRIPTIVE RESEARCH

Descriptive research is distinguished from predictive research based on the techniques used to test a hypothesis. Very briefly, a hypothesis is a "testable assertion," or a tentative statement that proposes "causal relations between various sets of facts." In descriptive research, testing a hypothesis usually involves searching for evidence that supports or refutes it. A historian (or an intelligence analyst), for example, might postulate a hypothesis to account for the occurrence of an event. He would test his hypothesis by searching for information that would support his hypothesis as well as for information that would refute it. His hypothesis could be said to be valid if the evidence obtained (and presumably, all of the evidence that existed) supported his hypothesis more plausibly than any alternative hypothesis. *Plausibility* in this instance would imply possibility and consistency with other facts and theories, and it might also imply simplicity. For example, in cases in which all other things were equal, the simple explanation (hypothesis) would be preferred over the complex.

In those instances in which a historian (or a sociologist or an anthropologist) might attempt to formulate a principle based on recurring conditions or events,[4] he would attempt to test his hypothesis by searching for other instances comparable to the event under consideration in which certain precedent conditions were followed by certain subsequent events. Should he discover comparable instances in which the relationship of precedent to subsequent conditions existed, these instances would tend to corroborate his hypothesis. The more instances he found that corroborated his thesis, the stronger his confidence would be that his thesis was valid. The researcher would also search for instances in which the same precedent conditions were not followed by a certain subsequent event. Should he find such instances, his hypothesis would be invalidated. Obviously, the historian cannot cause a historical event to occur again; thus, he cannot replicate his test. He can only search for, and hope to find, conditions similar to the one under consideration. The extent to which conditions are comparable is the extent to which his confidence in a hypothesis is maintained.

NATURE OF PROOF IN PREDICTIVE RESEARCH

Predictive research attempts to explain or to account for a phenomenon, but in addition, predictive research also attempts to formulate new principles (or natural laws) that foretell what the effects of the interaction of specified variables will be. Principles are fundamental truths or general laws based on observed regularities of the external universe. Principles are the foundation of modern scientific thought because they permit predictions to be made with a high degree of accuracy. Predictive research, of course, is most applicable to recurring phenomena. Disciplines that best exemplify predictive research in its purest form are the physical sciences.

In contrast to the historian and the typical intelligence researcher, who must search for whatever evidence exists to test their hypotheses, the physical (or experimental) scientist can manipulate independent variables in his laboratory according to plan. Thus, he can create the very conditions upon which his prediction (hypothesis) is based, and he can compare almost immediately the actual outcome of his manipulation of conditions (variables) with his predicted outcome (his hypothesis).[5] If the actual outcome of the experiment compares favorably to the predicted outcome, the scientist's hypothesis is validated.[6]

The test procedure used for validation in its broadest sense is the experiment. Again, in its broadest sense, an experiment may range from a mental exercise of eliminating alternative hypotheses (as a historian or an intelligence researcher might do) to a laboratory manipulation of controlled variables. Rarely can the intelligence researcher perform controlled experiments, but often he can make numerous observations of the same kinds of phenomena. Although not as good as observations of controlled situations, these observations nevertheless can be used as inputs to predictive models.

For the sake of comparison, the scientist's procedures were simplified. The point that should be noted, however, is that the scientist can replicate his experiment dozens of times. Perhaps more important, other scientists can also replicate the same tests. Herein lies the difference between squishy predictions evolving from descriptive research of unique events and "hard" predictions evolving from many repetitions of the same tests by independent researchers. The former type of prediction is usually based on a very limited sample—sometimes a sample of only one. Rules for accepting hypotheses in these cases are different from rules for accepting hypotheses based on a sample of, say, one hundred. In the former case, possibility and plausibility enter into the picture, as well as the persuasive power of the person formulating the hypothesis—his knowledge, experience, and past history of successful predictions. In the latter case, acceptance or rejection of a hypothesis is dictated almost entirely by statistical tables.

Although the nature of proof differs between descriptive and predictive research, this does not imply that one type of proof *necessarily* approaches "truth" more closely than the other. Both types of proofs are appropriate in their respective domains and are equally inappropriate in the other. Gregor Mendel's principles of genetics would have been meaningless without supporting statistics, but it is difficult to see how Edward Gibbon's explanation of the decline and fall of the Roman Empire could have been enhanced by any experimental treatment. Courts of law also have their own rules of evidence for establishing proof. For the sake of accuracy, it is better to reserve the term *proof* for mathematics and to use the terms *validity* and *validate* in the context of hypothesis testing. *Proof* denotes certainty, which is contradictory to the tentative nature of hypotheses and theories.

THEORY VALIDATION IN A CONFLICT SITUATION

Before the reader concludes that experimentation and theory validation have nothing to do with intelligence and intelligence research, he or she would do well to consider what takes place when one nation attempts to ferret out the operational pattern of another country's aircraft early warning system. The typical method involves sending aircraft loaded with electronic gear close to or across another country's border and recording the number, types, locations, and characteristics of the radars that the enemy activates.

Having executed this maneuver a number of times, a picture of the other side's aircraft early warning network evolves. Invariably, gaps exist in the picture. These gaps are filled initially with inferences or calculated guesses of the types of devices that should be covering a certain area based on observed regularities in other areas in the past. These inferences are testable hypotheses, and if time permitted, attempts would be made to provoke the enemy into turning on the radars in the "untested" territory so that the hypotheses could be validated. If it weren't for the fact that the enemy had the option of not turning on his radars (that is, was not bound by any natural law), this type of operation would qualify as predictive research in the most rigorous sense of the word.

Observed regularities of any enemy activity create the framework in which numerous kinds of quasipredictive research activities can be performed. Recurring activities, as mentioned previously, include standing operating procedures in communication, similar patterns in conducting field operations, and similar patterns of weapons systems research, testing, and development. But all of these activities are governed by choice on the enemy's part, and not by some inviolable law of nature. Hence, the strength of a prediction made on the basis of recurring activities in the past is never as strong in human affairs as it is in, say, the physical sciences. Confounding the issue, sometimes the enemy deliberately maintains a pattern of activities to conceal some other activity or to mislead or deceive.

Despite inherent limitations, validating predictions and attempting to establish "working principles" are fairly common activities in intelligence and intelligence research, and consideration of the nature of proof is by no means a mere academic exercise.

MODELS AND THE SCIENTIFIC METHOD

A concept that evolved in the physical sciences, but one that has application in many other nonscientific investigations and particularly in intelligence analysis and research, is the concept of the model. In its simplest sense, a model is an abstraction or representation of reality. For example, chessmen are models (representations) of combatants, and a chess game is a model of conflict; a chemical formula is a symbolic representation (model) of a substance; a model airplane is a miniature representation of the real thing (with many parts missing, of course); the naval war game described at the beginning of the chapter was a model of the actual conflict; and game theory is a model of political, military, or economic conflict, again with irrelevant parts deleted. Scientific theories are also models. The advantage of models is that they enable one to predict outcomes by manipulating only symbols rather than elements of the real world. The most common type of symbol manipulation for predictive purposes is simulation.

Whenever a researcher formulates a hypothesis that attempts to account for the interaction of variables, he is constructing a model. The formulation of the model is a creative act, hence the necessity for imagination discussed earlier. The quality of a model is a function of how well it accounts for the interaction of variables. In scientific models, quality is the extent to which the model predicts accurately. It is the act of determining how well a model explains or predicts that constitutes the scientific method.

Very briefly, the scientific method involves the following steps: (1) the researcher makes observations either directly or vicariously by studying reports of earlier observations and measurements; (2) the researcher formulates (postulates) a model that attempts to account for the phenomenon observed; (3) the researcher subjects his model to a test (the experiment). He checks his measurements, examines his logic (which is reflected in the model he postulated as well as in the design of his experiment), and compares results obtained against results predicted by his model; (4) if the results of his test are comparable to the results predicted by the model, his model may be said to be valid. If the obtained results are inconsistent with his model, and if the researcher ascertained that he made no error in measurement or observation, he may either revise his model or subject it again to the same series of tests, or he may simply discard the model and attempt to formulate a new hypothesis. The steps of the scientific method are shown in figure 3.1.

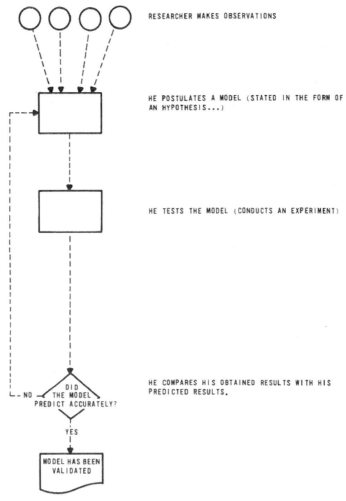

Figure 3.1.   Model Validation and the Scientific Method

It should be noted that the "basic" scientist is primarily concerned with establishing the quality of the model; he is not concerned with making specific predictions. Once models are validated, however, they can be used for making any number of predictions at any future time.[7] The "applied" scientist (like most intelligence researchers), on the other hand, is concerned with making specific predictions by applying the model in real situations.

THE SCIENTIFIC METHOD IN NONSCIENTIFIC RESEARCH

A historian or an anthropologist who postulates a hypothesis to account for a historical event or to describe the uses of a cultural artifact also constructs a model. Unlike the scientist's model, validation of a historian's hypothesis does not involve comparing actual events or conditions with predicted events or conditions. The canons or criteria for accepting a hypothesis, as pointed out earlier, are instead a matter of how well existing data fits the theory. But the point that should be remembered is that the steps in the scientific method are as relevant to nonscientific research as they are to validating a scientific predictive model. And with certain qualifications, the scientific method is a most appropriate methodology for intelligence research as well.

Typically, intelligence research or analysis begins when the researcher makes observations. Unlike the physical scientist, who may observe his phenomena directly, the intelligence researcher or analyst usually makes his observations vicariously; that is, he studies documents, reads intelligence reports, studies photographs, or interviews participants or other observers. Based on his observations, he postulates tentative explanations of what is taking place or why something is occurring. These initial tentative explanations are called working hypotheses. These working hypotheses are examined in terms of possibility and plausibility, and the hypotheses that seem most plausible are retained for further validation.

The retained hypotheses are tested against new input, and the hypothesis that is supported best by the new input (i.e., is most consistent with the new input) becomes the basis for the researcher's conclusions. In general, this procedure is not too dissimilar from the methods used by the physical scientist. But there are a number of important differences that may occur in intelligence research. For instance, whereas the experimental scientist limits his hypotheses to one, the intelligence researcher, in order to exhaust all logical possibilities more quickly, will attempt to postulate as many possible and plausible hypotheses as he can, and he may very well test several hypotheses simultaneously.[8] He is forced to do this because the variables cannot be replicated in the real world as they can be in the laboratory. Whereas the physical scientist can methodically test one hypothesis, then replicate the variables and test another hypothesis, and so on until he has exhausted all of his hypotheses or until he has validated one, the intelligence researcher cannot reconstruct the situation. Actors change, conditions change, and above all, time changes. Although it might be possible to recreate the physical conditions surrounding an event, it is impossible to recapture the event without taking into account the learning or experience that has been gained by the participants since the original event occurred.

Ideally, hypotheses should not be tested against information used to formulate the hypotheses initially. Using the same information for both hypothesis generation and hypothesis testing may give rise to circular reasoning. However, in historical research, it may not be possible to obtain additional information; thus, the test of a hypothesis is simply the extent to which the existing facts fit the theory.[9] Another difference between intelligence research and research that relates to establishing scientific principles is the role that prediction plays in validation. A scientific hypothesis is said to be valid only when a predicted event occurs. However, much intelligence research and analysis is performed for the very purpose of precluding an event's occurrence; hence, it is often impossible to use an actual event for the purposes of validating a prediction.

Finally, research conducted to establish scientific principles seeks to uncover relationships that permit the prediction of outcomes of classes of events.[10] Intelligence research, on the other hand, when it addresses prediction, is more concerned with predicting specific events. The general plan that would be followed for validating hypotheses in intelligence research is shown in figure 3.2.

PREDICTIVE MODEL VALIDATION IN INTELLIGENCE RESEARCH

Predictive model development and validation make up a significant portion of intelligence research activities. Economic intelligence researchers and analysts, for example, employ predictive models quite frequently, and model validation may constitute a major portion of their analytical or research activities. For instance, agricultural economists may devise algorithms (or formulas) for predicting grain yields given certain variables such as acreage under cultivation, availability of fertilizer, growing season, and precipitation. The initial algorithm is a model—a model that must be validated and refined by comparing predicted yields with the actual yields. In terms of armament produc-

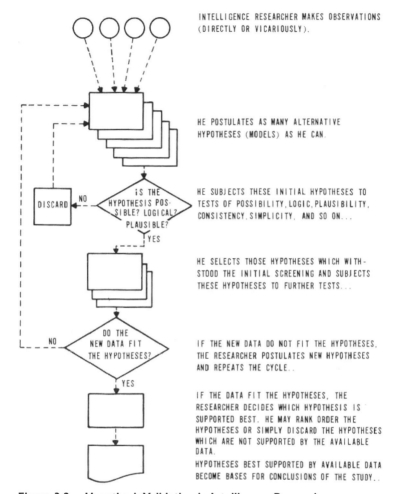

Figure 3.2.   Hypothesis Validation in Intelligence Research

tion, economists may again devise an algorithm for estimating the production capabilities of a manufacturing facility given variables such as the number of furnaces, storehouses, floor space, and available transportation nets.

In transportation intelligence, models or algorithms are used for estimating the amount of material that can be moved over selected rail lines, given such variables as transloading facilities, availability of single- or double-tracked lines, availability of rolling stock and locomotives, train length, and so on. Manipulating these variables by means of computer simulation permits analysts to estimate (predict) how much could be carried under varying conditions and configurations.

Sometimes the intelligence community enjoys a windfall, and an already validated model of the enemy (or his operations) becomes available for operational application. An example of this took place in World War II when U.S. intelligence analysts were able to estimate the size of the Japanese garrison on Betio (Gilbert Islands) based on the number of privies constructed out into the lagoon. The "models" that the analysts used were captured Japanese documents containing army doctrine that specified the required ratio of sanitation facilities per number of men. The estimated size of the garrison number differed by only 64 men (out of 4715).[11]

SEMANTIC PROBLEMS OF TECHNICAL TERMS

Language plays tricks on the unwary. For example, an investigation being nonscientific does not (or should not) imply that an investigation is unscientific. Science relates to activities that attempt to establish verifiable general laws. But in the sense that science is also organized knowledge, it is not distinct from any other discipline such as history, anthropology, or archaeology. As a matter of interest, many disciplines classified as sciences include branches that deal with the establishment of natural laws or principles in only the most remote manner. Taxonomy in botany, zoology, and geology are cases in point. These disciplines are essentially descriptive, not predictive. And whether or not the most rigorous experimental scientist admits it, all science started as descriptive research.

But one of the more unfortunate tricks that language may play on the uninitiated researcher is that it might suggest that the scientific method is a technique used only by the scientist. This, of course, is not true. The scientific method can be applied to a range of activities from predicting movement of the earth's surface to performing maintenance on a motorcycle.[12] The scientific method is *not* a body of arcane procedures that unerringly reveal truths. The scientific method is simply a tried and tested set of procedures for seeing how well a theory works. As such, the scientific method can be applied to any type of inquiry in which theories are developed and tested. In this sense, the scientific method is a most appropriate set of procedures for intelligence research.

SUMMARY

- Predictive research and descriptive research are the two types of activities that constitute the major portion of intelligence research and analysis activities.

- Descriptive research attempts to reconstruct, explain, interpret, account for, or describe a phenomenon. Proof in descriptive research involves searching for data that support or refute a hypothesis or theory.
- Predictive research attempts to formulate new principles (or natural laws) that would enable the researcher to predict, anticipate, or foretell what the results of the interaction of variables will be. Proof in predictive research involves comparing a predicted outcome against a real outcome.
- As the term is used in this book, *predictive research* will relate primarily to the process of developing and validating predictive models.
- Procedures for developing and validating predictive models are sometimes referred to as the scientific method.
- The scientific method involves four steps:
  - The researcher makes and records observations.
  - The researcher formulates a conceptual model that attempts to account for the phenomenon (postulates hypotheses).
  - The researcher tests the model (in laboratory situations, he would experiment).
  - The researcher compares the predicted outcome from his model with the real outcome. If the results are comparable, the model is said to be valid.
- The scientific method, with modifications, is applicable to nonscientific investigations as well.
- Theory validation in intelligence research differs from theory validation in scientific research in the sense that many hypotheses may be tested at the same time. Furthermore, rarely can the intelligence researcher control variables in the sense that a scientist in a laboratory can. For the greater part, intelligence researchers must search for conditions or events that would permit them to test a theory. Physical scientists and other experimental scientists can create the conditions needed to test a theory.

NOTES

1. Emile Gauvreau, *The Wild Blue Yonder* (New York: E. P. Dutton, 1944), 169–171.
2. Some writers would classify explanation as a separate type of research. However, many "explanations" are merely descriptions of the interaction of variables. Explanations of events, for instance, are often descriptions of antecedent conditions that purportedly give rise to the subsequent events.

3. For example, it became necessary to develop quantum mechanics to account for the movement of subatomic particles because these phenomena were not adequately addressed by Newtonian mechanics.

4. Studies of "national character" would be examples of intelligence research that attempt to formulate principles of group behavior.

5. Immediate, as opposed to the length of time required to test Malthus's theory of the world's population outstripping its food supply and Spengler's theory of the decline of the West.

6. This is an oversimplification, of course. In reality, the scientist tests the null hypothesis—the hypothesis which says in effect that any results obtained could have been obtained by chance. When data do not support the null hypothesis, it is rejected, and the rejection of the null hypothesis is tantamount to the acceptance of the original hypothesis.

7. Provided, of course, that the observed relationships among variables do not change.

8. In reality, hypotheses are never tested singly. At a minimum, as pointed out earlier, there is always a null hypothesis for any hypothesis postulated.

9. In hypothesis formulation one attempts to fit a theory to the facts. In hypothesis validation, however, the test is how well the facts fit the theory.

10. As an oversimplified example, theories of gravity apply as much to apples as they do to ballistic missiles.

11. Samuel Eliot Morison, *History of United States Naval Operations in World War II*, vol. 7, *Aleutians, Gilberts and Marshalls, June 1942–April 1944* (Boston: Little, Brown and Company, 1961), 149.

12. For a nontechnical discussion of the scientific method applied to everyday problems, the reader is advised to peruse Robert M. Pirsig's *Zen and the Art of Motorcycle Maintenance: An Inquiry Into Values* (New York: William Morrow and Company, 1974)—a book that, in reality, says virtually nothing about Zen, and very little about motorcycle maintenance. Despite the title, the book is essentially a critique of rational thinking.

The Relation of Induction and Deduction to Theory Building in Intelligence Research

On November 3, 1943, Adolf Hitler issued an order for the defense of the western approaches to Festung Europa. All indications, according to Hitler, pointed to an Allied invasion of France by 1944. The most likely place for the invasion was the Strait of Dover. Defenses were to be strengthened to the maximum in the areas along the strait and Field Marshals Gerd von Rundstedt and Ervin Rommel were assigned the mission of defeating the enemy invasion forces. Von Rundstedt, like Hitler, believed that the Allied invasion would take place between Le Havre and Dunkirk, despite the concentration of German coastal defenses, because an invasion here would permit the Allies to deploy in the plains of Picardy and drive eastward to the Ruhr. Very few German generals thought that the Allies would be foolish enough to risk getting bogged down in Normandy. Furthermore, the launching platforms for the V-1 and V-2 bombs and rockets that Hitler was preparing to use in mass attacks on England were close to the Strait of Dover.[1] In short, it was only "logical" that the Allies would launch their inevitable invasion across the Strait of Dover, the classic invasion route for Alfred the Great and the route specified in the aborted plans of Napoleon Bonaparte and later Hitler himself in 1940.

The Allied invasion did not take place across the Strait of Dover, of course. On the basis of assumptions, generalizations based in part on elaborate deceptive measures by the Allies, and faulty deductions, the German High Command made one of the most fateful decisions of the war. The errors made by the German High Command were errors of induction. Unfortunately, for commanders in the field, for intelligence analysts at their desks, and for intelligence researchers in general, there are no safeguards against drawing faulty generalizations—no rules to follow and no exercises to "strengthen" one's mental faculties so that correct generalizations necessarily follow from observations.

This chapter will discuss the reasoning processes involved in intelligence research and analysis. More specifically, the chapter will discuss the reasoning processes as they relate to different steps in the scientific method. In this chapter, the term *hypothetico-deductive method* will be used in place of *scientific method*. Both terms mean the same thing. Although *hypothetico-deductive method* is not as familiar as the term scientific method, the term describes the problem-solving process more accurately and avoids the connotation that a procedure may be limited only to scientific inquiry.

Initially, the chapter will discuss the mental processes by which vague concepts are translated into hypotheses that can be tested. Then the chapter will discuss the mental processes involved in testing hypotheses. With respect to formulating hypotheses, however, a word of warning is appropriate at the outset: there is little advice that can be given to the researcher at the hypothesis formulation stage of his inquiry. Much of the activity that precedes the formulation of testable hypotheses is unstructured, amorphous, and perhaps even chaotic.

The processes that a researcher performs at the prehypothesis stage defy generalization, and the stereotyped notion of the researcher moving unerringly from a vague concept to a refined and validated theory is largely a myth. In fact, it may come as a surprise to the new researcher that the most agonizing phase of a research activity is the prehypothesis stage. Once the researcher has formulated testable hypotheses, the avenue of progression for the researcher is clear. He can delineate what must be accomplished, he can specify the sequence of events, he can predict the form of his final product, and with experience, he can probably tell how long it will take to complete his inquiry. But it is indeed the rare individual who can anticipate what conditions and how much time will be required to formulate the hypothesis.

DEFINING INDUCTION

Induction is the intellectual process of drawing generalizations on the basis of observations or other evidence. Induction takes place when one learns from experience. For example, induction is the process by which a person learns to associate the color red with heat and heat with pain, and to generalize these associations to new situations. Obviously, induction is essential not only for the transmission of knowledge, but also for survival.

Induction is a process of discovery. Induction occurs when an analyst or researcher begins to see certain relationships in the phenomena he is observing. For example, an analyst or researcher might notice from his systematic examination of open-source reports that unusually bellicose public statements were uttered by spokesmen of country Z prior to the time when arms agreements, concluded with country Y, were announced formally. Or the analyst may have noted that an invariant sequence of events preceded country Z's nuclear tests.

Induction occurs when one is able to postulate causal relationships. Intelligence estimates are largely the result of inductive processes, and, of course, induction takes place in the formulation of every hypothesis. Unlike other types of intellectual activities, such as deductive logic and mathematics, there are no established rules for induction. Describing how induction takes place is tantamount to describing how one conceives ideas. Obviously, knowledge and experience are important for one to generate ideas, and certain personal traits of the investigator, such as curiosity or an obsession with a lack of closure, are important contributors to induction. Imagination and "powers" of observation clearly figure into the inductive process.

Physical and social environments that are conducive to induction can also be created—environments in which a researcher may try out ideas without fear of ridicule from his colleagues, for example—but different people react differently to various conditions, and for some researchers an element of stress, anxiety, or discomfort is conducive to sharpening creative powers. Observations usually precede all valid generalizations. Although one cannot guarantee that making numerous observations will necessarily yield generalizations, one can state that without observations, the likelihood of developing valid generalizations is indeed remote.

The objective of the inductive phase in the hypothetico-deductive process is to arrive at a number of testable hypotheses. Since the quality of the hypotheses is a function of the knowledge and experience of the observer, one way of improving hypotheses is to involve several people in the hypothesis formulation (inductive) phase. At times, it may also be profitable to employ a naive observer—one who is not deeply involved in the problem at hand. Naive observers contribute by questioning basic assumptions, assumptions that those deeply involved in an activity may take for granted. The inductive phase of the hypothetico-deductive process ends when testable hypotheses are formulated.

DEFINING DEDUCTION

Deduction is the process of reasoning from general rules to particular cases. Deduction may also involve drawing out or analyzing the premises to form a conclusion.[2] In the example of induction mentioned earlier, an analyst noted a pattern of events relating to country Z's nuclear tests. His generalization at that point may have taken the form, "events 1, . . . , n always precede nuclear tests in country Z." After arriving at this generalization, the analyst may have received reports that events 1, . . , n were occurring in country Z. On the basis of this information, the analyst would conclude that country Z was about to test another nuclear device. Initially, the analyst reasoned inductively from numerous observations to a generalization. When the analyst reasoned from a generalization to a specific case, he reasoned deductively. His reasoning progressed from premises to a conclusion. The major premise was that events 1, . . . , n always preceded nuclear tests in country Z. The minor premise stated that events 1, . . . , n had been reported. Assuming that events 1, . . . , n were not associated with any other activity, the logical conclusion that would be reached was that country Z was about to test a nuclear device. The example just cited was overly simplified, and like most simplifications, it glossed over points that might make a significant difference in intelligence research.

Deduction works best in closed systems such as mathematics, formal logic, or certain kinds of games—war games played on a computer, for example, in which all the rules for playing the game are clearly spelled out. In the statement, "This is a triangle; therefore, the sum of the interior angles will equal 90 degrees," the validity and truthfulness of the conclusions would be apparent to anyone with a knowledge of geometry. If drawn correctly, conclusions in closed systems are always valid.

But intelligence research rarely deals with closed systems; thus, conclusions may still be drawn correctly, but the premises from which they are drawn may not be true. In the example of the nuclear tests, for instance, country Z may have assumed that its activities were being monitored and, for strategic reasons, embarked on a large-scale deception program. In this case, the premise that events 1, . . . , n always precede nuclear tests in country Z would be false, and consequently, even if the researcher or analyst reasoned validly from the premises, the conclusions would still be false. The implication for intelligence research is apparent: human activities rarely involve closed systems in which conclusions necessarily follow certain premises. Therefore, in intelligence research, deduction must be used carefully with a full awareness of the limitations of the processes and with an awareness of potential errors in the premises.[3]

INDUCTION AND DEDUCTION IN THE HYPOTHETICO-DEDUCTIVE PROCESS

It was mentioned previously that in the hypothetico-deductive process, induction ended with the formulation of testable hypotheses. Hypotheses, it will be recalled, are theories or unproved assumptions that relate or explain different facts. The purpose of a hypothesis is to guide the researcher in his search for evidence. Without hypotheses to delimit the boundaries of the search, the researcher would be unable to ensure that any collected data were relevant or germane to his purposes. As Darwin pointed out, "all observation must be for or against some point of view [a hypothesis], if it is to be of any service." Again, the greater the number of hypotheses formulated, the greater the chance that one of the hypotheses will prove to be the correct one. This is important to remember because there is a tendency among many researchers to "lock in" early on a favorite hypothesis to the exclusion of others. The number of hypotheses that might be generated is infinite, but at the minimum, the researcher should formulate at least three.[4]

Typically, hypotheses in problem-solving contexts are stated in the form of a syllogism, that is, "if, then." This first statement constitutes the major premise or the generalization. The next statement (the minor premise) would include the actual evidence to date. To return to the nuclear test example, the syllogism would look like this:

- *If* events 1, . . . , n, then a nuclear device will be tested (major premise).
- Events 1, . . . , n have been reported in country Z (minor premise).
- Therefore, a nuclear test is imminent in country Z (conclusion).

The relationship of inductive and deductive reasoning to the hypothetico-deductive process (the scientific method) is shown in figure 4.1.

As critical as these two reasoning processes may be, it should not be assumed that every research program will necessarily require that both processes be performed. Nor must the researcher formulate hypotheses for every type of intelligence research project. Certain types

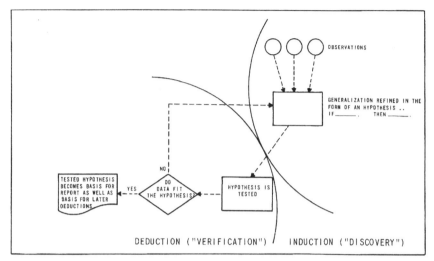

Figure 4.1.   Relationship of Inductive and Deductive Reasoning to the Hypothetico-Deductive Method

of intelligence problems will require only the addition of new information. In other cases, the hypotheses may be given to the researcher for testing as part of his assignment, thus eliminating the need for the researcher to draw initial generalizations. Sometimes a research project will involve only the inductive phase and the product will consist of a generalization that was not yet tested. However, in the case of self-initiated intelligence research efforts, it is difficult to see how one could progress systematically and not employ the hypothetico-deductive process.

SUMMARY

- Induction is the intellectual process by which one arrives at generalizations on the basis of observations or other evidence. Induction is the process by which testable hypotheses are formulated.
- Deduction is the process of reasoning from general rules to particular cases. Conclusions drawn deductively (and correctly) in closed systems such as mathematics and formal logic are always valid. Unfortunately, rarely does intelligence research involve closed systems.

- Induction is involved in the process of discovery, for example, noting certain relationships among phenomena that previously were not known to exist. Deduction is involved in testing and verifying the generalizations formed inductively.
- Not all research requires both induction and deduction. Sometimes a research project (assigned or self-initiated) may conclude with a set of generalizations. Other times a research program may be initiated to test a set of generalizations.

NOTES

1. Samuel Eliot Morison, *History of United States Naval Operations in World War II*, vol. 9, *The Invasion of France and Germany, 1944–1945* (Boston: Little, Brown and Company, 1962), 39–49.

2. The word *deduction* comes from the Latin *deducere*, which means to draw out.

3. Rules for deduction can be found in most textbooks of logic.

4. The three are the original hypothesis, the null hypothesis (which is essentially the refutation of the original hypothesis), and one more hypothesis that is completely independent of the other two.

5

Planning the Research Program: Problem Definition

Every well-performed research project involves four major phases: problem definition, data collection, data analysis, and report preparation. The normal sequence of events progresses from the translation of an identified need into a plan of action, the execution of that plan of action, and the submission of the results of the planned research activities. There is nothing sacrosanct about the sequence in which the steps are performed. In many instances in intelligence research, data collection may occur before a problem is defined or becomes apparent. Very often data analysis begins before all of the data are collected, and report preparation usually begins before all of the data are analyzed.

This chapter discusses the steps that should take place in the problem definition phase of a research project. This is a critical phase of the project because decisions made at this phase affect the manner in which the entire project will be conducted. At the outset, it should be noted that the problem definition phase involves more than merely selecting a research topic. The problem definition phase is, in reality, a planning phase in which all of the factors that would influence the successful completion of a proposal effort must be considered.

The problem definition phase involves two major functions: (1) defining the problem and (2) determining the feasibility of the proposed approach for attacking the problem. These functions are interrelated. The nature of the problem determines what resources are required by the researcher. The available resources, time, funds, and manpower determine whether or not the problem as stated can be addressed effectively. Problem definition is an iterative process of selection and refinement. Based on need and the capabilities and interests of the researcher, general problem areas are identified. Within these larger problem areas, a number of tentative topics may be chosen. These topics, in turn, are examined initially with respect to their value to the intelligence community and to the researcher, and then with respect to the feasibility of actually conducting the research.

DEFINING THE PROBLEM: SOURCES AND ORIGINS OF RESEARCH PROJECTS

The objective of this step is the identification of a research topic. This section will discuss the factors that should be taken into account as the research problem is defined and the topic selected. The factors include the sources and origins of problem areas, the need, and the many decisions that must be made in delineating the scope of the proposed research project, such as specifying terms of reference and operational definitions.

Research projects evolve from recurring needs of a sponsoring agency or headquarters, from specific nonrecurring needs of an agency or headquarters, or from problem areas perceived by the researcher himself. Examples of research projects that are assigned are periodic reports and updates. Usually these types of research projects are scheduled and generally pose no special problems to the researcher. Another type of assigned research project is special ad hoc studies. This type of project might cause problems because deadlines are often short, the issues are critical, and data may not be available. An advantage of all assigned projects, however, is that the terms of reference are spelled out in the assignment. Thus, the researcher need not ponder the scope, length, complexity, operational definitions, availability of funds, need, or the feasibility of the project as he must do with self-initiated projects.

Self-initiated research projects might evolve from a problem an intelligence staff officer encountered on his last tour of duty, or from chronic problems facing the organization to which he will be assigned. Perennial problems facing the intelligence community are always potential sources for research topics. These problem areas can be spelled out in detail in discussions with various agency spokesmen. Conceivably, a research project currently underway at an agency might be enhanced by a supplementary effort, provided that the supplementary effort could be completed in time to be of value. Current intelligence reports and even collection requirements or statements of intelligence interest (SIIs) might suggest topics for self-initiated research programs.

IS THERE A NEED?

A proposed self-initiated project that addresses a critical need stands an excellent chance of being approved and funded. Projects that address peripheral needs or potential future needs require that the researcher explain where and how the results of the effort would be of value to the intelligence community. At least part of this justification would include ascertaining whether or not the study has already been done. This should entail a search of the various agencies' classified holdings as well as an initial survey of the open literature. This initial literature survey also helps the researcher determine whether or not there is sufficient information available to conduct the study.

Simply because a study had been done in the past does not mean that the researcher must rule out the possibility of repeating the study or carrying out a similar research project. Certain types of subject matter have short shelf life. An example would be a general population's attitudes toward a specific issue. As conditions change, public attitudes may change accordingly and, therefore, may warrant reexamination. Personal, military, and political alignments change, sometimes in a surprisingly short time, and findings produced by an earlier study may be sufficiently obsolescent five years later to warrant reconsideration.

Studies in which methodological problems hampered data collection or analysis are always logical candidates for reexamination when new techniques become available or when military or political conditions change so that the researchers have access to areas that were formerly denied. Sometimes the discovery of new information such as diaries, memoirs, or private correspondence may cause earlier findings to be reexamined. The same is true when formerly highly confidential official documents are made public.

Experiments in which the original researcher failed to consider certain factors, or experiments in which the then-existing technology did not permit accurate observation and measurement, are candidates for reexamination, as are studies in which bias on the part of the original researcher is suspected. In short, because a study was done in the past does not rule out the possibility of doing it again. The criterion to consider in repeating earlier studies is the likelihood of producing new knowledge of value to the intelligence community.

DEFINING BOUNDARIES: A SCOPE

Limiting the scope of the research project is one of the more critical early tasks the researcher must perform. Typically, the researcher underestimates the magnitude of his proposed effort. For example, he may not be aware of the vast quantity of data he must screen in order to obtain only a few kernels of useful information. Furthermore, unless a topic is delineated carefully, the researcher may find that his topic has no realistic bounds. For instance, a researcher examining the causes of the Bolshevik Revolution in Russia could very easily progress backward through the decline of the Romanovs, to the decline of the Roman Empire, to the rise of Constantinople, and to the birth of Christ!

An intelligence researcher with an interest in history and geography might select initially as a research topic the strategic significance of the Dardanelles only to discover that without addressing the who and when questions, adequate coverage of the topic would require at least some consideration of the Greco-Persian wars and of all intervening conflicts since the fifth century. Interesting, perhaps, but this background coverage would probably be of little value today.

The cast of characters expands exponentially in historical research, and without limits or guidelines for determining who will be studied, the researcher may be soon overwhelmed by the comprehensiveness and magnitude of his poorly defined topic.

TERMS OF REFERENCE

Delineating the scope involves establishing terms of reference. Terms of reference are descriptors that define the boundaries of the research effort. Terms of reference can be established with respect to time periods, specific geographic locations, events or movements, and significant personalities to be considered in the study.

Defining terms of reference also includes:

- stating the problem,
- stating assumptions relating to the subject matter,
- stating the hypotheses, if the nature of the research is such that hypotheses must be tested,[1]
- formulating operational definitions,
- proposing a title (which may contain many of the same terms used in the statement of the problem),[2]
- describing briefly the methodology to be used (either in data collection or data analysis),
- describing sources of data if the sources are unusual,
- indicating completion dates (anticipated dates, if the project is self-initiated),

- estimating the man-hours required (if the project is assigned), and
- identifying coordination required and any additional assistance needed from support groups (imagery interpreters or translators, for example).

In the case of an assigned project, or in the case of a project that is essentially a replication of an earlier project, an initial outline of the anticipated final product might also be submitted as a term of reference. An outline makes explicit to those who must approve a proposed effort the breadth of coverage and the extent of detail that the researcher proposes to provide. In the case of self-initiated projects, however, the researcher will more than likely be forced to revise the outline constantly as his project progresses, hits unanticipated snags, and employs alternative collection or analysis procedures.

The nature of the outline also depends upon the number of researchers working on the effort and the experience and personal preferences of the researcher. Generally, efforts involving the contributions of several researchers require a more structured outline than would an effort staffed by one person. Then, too, there are individual preferences. Some researchers prefer to initially synthesize a highly detailed skeleton of the report and then flesh out the skeleton with specific information and transitions. Other researchers prefer to work with only a very general outline, which is refined and revised as data are collected and analyzed and as implications of the analyzed data become evident.

Certainly the experience of the researcher is a factor to consider in deciding how detailed an outline should be. Experienced newspaper reporters, for example, can write a story quickly without preparing a detailed outline simply by stating the most important fact first, followed by the next most important fact, and so on. The outline is a tool for preparing a report; it is not the report itself. Consequently, the amount of time spent preparing the outline should be proportional to the scope of the overall effort.

OPERATIONAL DEFINITIONS

Operational definitions must be made at this stage. An operational definition is the writer's translation of a concept into observable (empirical) terms. To put it another way, an operational definition is a concept stated in terms of that which can be observed and, ideally, in terms of the means by which the concept can be measured or quantified.

The concept of *net capabilities* is an example of a term requiring operational definition. With respect to net capabilities, the question must be raised: to what specific action do the net capabilities relate, and in what units are the capabilities to be expressed? *Power, revolt,* and *instability* are also common terms that require operational definitions.[3]

There need not be universal agreement on the operational definition (although it helps), but the writer must make clear what he means when he uses abstract terms such as *leadership, power structure, revolt, strategic significance,* and so on. Again, this process of spelling out operational definitions also helps delineate the scope and establishes the referents by which conclusions can be arrived at and evaluated.

BROAD TOPICS OR LIMITED TOPICS: DETERMINING THE FEASIBILITY OF THE APPROACH

Delineating the scope of the effort requires the researcher to decide if he intends to treat a broad topic in general terms or a limited topic in precise terms. It is the broad topic that causes problems. Typically, the scope of a broad topic is so great that it exceeds the constraints of cost, time, and manpower. Another problem with broad topics is that often the treatment tends to be superficial and, thus, of little value to anyone who needs substantive information. To produce useful, substantive information about a broad topic area, the researcher must know his topic well before he begins his project, and this criterion excludes most students.

This is not to rule out categorically any consideration of broad topic areas. At times, coverage of a wide topic area can provide very useful information. Examples of broad topic coverage might be evaluations of previous research, or surveys of literature relating to a specific topic. Generally, broad topic coverage is appropriate in new areas or in areas in which little is known. The use to which the product will be put would also be a factor in determining whether the researcher should opt for broad coverage or detailed specific coverage.

The objective of this step in the problem definition phase is to determine whether or not the topic can be addressed in light of constraints of time, manpower, available resources (including information), and the capabilities and interests of the researcher.

Testing the Limits of Time

The constraint that permeates every type of intelligence research is time. Even the student in the academic environment has time limitations within which his research must be completed. Researchers in an operational environment typically have shorter response times, but these research projects are often team efforts, and in many cases the addition of other researchers can compensate for limited time. Nevertheless, the length of time available is a major determinant in the scope of a proposed project, and this constraint makes realistic scheduling and planning all the more critical.

Again, inexperienced researchers typically underestimate the amount of time that will be required to carry out their proposed program. Most government-sponsored research necessitates coordination. If the research involves contact with foreign nationals, coordination requests may have to be transmitted from the U.S. Department of State (or Defense) through the hierarchy of another government. The researcher may have to spend many hours explaining the nature of his request to headquarters of every echelon through which the request passes. Protocol is important, chains of command may not be bypassed, and all of this takes time.

Admittedly, access to remote computer terminals may save time in collecting archival data, but trips to archives may be required nevertheless. Again, procuring travel funds, forwarding clearances, establishing points of contact at the visited agency, and making protocol visits take up valuable time. Especially frustrating are instances in which leads fail to yield any substantive information, or instances in which archives that should contain the required information yield little of value. Blind alleys are encountered in every research project. They are exasperating, costly, and time-consuming. But they must be anticipated.

Capabilities and Interests of the Researcher

The researcher must not overlook his personal knowledge, skills, and interests when he selects a research topic. For example, a researcher with no knowledge of research design or of basic statistics would be well advised to stay away from programs involving laboratory experimentation. Researchers who require extensive use of data processing equipment need certain skills and knowledge if they are to use these facilities effectively. Admittedly, research is a learning process, but without a minimal level of background knowledge or skills, the researcher is in a poor position to make even a modest contribution. In an academic environment, the researcher may have to take time to develop requisite skills or acquire sufficient background in a subject area in order to address it effectively, but in light of the time constraints in intelligence, this is rarely feasible in an operational environment.

Because of dispositions, personal proclivities, and so on, certain types of research activities or subject matter may be distasteful to the researcher. Nothing can be more stultifying than poring over screed that is tedious, monotonous, and uninteresting. Invariably, the research product reflects the enthusiasm and interests of the researcher; therefore, selecting an interesting topic is one method of maintaining quality control.

Feasibility: The All-Inclusive Issue

Throughout all of the initial planning steps of a project, one question must be asked constantly: is the proposed effort feasible? Limiting the scope, ensuring the availability of funds, and planning for sufficient lead time increase the likelihood that the program can be completed successfully. But these factors cannot guarantee success.

Likelihood of successful completion is an important criterion in gaining approval for a self-initiated project. If any government funding is involved in the self-initiated project, intelligence managers (and faculty advisers) want some reasonable assurance that the effort will be worth the expenditure. Even if funding is not involved, the researcher is making a large investment of his own time and energy. Every graduate student has heard horror stories of advanced degrees being withheld for years until some major stumbling block had been removed and the research had been completed successfully. Delays are burdensome to the researcher and nonproductive to the intelligence community.

Aside from a topic that may be too broad with respect to available time and resources, the factor that contributes most to making a project unfeasible is nonexistent or unavailable data. Therefore, the researcher should pay especially close attention to primary and alternate methods for collecting the data he needs. Data relating to a specific topic may not exist in any archive or in a form in which they can be used. This is nothing new, and this is why data collection typically takes up such a large portion of a research effort. But unavailable data is another problem.

Data may be unavailable for a number of reasons: there may not be any sensor capable of detecting a certain emanation, or the state of the art may be such that a sufficient degree of resolution has not been attained to make a detected emanation useful. But these are secondary conditions relating to a larger problem, namely, inaccessibility to the target of interest. A target of interest may be a fortification, a production facility, or a weapons system. But the target of interest may also be a sample of the opposition's general population or the party cadre in a capital city. In sensitive political environments, even friendly populations may be inaccessible to the researcher, and the likelihood of his acquiring data directly from these "denied" groups is very remote. Problems in obtaining information about denied groups may be so great as to warrant research in their own right.[4]

In other cases, data might be obtainable, but only at great risk to the collectors. Here a judgment must be made as to whether the data are worth the risk entailed in collecting them. It is highly unlikely that any self-initiated program involving risks to lives or equipment would be approved. If the topic addressed were indeed so critical, the project probably would have been assigned in the first place. The researcher should consider that even when he has direct access to the data, political or military conditions may change suddenly and the data may become inaccessible. One method of increasing the feasibility of the proposed effort is to plan a series of alternative data collection procedures. Ideally, the data collection procedures would range (initially) from those in which the researcher could make direct observations, to those in which the researcher could make only inferential judgments. As undesirable as inferences may be, compared to direct, firsthand observations, making decisions on inferences when facts are not available is not uncommon in intelligence.

PROBLEM DEFINITION: THE FIRST BUT NOT FINAL PHASE OF THE PLANNING ACTIVITY

It should be apparent that the process of defining the research problem involves more than simply picking a topic. Defining the problem involves consideration of every phase of the entire research program. Defining the problem is, in fact, a micro research program in its own right. Factors that determine whether a proposed program is relevant and feasible are interrelated, and any one factor in a self-initiated program might impact on the others sufficiently to make the entire program unfeasible.

Defining the problem is the first phase in the planning process. But this phase does not end when the next phase begins. Throughout the conduct of the overall project, the original problem may be further refined and delineated. It is not unusual to discover in the course of a research program that certain questions subsumed under the larger original question were more important than the initial topic. The distillation process is common (and desirable) in self-initiated research programs, and the more specific a topic becomes, the greater the likelihood that the researcher will be able to conclude his project successfully. Steps in the problem definition phase are shown in figure 5.1.

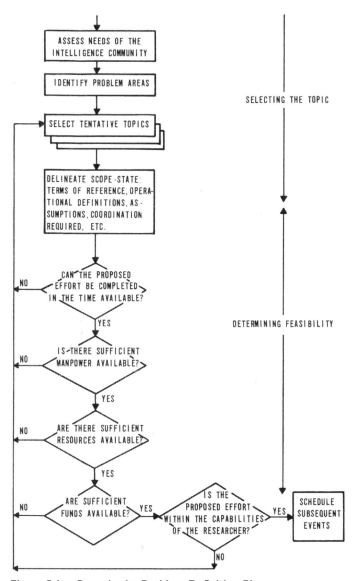

Figure 5.1.   Steps in the Problem Definition Phase

SUMMARY

- Most research projects involve four phases: problem definition, data collection, data analysis, and report preparation. Planning is essential in all phases.
- The problem definition phase of a research project involves two major functions: defining the problem and determining the feasibility of the proposed approach for attacking the problem.

- Defining the problem involves considering the need for the study, delimiting the scope, defining terms of reference, and stating operational definitions.
- In self-initiated research projects, the researcher may further refine his topic throughout the problem definition, data collection, and analysis phases of his project.
- The ultimate criterion in selecting a research topic is *need*. The ultimate criterion in determining if and how a research topic should be addressed is *feasibility*.

NOTES

1. Not all research requires hypotheses. For example, a survey to determine the status quo, or to establish what exists at present, would not necessarily involve hypotheses.

2. Writing titles is an art. Intelligence reports, unlike literary works produced for public consumption, do not (or should not) depend upon a provocative title to attract readers. Numerous problems arise when a title does not accurately reflect the content of a report. The amount of time and money wasted in cataloging, retrieving, and examining documents whose titles are misleading is mind-boggling. If possible, the title should contain the what, where, when, or who, if important individuals are discussed in the report. In the process of delineating the problem, the title may be revised several times before a research project is completed.

3. Degrees of instability, for example, can be expressed in terms of events corresponding to points on a Guttman scale—events such as the resignation of cabinet officials (at one end of the scale) and a coup d'etat and civil war at the other end of the scale.

4. A case in point would be the studies funded by the Department of Army to devise techniques for assessing the effectiveness of psychological operations directed toward denied audiences.

6

Planning the Research Program:
Locating Information

In order to determine the nature and extent of the data collection activities to be performed, the researcher must know what data exist and where and how data can be obtained. This chapter will discuss characteristics of various types of data and places where data can be obtained.

PRIMARY AND SECONDARY SOURCES

Primary sources of information are *firsthand* observers, participants, or recorders. For example, a participant in a military operation would be a primary source, and any account he prepared pertaining to the operation, such as an after action report, would be a primary source document. An attaché who observed a training exercise would be a primary source; so would an agent or a defector who made firsthand observations be a primary source. The outputs of various sensors (ELINT receivers, other receivers, radars, cameras, and scanners) are primary source data.

Secondary sources are documents prepared on the basis of primary sources. Thus, if an analyst prepared a report based upon evaluated information derived from interviews with agents or defectors, his document would be considered a secondary source. Many researchers assume that primary sources or primary source documents are *necessarily* more reliable than secondary sources. This assumption is unwarranted. In evaluating any information, both the competency and the motivation of the source must be taken into account. In certain instances, observers are not competent to report what they observed. For example, an untrained observer might report an armored car as a tank, or a company-sized unit as a battalion.

Sometimes people see only what they want to see. For example, in World War II an enemy fighter plane downed while attacking a formation of bombers might be claimed as a "kill" by nearly every gunner in the bomber formation. Inflated estimates of enemy aircraft involved in a battle and inflated reports of the number of kills plagued intelligence organizations on both sides during World War II. Motives of the writer must be taken into account when primary source documents are used. If a writer realizes that his personal records will be used by others, he may deliberately portray himself in a favorable light. Even the most candid memoirs tend to be self-serving to some extent. Researchers using statements made by prisoners of war must pay especially close attention to the motives of the source. Prisoners of war (PWs) may lie or exaggerate in order to appease their captors, or to justify their behavior, or to deceive. During the Korean War, for example, Chinese Communist troops would permit themselves to be captured in order to organize other PWs detained in United Nations prison compounds. It was not unusual for North Vietnamese Army (NVA) prisoners in Vietnam to report the favorable reception of United States-produced psychological operations (PSYOP) leaflets in areas where none had been dropped. Rarely do prisoners give fear as a reason for surrendering, but instead cite ideological reasons or lack of resources with which to fight as reasons for their capture.

People under stress are *often* poor observers or reporters (except of their own emotions, perhaps), and memories sometimes fail in recalling significant details. General S. L. A. Marshall found that descriptions by individual participants in battle were notoriously unreliable and that only by collating the accounts of many participants could a valid picture of what actually occurred be constructed.[1]

Furthermore, cultural traits may impair the usefulness of primary sources. For example, in the East, it is not unusual for a courteous respondent to report only what he thinks the researcher *wants* to hear, and for this reason it is sometimes necessary to devise a number of stratagems to corroborate various responses to a single question. In short, primary sources and primary source documents are not necessarily the best sources of reliable information.

INTENTIONAL AND UNINTENTIONAL TRANSMITTERS OF FACTS

In addition to being classified on the basis of source, research data may also be classified on the basis of whether or not the medium by which a fact is transmitted was created intentionally or unintentionally as a conveyor of information. Intentional transmitters of facts, according to Barzun and Graff, would include all records (both verbal and nonverbal). Unintentional transmitters of facts would include relics, such as remains, language, customs, tools, and artifacts.[2] Interestingly, this listing of transmitters of historical facts has a corollary in intelligence (table 6.1).

The listing of intelligence transmitters of facts makes it clear that the researcher who limits his data only to printed documentation is overlooking other potentially valuable types of input. Admittedly, nondocumentary input must be transformed into some documentary form before it can be used, and formatting and structuring of the data may be necessary. But even when large amounts of printed data are used, the data must also be formatted for ease in tabulation or interpretation and analysis.

DATA SOURCES AND POTENTIAL FOR BIAS

Concern for bias should enter into the researcher's selection of any type of data. Bias may be of two types: that which is inherent in the data, and that which may be introduced by the researcher. One would anticipate, for example, that intentional transmitters of facts would very likely contain bias introduced by their author or creator. Biographies of Premier Kim Il-sung deliberately confuse the details of his birth and imply that he and the legendary hero Kim Il-sung are one and the same. Similarly, biographies of President Park Chung-hee treat very cursorily Park's military training in the Japanese Army. Even purportedly "objective" documents may be biased; for example, field reports sent to higher headquarters by the Japanese in World War II often contained fantastic claims of success, and the Japanese High Command became a victim of its own propaganda.[3]

But researchers often fail to take into account the bias they may introduce themselves. As mentioned earlier, inexperienced researchers categorically reject as "mere propaganda" any statement carried over state-controlled broadcasting systems. For instance, broadcasts from mainland China and from North Korea have alluded to industrial production problems and to instances of internal dissent. And in the case of China, often these references were precursors to major changes in the party or military hierarchy.[4]

One of the major sources of researcher-introduced bias involves the manner in which the researcher selects and analyzes his data. For

Table 6.1. Premeditated and Unpremeditated Transmitters of Facts

HISTORIOGRAPHICAL TRANSMITTERS OF FACTS (BARZUN AND GRAF)	INTELLIGENCE TRANSMITTERS OF FACTS
RECORDS (INTENTIONAL TRANSMITTERS OF FACTS)	**RECORDS** (INTENTIONAL TRANSMITTERS OF FACTS)
1. CHRONICLES, ANNALS, BIOGRAPHIES, GENEALOGIES	1. OFFICIAL STATE HISTORIES, BIOGRAPHIES, GENEALOGIES (e.g., THE OFFICIAL BIOGRAPHY OF KIM IL-SONG, HO CHI MINH, AND MAO TSE-TUNG; THE REVISED BIOGRAPHY OF STALIN.)
2. MEMOIRS, DIARIES	2. KHRUSHCHEV'S MEMOIRS; THE PENKOVSKY PAPERS; CAPTURED DIARIES OF PRISONERS; NON-FICTION NOVELS, e.g., THE GULAG ARCHIPELAGO.
3. CERTAIN KINDS OF INSCRIPTIONS	3. FACTORY MARKINGS ON MILITARY EQUIPMENT; INSIGNIA; PRINTED SLOGANS.
ORAL	ORAL
4. BALLADS, ANECDOTES, TALES, SAGAS	4. PATRIOTIC SONGS; PATRIOTIC SLOGANS; CHEERS; MOTTOES
5. PHONOGRAPHS AND TAPE RECORDINGS	5. RECORDINGS OF OPEN PROCEEDINGS OF CONGRESSES;SPEECHES OF THE LEADER; TRANSCRIPTIONS OF PRESS CONFERENCES
WORKS OF ART	WORKS OF ART
6. PORTRAITS, HISTORICAL PAINTINGS, SCENIC SCULPTURE, COINS AND MEDALS	6. STATE-COMMISSIONED DRAMAS, DANCES, MUSICAL COMPOSITIONS; PAINTINGS AND STATUARY; NATIONAL SHRINES; TOMBS OF GREAT LEADERS, e.g., LENIN'S TOMB.
7. CERTAIN KINDS OF FILMS, KINESCOPE, ETC.	7. STATE PRODUCED RADIO AND TELEVISION DRAMATIZATIONS; PROPAGANDA FILMS, ETC.
RELICS (UNPREMEDITATED TRANSMITTERS OF FACTS)	**RELICS** (UNPREMEDITATED TRANSMITTERS OF FACTS)*
8. HUMAN REMAINS, LETTERS, LITERATURE, PUBLIC DOCUMENTS, BUSINESS RECORDS	8. INTERCEPTED CORRESPONDENCE AND OTHER COMMUNICATION: CAPTURED PLANS, ORDERS AND REPORTS; BILLS OF SALE; SHIPPING DOCUMENTS; PRODUCTION FIGURES; BUDGETS; ORGANIZATION CHARTS.
9. LANGUAGE, CUSTOMS, AND INSTITUTIONS	9. CREATION OF NEW WORDS (TECHNICAL VOCABULARY): CAREFUL AND SELECTED USE OF DIPLOMATIC LANGUAGE;ATTEMPTS TO EXPUNGE THE WORKS OF EARLIER SPOKESMEN.
10. TOOLS AND OTHER ARTIFACTS	10. CAPTURED WEAPONARY, UNIFORMS AND EQUIPMENT

* TO THE LIST OF UNPREMEDITATED TRANSMITTERS OF INTELLIGENCE FACTS SHOULD BE ADDED RADIATIONS AND EMISSIONS: e.g., LIGHT, ELECTROMAGNETIC RADIATIONS, HEAT (IR), PARTICLES, ACOUSTIC, AND SEISMIC.

example, he may limit his input to only one source and thus exclude other potentially valuable collateral information. He may be unsystematic in his selection and collection of data, or he may use analysis techniques that are inappropriate for his data.

For example, one of the authors noted that propaganda analysts were performing statistical analyses of North Korean propaganda when the initial assumptions of the statistics were not satisfied. Frequency counts, means, and standard deviations were calculated on data that were not obtained in any systematic manner. In order to perform statistical analyses, the data has to be obtained from the same source, at the same times, for a specified period. However, even "random" sampling must be done systematically if any meaningful statistical analyses are to be performed on the data.

Anticipating the existence of bias permits the researcher to take appropriate safeguards and, at the minimum, to treat his data with skepticism. Much harder to anticipate are potential biases inherent in the researcher himself, particularly cultural biases, which not only affect the way a researcher may feel, but may also affect the manner in which a researcher actually perceives reality.[5] One method of possibly reducing the effects of bias is to use a variety of sources as rigorously and as systematically as possible.

SOURCES OF RESEARCH DATA: PEOPLE, OBJECTS, EMANATIONS, AND RECORDS

Sources of research data may be people, objects, emanations, and records. As mentioned earlier, the sources may be primary or secondary. Regardless of the nature of the source, all data from all types of sources must be transformed ultimately into some symbolic form, typically words or numbers.

People

Human sources of research data may be subject matter specialists, or they may be "information specialists." Examples of subject matter specialists would be analysts at various desks in the different governmental agencies, journalists, scientists and engineers (employed by the U.S. government or under contract), scholars, émigrés, defectors, eyewitnesses, or participants (in an event, a movement, an organization, or an operation). These specialists can help the researcher by providing substantive answers to specific questions and by indicating additional sources of information. These additional sources could be other human sources or documentary sources.

Sometimes the human sources of data are also the subject of the research. For example, the former KGB agents interviewed by John Barron for his book *KGB: The Secret Work of Soviet Secret Agents*[6] were both primary sources of information about the KGB's organization and operations as well as the primary subjects of the book.

Analysts, scholars, or journalists who specialize in certain subject matter areas know the literature in their field and can save the investigator many hours of searching by indicating the best or most recent literature relating to the researcher's needs. When time is critical, this preliminary literature screening is invaluable.

But for increasing research *efficiency*, the information specialist excels. Information specialists are those who are intimately familiar with the holdings of various repositories and who are trained in the techniques of retrieving information. Information specialists include those whose tasks include procuring, cataloging, and retrieving documents (i.e., librarians, in the traditional sense) and those who specialize in retrieving data from automated systems. These resource personnel can assist the researcher, again, by indicating likely sources of information, but equally importantly, by helping the researcher devise efficient search strategies. For example, the librarian can identify indexes relating to various subjects, and use of these indexes can save the researcher many hours of poring through card catalogs. The librarian may also be able to identify special holdings, for example, certain kinds of classified information or private or public collections of works relating to a specific topic, and again save the researcher time. Data processing experts can help the researcher formulate queries for machine processing so that the response is tailored to the researcher's specific requirements.[7]

Not to be overlooked are research assistants. Admittedly, research assistants may not be available for student use, but major commands and the larger intelligence organizations may have personnel available who are well trained in gathering documentation from various libraries and other repositories.

Objects

Objects are more often the subject of research than they are a source of research information. However, the characteristics of an object may suggest something about its origin and intended use, and in this sense, an object is at least a source of inferences if not an actual transmitter of facts. A change in the composition of a piece of personal equipment, for example, may indicate a shortage of certain materials, a change in quality or design sophistication may indicate a lack of sufficiently trained production personnel, the absence of certain equipment on later models may indicate that problems were encountered with the equipment on earlier models, and machine stampings indicate the country that produced the item.

In intelligence research, the objects of concern are weapons, weapon platforms, and equipment—configurational, navigational, logistical, medical, transportational, and personal. Unless the intelligence researcher is technically competent to "exploit" a piece of equipment himself, he will require assistance from other human sources. Where appropriate resource personnel could be located would depend upon the service to which the piece of equipment would be of primary concern. Equipment specialists in various branches of the Army could also provide consultative assistance.

Exactly where to go for what type of assistance is difficult to spell out. For example, fire direction radar on an antiaircraft weapon might be considered the purview of the Air Force, whereas radar used for battlefield surveillance would be of primary interest to Army electronics specialists. Furthermore, one technical intelligence organization may be concerned only with selected aspects of a piece of equipment. Coordination with the appropriate agencies must follow established chains of command. Agency liaison and service personnel at the Defense Intelligence School can provide guidance in coordinating contacts with the various agencies. Information for coordinating visits can be obtained directly from the agencies or organizations to be visited.

Emanations

Emanations refer to those detectable phenomena given off or radiated by natural or man-made objects. Since virtually every war-making device gives off certain emanations, the detection and classification of these phenomena are critical to the intelligence community. Emanations are essentially bias-free. But bias may be introduced when the human attempts to give meaning to a specific radiation or emanation.

Emanations are unintentional and unpremeditated transmitters of facts, and adversaries often go to great pains to reduce or eliminate them. For example, in the early part of World War II, the German navy began to sustain very high losses in its submarine fleet. Convinced that British airborne radars were detecting waves that were reradiated from the submarines' receivers, the Germans curtailed the use of the receivers. But the casualties continued to mount because the British had developed microwave radars whose signals could not be detected by German receivers, even if they had continued to be used. The fact that British radars operated on frequencies and power output unknown to the Germans forced the Germans to develop methods by which subs could remain submerged, and this gave impetus to the development of the snorkel, a device that permitted submarines to recharge their batteries without surfacing.[8]

Data about emanations are obtained from the outputs of various sensors, and the type of sensor determines the nature of the output. For example, the output may take the form of imagery (photographic, infrared, or multispectral) or magnetic tapes. Exploitation of these data requires highly specialized skills. Furthermore, before the data can be used by the nontechnical analyst or researcher, they must be converted into another form, usually verbal or pictorial.[9] Collection and analysis of emanations constitute some of the most highly classified operations of the intelligence community. Access to these data requires special clearances.

Records

Records exist in symbolic and nonsymbolic forms. Symbolic forms of records include all verbal reports (written and oral, e.g., tape-recorded interviews) and numerical tabulations. Nonsymbolic forms of data include photographs (without annotations) and outputs of other sensors, which are usually contained on magnetic tape. Until the nonsymbolic forms of records are converted to some symbolic form, they must be considered "raw," unevaluated data. Even many of the symbolic records at the disposal of the intelligence researcher are raw data; for example, the unevaluated intelligence reports.

Using nonsymbolic raw data requires a high degree of specialized technical training, and separate organizations have been created specifically for exploiting these types of data.

Unless the researcher has the appropriate training and skills necessary to work with raw nonsymbolic data, he is advised not to attempt to use them. Raw *symbolic* data are a different matter. Use of these data requires only the skills that all researchers should have developed—skills in establishing the credibility of the source and the plausibility of the contents. Evaluated symbolic data constitute the bulk of the materials with which most researchers work. These data are stored in libraries, archives, repositories, and databases.

SUMMARY

- Knowledge of real or potential sources of data is essential for project planning purposes. The nature and extent of the subsequent data collection effort will depend upon the availability of sources.
- Sources are classified as *primary* or *secondary*. A primary source would be a firsthand observer, participant, or recorder of an event or activity. A secondary source is a document prepared based on a primary source. Primary sources are not necessarily better than secondary sources, because some firsthand observers or participants may be poor observers, may be poor recorders, or may deliberately report only that which tends to reflect most favorably on themselves.
- Data or information may be classified also on the basis of whether or not the medium by which a fact is transmitted was created intentionally or unintentionally. Examples of intentional transmitters of facts would be diaries, chronicles, and annals. Examples of unintentional transmitters of facts would be customs, tools, relics, and artifacts.
- The concern for possible bias should be taken into account when selecting sources of data. Bias may be inherent in the data, or may be introduced inadvertently by the researcher.
- Sources of research data include people, objects, emanations, and records.
- The researcher's tasks in the planning (or problem definition) phase are to determine what kinds of data he needs, who or what are the best sources of these data, and where the data are located.
- For archival data, the librarian can provide invaluable assistance. In addition to actually procuring needed reference material, the librarian can also assist the researcher by helping him define his data requirements more precisely.

NOTES

1. The Late Cornelius Ryan, author of *The Longest Day*, *The Last Battle*, and *A Bridge Too Far* (New York: Simon and Schuster), used the same technique as Marshall, interviewing literally hundreds of participants in order to reconstruct an accurate account of what happened at Normandy, Berlin, and Arnhem, respectively.

2. Jacques Barzun and Henry F. Graff, *The Modern Researcher*, 1st Harbinger Books edition (New York: Harcourt, Brace and World, 1962), 147–148. Strangely, Barzun and Graff classify letters, public documents, and business records as "unpremeditated transmitters of facts." Yet it seems that the only purpose for which most of these "relics" would be produced would be to record for later use an account of that which took place at the time the record was made.

3. Morison states that the Japanese Navy section of the Imperial General Headquarters accepted their pilots' reports of U.S. losses at face value and issued a communiqué prior to the invasion of Leyte that U.S. Third Fleet losses included eleven carriers, two battleships, three cruisers, and one destroyer. In addition, eight carriers, two battleships, four cruisers, and thirteen unidentified other ships were reported as damaged and set afire. Although Japanese naval officers said after the war that they did not believe these claims, the Army section of the Imperial General Headquarters did believe them, and had begun to modify the defense plans of the Philippines accordingly. Samuel Eliot Morison, *History of United States Naval Operations in World War II*, vol. 12, *Leyte, June 1944–January 1945* (Boston: Little, Brown and Company, 1961), 108–109.

4. Interestingly, a two-page advertisement in *The New York Times* (March 16, 1975) paid for by the Information Section of the Office of the Permanent Observer of the Democratic People's Republic of Korea, mentioned the existence of a black market and a "peasant market" in the otherwise utopian socialist society of North Korea.

5. Benjamin Lee Whorfs, "The Relation of Habitual Thought and Behavior to Language," is a masterpiece in this respect. The essay discusses the effects of language, one of the more profound manifestations of culture, on perception. The essay can be found in Leslie Spier, ed., *Language, Culture and Personality: Essays in Memory of Edward Sapir* (Menasha, WI: Sapir Memorial Fund, 1941).

6. John Barron, *KGB: The Secret Work of Soviet Secret Agents* (New York: Reader's Digest Press, 1974).

7. An intelligence analyst queried his system for information relating to underground structures. Unfortunately, the "structure" part of the query was not made clear, and the machine "dumped" everything relating to underground organizations, the French Maquis, guerrilla warfare, unconventional warfare, and so on since World War II.

8. Jerome A. O'Connell, "Radar and the U-Boat," *United States Naval Institute Proceedings* 89 (September 1963): 53–65. This anecdote also illustrates the dangers of faulty assumptions. German electronic specialists assumed that since they had not been able to develop radars in certain frequencies, neither could the Allies.

9. Infrared (and other) imagery may be converted to digital data for certain types of analysis, then back into some pictorial form for other types of analysis.

7

Foundations of Analysis: Some Basic Concepts

On the night of March 20, 1935, Berthold Jacob, a German journalist living in London, was kidnapped from a restaurant in Basel, Switzerland, and taken to Gestapo headquarters in Berlin. Jacob's offense: publishing a book about the German General Staff, a book so detailed that even rifle platoons constituting the newly formed Panzer divisions were identified.

How did he get his information? Who were his sources? Where was the security leak? These were questions the interrogators asked Jacob. The answer, to the consternation (and grudging admiration) of the interrogators, was the German press. Over a period of months and years, Jacob noted, recorded, and compiled press releases, obituaries, wedding announcements, and articles from Geffilan military journals. No leaks existed; no agents and no informers were involved—only a body of "open" source material available to anyone with an "analytic mind."

Data collected in the preceding phase are mobilized in the analysis phase of a research program. This phase constitutes the moment of truth of any research project. It is in this phase that assumptions, hypotheses, and guesses are put to the test. It is in this phase that interpretations, significance, and meaning are ascribed to the data. This chapter discusses basic concepts that underlie *all* types of analytic processes, regardless of whether the processes are performed by an intelligence analyst or performed in the larger context of intelligence research. Topics covered in this chapter include rules for verification, causality and correlation, canons (or rules) for establishing causality, and the sometimes nebulous distinction between quantitative and qualitative approaches to analysis.

ANALYSIS

Analysis has been defined as the process of breaking down a problem into its component parts and studying the elements separately; as the mental process of "handling of data by the analyst for the purpose of incorporating the data . . . into the text of a report"; and as the "minute examination of related items to determine the extent to which they confirm, supplement, or contradict each other and thereby to establish accepted facts and relationships."[1]

There are subtle distinctions between the use of the term *analysis* in intelligence production and the use of the term in research, but essentially the term connotes breaking down larger components or elements of a problem into smaller units, performing mental (and sometimes physical) operations on collected data, and, on the basis of the operations performed, arriving at a generalization or conclusion about the larger problem that is being addressed. In the technical terminology of intelligence, *analysis* is usually the term that is applied to all activities and processes performed on collected data, including the formulation of hypotheses, the determination of the relevance and validity of the data, and the collation and classification. In conventional research terminology, some of these activities would be performed in different phases of a research program. For example, hypotheses would be formulated during the problem definition phases, and relevance of data would be addressed during the data collection phase.[2] Interestingly, the term *analysis* is derived from the Greek words *ana*, which means "up," and *lyein*, which means "to loosen," hence, "to loosen up" the data, a most appropriate description of the operation.

INDUCTION AND DEDUCTION: A SHORT REVIEW

It will be recalled from the earlier chapters that deductive reasoning is the act of drawing conclusions from previously formulated premises. It is the type of reasoning that is used, for example, when mathematical proofs are established. And when used in closed systems such as mathematics, deduction is "safe, beyond controversy, and final." Deduction is sometimes referred to as *demonstrative* reasoning because it is used to demonstrate the truth and validity of a conclusion given certain premises.

In contrast to deduction is induction. Induction, it will be recalled, is the process of arriving at a generalization on the basis of one or more observations. Unlike deduction, which simply makes clear what is already known, induction provides new knowledge. Furthermore, induction or *plausible reasoning* invariably precedes deduction, and it is the type of reasoning that analysts and researchers are required to perform more frequently. Induction involves the processes of discovery and verification. With respect to the act of discovery, general rules or guidelines are nonexistent. For example, Polya states, "The first rule of discovery is to have brains and good luck. The second rule of discovery is to sit tight and wait until you get a bright idea"—hardly comforting admonitions to the analyst or researcher facing a deadline.

However, with respect to verification, the second part of the inductive process, there are certain guidelines that the researcher may find useful. Induction can never yield "truth" with the rigor that deduction can demonstrate. Induction, on the other hand, can yield highly plausible conclusions that can be tested over time. Since verification constitutes an important part of the analytic process, general "rules" for performing verification are discussed below. These general rules for verification apply equally to the use of qualitative or quantitative data as well as to every type of analysis in which an analyst or researcher is required to arrive at some conclusion.

SEVEN GENERAL RULES FOR VERIFICATION

The product of the process of induction is a generalization. Having arrived at a generalization (guess, conjecture, hypothesis), the researcher's problem changes from one of *discovery* to one of *verification*. Described below are seven general rules for determining the *plausibility* of a generalization. Note: the rules are methods for establishing *likelihood*, not *certainty*, that a generalization is true. The general rules are paraphrases of Polya's rules for plausible reasoning.[3]

1. *A generalization is more believable when a consequence of that generalization is verified.* For example, an analyst might generalize on the basis of earlier observations and information that a new missile being developed by a foreign country was nearing an operational stage. This generalization would be strengthened should photographs of a test facility reveal burn marks on the concrete apron where a missile's propulsion system was tested. Clearly, the burn marks do not prove that a missile's propulsion system was working well, but the marks are *not inconsistent* with a successful test on the pad.

2. *The credibility of a generalization increases as the different means used to test the generalization support it.* To return to the operational status of a missile, should a country declare the airspace near its missile test range off-limits for a certain period, the credibility of the initial generalization of the researcher or analyst that the missile was nearing operational status would increase. The observation of increased activity at the test range would further tend to support the initial generalization, as would increased communication traffic on the nets used for test purposes.

3. *Confidence in a generalization increases as the observable bits of evidence that support the generalization bear some proximity to each other.* Proximity can be expressed in terms of time or geographic location. In the example above, increased activity at a test range and the declaration that the airspace over the test range was restricted bore both chronological and geographical proximity to each other.

4. *The credibility of a generalization is directly proportional to the number of instances in which the generalization was supported.* Stated somewhat differently, every time a generalization is supported by new bits of evidence, the strength (plausibility) of that generalization increases.

5. *Confidence in a generalization increases when an incompatible and rival conjecture is refuted.* In the example of the missile test above, the burn marks on the concrete apron could have been caused by an accidental explosion. However, if the test facilities around the test stand showed no indication of damage, this hypothesis would be discounted and the original conjecture would be strengthened.

6. *Confidence in a generalization increases to the extent that it is consistent with another generalization that is highly credible.* For example, if the country in which the status of the missile was in question invariably followed the same sequence of test and development phases that another country followed about which more information was available, the researcher or analyst would tend to have more confidence in predicting the next event in the missile's developmental cycle. This is tantamount to reasoning by analogy, and although this is a fallacious type of reasoning *in logic*, it is a very practical and common procedure in intelligence research and analysis.

7. *In instances in which observables support two different generalizations, the simpler generalization stands a better chance of being true.* In the missile test example cited earlier, it would be

conceivable that the missile's propulsion system had failed during the tests, but, in order to convey the impression that development was progressing according to schedule, spurious positive indications had been generated intentionally. This is certainly not an impossibility, but the simpler explanation (that the test had been successful) intuitively appears more plausible.

CAUSALITY AND CORRELATION

A fundamental concern in intelligence research and analysis is the identification of causal factors.[4] Intelligence research is concerned with identifying causal factors because these factors permit one to predict or to anticipate results and effects. In certain types of intelligence analysis, causal factors can be identified readily, and the effects of these causal factors can be predicted accurately. Not surprisingly, these are the areas of scientific and technical intelligence. For example, the range of a missile is proportional to the velocity of the missile at burnout. Thus, given the velocity of a new missile at burnout, the range of that missile can be estimated.

In the "softer" types of intelligence, analysts are not so fortunate. Not only are the effects of certain variables unpredictable, but there may also be little agreement as to what constitutes the causal or contributing factors in the first place. It is because of this basic inability to establish causes rigorously that intelligence is (and probably always will be) referred to as an art or a craft rather than a science. The case for causality is not hopeless, of course, and there are many instances in which at least a plausible if not a definitive case can be made for stating that a certain event, condition, or phenomenon brought about another phenomenon, or that a given event will bring about a certain type of response or reaction. Because this function is so basic to intelligence research and analysis, attention will be paid to procedures by which causal factors can be determined.

Perhaps one of the most common methods for establishing causality is to consider initially those events or conditions that are correlated. Correlations may be said to exist when two or more phenomena occur or vary in relation to each other. Obviously, because two phenomena occur or vary together does not imply that one phenomenon is the cause of the other. For example, there may be a positive correlation between height and weight, but, obviously, one trait is not the cause of the other, because some people are tall and light and others are short and heavy. But the ability to establish correlations is often a first step in establishing causes, and established correlations permit one to generalize from characteristics of a known phenomenon to characteristics of an unknown (but correlated) phenomenon.

Correlations are used very often in current intelligence and estimative/predictive intelligence analysis. "Indicators," for example, are signs or manifestations that are associated (correlated) with certain events. Certain events or conditions are titled "precursors" because they had been correlated with other events that occurred later. Certain precursors are not only related factors, but may also be causal factors. When two events, conditions, or characteristics vary together and in the same direction (e.g., an increase in weight correlated with an increase in size), a *positive* correlation is said to exist. When two events vary inversely to each other (e.g., an increase in size correlated with a decrease in speed), a *negative* correlation is said to exist. From the standpoint of inferring an unknown characteristic on the basis of a known and correlated characteristic, it does not matter which type of correlation exists. What is important, of course, is to understand (1) that two phenomena are directly related, and (2) the manner in which they are related, negatively or positively.

Reliability refers to the extent to which successive measurements of the same phenomenon would yield the same results (negatively or positively) of how they are related.[5] Perhaps this point is obvious, but the authors have encountered many researchers who expressed dismay when their tests revealed negative correlations. Yet, from the standpoint of predicting or inferring from a known to an unknown, a negative correlation may be as useful as a positive correlation.

As an aid to analysis, the establishment or identification of correlated events, activities, conditions, or other phenomena may permit other inferences to be drawn, often with a high degree of predictability. And, as will be discussed below, the identification of correlates is basic to the identification of causal factors.

CANONS OF CAUSALITY

The ability to establish causality is essential to valid prediction. As W. Stanley Jevons put it, "a cause is defined as the necessary or invariable antecedent of an event, so that when the cause exists the effect will also exist or will soon follow. If then we know the cause of an event, we know what will certainly happen."[6] Although intuitively the researcher may feel that certain factors "caused" or brought about a certain result, it is essential that at some point in his analysis he replaces his intuition with stronger, more "public" evidence. In short, it is necessary that he subject his speculations to certain tests. One set of tests of causality are the rules set forth by the utilitarian philosopher John Stuart Mill. The rules are commonly referred to as "Mill's Canons." They epitomize the scientific method (most experimental designs incorporate them in one way or another), and although they are not without their detractors (Jevons being one), they are most relevant to intelligence analysis. The "canons" are paraphrased below.

1. *If two or more instances of a phenomenon have only one characteristic or feature in common, the single characteristic or feature that exists in all instances is the cause (or effect) of the given phenomenon.* Applied to intelligence research or analysis, this canon might be applicable in instances in which, for example, the presence of a Soviet missile expert had been noted at various test sites prior to the firing of a new missile. Diagrammed, this canon would look like this (figure 7.1).

2. *If an instance in which a phenomenon occurs and an instance in which a phenomenon does not occur have every characteristic or feature in common but one, and that one feature was present only when the phenomenon occurred, then that single characteristic (feature or circumstance) is the cause, an important part of the cause, or the effect of the phenomenon.* For example, in the case of the missile expert's association with test firings, this canon would apply when all conditions existed for a test firing *except* the presence of the missile expert (and, of course, the nonoccurrence of a missile firing). See figure 7.2.

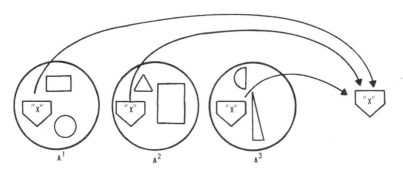

$A^{1,2,3}$ — DIFFERENT INSTANCES OF THE SAME TYPE OF PHENOMENON (e.g., MISSILE TEST FIRINGS)

"X" — THE SINGLE FEATURE COMMON TO ALL OCCURRENCES OF THE PHENOMENON, i.e., THE CAUSE, AN IMPORTANT PART OF THE CAUSE, OR THE EFFECT OF THE PHENOMENA

Figure 7.1. Mill's First Canon

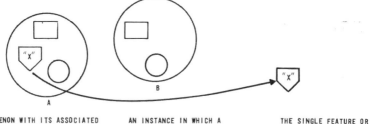

THE PHENOMENON WITH ITS ASSOCIATED
CHARACTERISTICS, FEATURES, OR
CIRCUMSTANCES..e.g., THE PRESENCE OF
A MISSILE EXPERT AT A TEST SITE, AND
THE FIRING OF A MISSILE.

AN INSTANCE IN WHICH A
PHENOMENON DID NOT OCCUR
(NO MISSILE WAS FIRED), BUT
IN WHICH ALL CONDITIONS EXCEPT
THE PRESENCE OF THE MISSILE
EXPERT EXISTED.

THE SINGLE FEATURE OR
CIRCUMSTANCE THAT IS
THE CAUSE, AN IMPORTANT
PART OF THE CAUSE, OR
THE EFFECT OF THE
PHENOMENON..

Figure 7.2.   Mill's Second Canon

3. *If two or more instances in which the phenomenon occur have only one feature, condition, or circumstance in common, while other instances in which the phenomenon does not occur have nothing in common except the absence of that single condition, the condition that sets the instances apart is the cause, an important part of the cause, or the effect of the phenomenon.* For example, if two instances were encountered in which the presence of a new radar could be associated with exceptionally accurate air defenses, and several instances were encountered in which these radars were not detected and in which the air defenses were no more accurate than usual, the cause of the increased accuracy of the air defenses could be attributable to the newly detected radars (figure 7.3).

4. *For any phenomenon, list all of the pertinent antecedent conditions. Then, determine which parts of the phenomenon were*

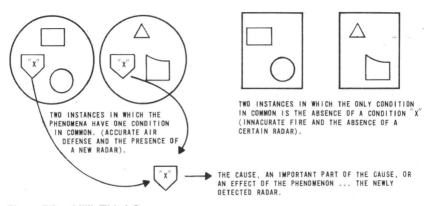

TWO INSTANCES IN WHICH THE
PHENOMENA HAVE ONE CONDITION
IN COMMON. (ACCURATE AIR
DEFENSE AND THE PRESENCE OF
A NEW RADAR).

TWO INSTANCES IN WHICH THE ONLY CONDITION
IN COMMON IS THE ABSENCE OF A CONDITION "x"
(INNACURATE FIRE AND THE ABSENCE OF A
CERTAIN RADAR).

THE CAUSE, AN IMPORTANT PART OF THE CAUSE, OR
AN EFFECT OF THE PHENOMENON ... THE NEWLY
DETECTED RADAR.

Figure 7.3.   Mill's Third Canon

caused by specific antecedents and subtract these parts from the overall phenomenon. The remaining parts of the phenomenon are the effects of the remaining antecedents. This canon is most appropriate for laboratory situations or in situations in which all pertinent antecedent conditions can be identified. But the identification of all relevant antecedent conditions may be extremely difficult in unstructured situations. As tenuous as this canon may appear, in reality it is applied quite often. For example, in scientific and technical intelligence analysis, the components and functions of a piece of captured equipment would be identified. Control devices would be associated with various functions. Functions for which control devices would not be identified initially would be controlled by the remaining devices not related to other functions. In layman's terms, this activity is referred to as the process of elimination (figure 7.4).

5. *When a phenomenon varies whenever another phenomenon varies, the first phenomenon is a cause of, the effect of, or is connected to the second phenomenon.* (This is a succinct statement of the relationship of correlation to causality discussed in the previous section.) For example, certain unknown telemetry signals might be associated with certain maneuvers of a missile that was being tracked by friendly radars. The extent to which the signals changed *invariantly* with maneuvers of the missile would be the extent to which those signals would be considered the cause of the missile's maneuvers (figure 7.5).

Obviously, causes always exist or occur *before* effects. Admittedly, the difference in time might be measurable in only nanoseconds, but

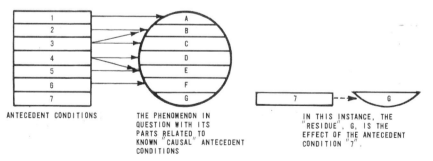

ANTECEDENT CONDITIONS

THE PHENOMENON IN QUESTION WITH ITS PARTS RELATED TO KNOWN "CAUSAL" ANTECEDENT CONDITIONS

IN THIS INSTANCE, THE "RESIDUE", G, IS THE EFFECT OF THE ANTECEDENT CONDITION "7".

Figure 7.4. Mill's Fourth Canon

Figure 7.5.   Mill's Fifth Canon

A must precede B if A is to be identified as the cause of B. Finally, it should be apparent that causal factors are always correlated factors, but not all correlated factors are causal factors.

"QUANTITATIVE" AND "QUALITATIVE" ANALYSIS: A NEBULOUS DISTINCTION

It is a truism to say that analysts and researchers are concerned with the rigor of their investigation. But what may not be so obvious is that one of the ways by which researchers attempt to attain rigor (or at least give the impression of rigor) may be fallacious. Specifically, naive researchers assume that the presentation of information in "quantitative" terms somehow enhances the quality of the information or increases the reliability and validity of the conclusions. This is erroneous, of course, but the mystique of numbers persists. Casting crude observations into some statistical form will not improve quality of the research, nor will highly precise quantification of badly classified information yield anything more substantive than what there was initially.[7]

A misunderstanding of the application of statistics to any type of studious inquiry is reflected in the persisting dichotomy between qualitative and quantitative research or between nonstatistical and statistical approaches. But qualitative and quantitative approaches are merely logical extensions of each other. For example, that which is measured or quantified is always a quality. Quantification is a method of expressing a quality with more precision *if*—and this is critical—*if* that quality is defined with sufficient clarity to permit reliable measurement.[8]

By the same token, there is implied measurement in many of the concepts that would normally be considered qualitative. For example, to say that one government is *more* belligerent than another implies a comparison of degrees of belligerency, a crude form of measurement. A political scientist who comments upon the high degree of political cohesiveness within a certain country is making a quantitative statement about a quality. When analysts or researchers couch their degrees of certainty about an event's occurrence in terms of "it is almost certain that," or "it is highly probable (or improbable) that," they are making qualitative statements that are in fact quantifiable in terms of probabilities. The Sherman Kent chart (figure 7.6) is a device for converting qualities of intelligence statements into quantitative expressions of likelihood.

CHANCES FOR - AGAINST	
100 – 0	CERTAINTY NO ESTIMATE
99 – 1 85 – 15	ALMOST CERTAIN. HIGHLY LIKELY.
84 – 16 55 – 45	PROBABLE. LIKELY. PROBABLY. WE BELIEVE.........
51 – 49	CHANCES JUST BETTER THAN EVEN. ON BALANCE......
50 – 50	CHANCES ARE EVEN.
49 – 51	CHANCES JUST LESS THAN EVEN.
45 – 55 16 – 84	IT IS DOUBTFUL. WE DOUBT. IMPROBABLE. UNLIKELY. PROBABLY NOT.
15 – 85 1 – 99	ALMOST CERTAINLY NOT. HIGHLY UNLIKELY. CHANCES ARE SLIGHT.
0 – 100	IMPOSSIBILITY NO ESTIMATE

Figure 7.6. Sherman Kent Chart, Converting Qualitative Judgments in Quantitative Terms (and Vice Versa)

The distinction between approaches becomes even more tenuous when the various scales used for measurement are considered. The nominal scale, for example, is essentially a nonquantitative scale for assigning elements to various categories, and ordinal scales are "quantitative" only in the sense that the elements measured are rank-ordered in terms of magnitude.[9] The important concern in any type of analysis is precision, but analysis cannot increase the precision of data that were collected "imprecisely," or of data that are poorly defined.

SUMMARY

- The term analysis has slightly different connotations in intelligence research and in academic research. Despite the subtle distinctions, *analysis* in both contexts refers to breaking down a large problem into a number of smaller problems and performing mental (and sometimes physical) operations on the data in order to arrive at a conclusion or generalization.
- Deduction and induction are two basic mental operations performed on data. Deduction is referred to as demonstrative reasoning because it is the process used to demonstrate the truth and validity of a conclusion. Induction is sometimes referred to as plausible reasoning. It is the type of reasoning one employs in discovering and verifying generalizations. It is also the process used most commonly in problem solving.
- Although formal rules exist for deduction, no formal rules exist for induction. Nevertheless, certain generalizations can be stated in terms of conditions that increase the plausibility of a generalization being true. These generalizations were stated as *rules for verification* or *rules of plausible reasoning*.
- The ability to establish the cause of an effect is basic to predicting outcomes. Therefore, scientists and intelligence researchers are very much concerned with establishing cause-and-effect relationships.
- A correlation always exists between causes and effects, but not all correlations are causal relationships.
- Commonly used rules for establishing causal relationships are John Stuart Mill's canons, which were described in this chapter.
- Distinctions between quantitative analysis and qualitative analysis become tenuous when it is recognized that what is quantified is always a quality, and that certain distinctions based on qualitative features often reflect a basic form of measurement or quantification.

- Simply because a phenomenon was expressed in quantitative terms does not necessarily imply that the research was rigorous. Even the most rigorous mathematical or statistical analysis cannot improve the quality of poor data.

NOTES

1. Armed Forces Staff College, "Intelligence for Joint Forces" (Norfolk, Virginia: Armed Forces Staff College, 1966).

2. In the technical terminology of intelligence, *analysis* is usually the term that is applied to all activities and processes performed on collected data, including the formulation of hypotheses, the determination of the relevance and validity of the data, and collation and classification. In conventional research terminology, some of these activities would be performed in different phases of a research program. For example, hypotheses would be formulated during the problem definition phase, and relevance of data would be addressed during the data collection phase.

3. George Polya, *Mathematics and Plausible Reasoning*, vol. 2, *Patterns of Plausible Inference* (Princeton, NJ: Princeton University Press, 1954), v. George Polya, the Stanford University mathematician, is perhaps the leading contemporary advocate of "plausible reasoning." In five separate but related works, Polya attempts to refine the science (or art) of problem solving or heuristics, as it is formally called. Polya is quick to point out that it would be naive to believe that any given set of rules of problem solving could be applied universally to all kinds of problems. He does make an excellent case, however, for developing rules of discovery and verification in his own professional field of mathematics. For the greater part, most of the examples Polya uses to illustrate his "rules" pertain to mathematics. But it takes very little imagination to see how his rules would apply to other domains as well; for example, to intelligence propaganda analysis, or law.

Some years ago, HRB-Singer researchers discussed with Polya the relevancy of heuristics to intelligence analysis. Polya's advice was essentially that heuristics had to be developed specifically for each separate domain. The rules of verification that are suggested in the following pages are attempts to begin structuring a heuristic approach for intelligence analysis. The contribution of Polya is obvious.

4. Nor is it surprising that this is the focus of much basic scientific research—particularly medical research.

5. Also important, of course, is the strength of the correlation (i.e., how well or to what degree two phenomena are correlated). The strength of correlation is partly a function of the sample size. Unfortunately, in intelligence research and analysis, sample sizes tend to be very small.

6. W. Stanley Jevons, *The Principles of Science: A Treatise on Logic and Scientific Method* (New York: Dover Publications, 1958), 222.

7. *Classified* in this context means being assigned to a category.

8. *Reliability* refers to the extent to which successive measurements of the same phenomenon would yield the same results.

9. Four types of scales are used in measurement: nominal, ordinal, interval, and ratio scales. The scales are defined as follows:

  1) Nominal Scale: This scale categorizes qualities. Applied to vehicles, for example, vehicles could be classified, categorized, or measured by their type of propulsion, for example, gasoline-powered or diesel-powered; or aircraft by the nature of their wings, for example, fixed, rotating, or swing. Nominal scales are the type of measurement scales used in classification, a basic step in the analytic process.

  2) Ordinal Scale: This scale categorizes (or classifies) on the basis of qualities that can be rank-ordered; for example, a tracked amphibious vehicle could be classified as being "more mobile" than a wheeled, non-amphibious vehicle. Foreign countries might be rank-ordered in terms of their strategic importance to U.S. national interests.

  3) Interval Scale: This scale has the characteristics of the ordinal scale in addition to numerically equal distances between points on the scale. Fahrenheit and Celsius thermometers are examples of devices using interval scales (the zero point on interval scales is arbitrary).

  4) Ratio Scale: This scale contains an absolute or true zero point in addition to equal units. Examples would be measures of weight, length, and height.

8

Classification: A Basic
Step in Analysis

Classification is the process of assigning information to classes.[1] The process is indispensable in research projects involving large-scale surveys where many cross-tabulations must be performed, and it is often useful in small-scale research studies, not only as a means for expediting data handling, but also as a means of problem solving. Two examples cited in this chapter deal with classification in the biological and physical sciences. Significant discoveries have been made in the sciences as a result of the process of classification, and conceivably, similar "discoveries" can also be made in intelligence.

CLASSIFICATION IN SCIENCE AND INTELLIGENCE

Scientists who are able to assign an object, an organism, an event, a condition, or an activity to a class are often able to infer qualities about the phenomenon that would not be apparent otherwise. For example, a zoologist may have noticed a track of an animal with a four-padded foot and retractable claws. With his knowledge of zoological categories, the zoologist would assign this animal to the class of mammals. (Amphibians have four toes, no claws; reptiles, five toes but non-retractable claws.) Having assigned the unobserved animal to the class of mammals, the zoologist could infer other characteristics about the unseen animal based on class characteristics, namely, that it is a hairy animal and that it nurses its young. The zoologist could infer that, since the animal has retractable claws, it eats meat. As a meat eater, the animal most likely has incisors, canine teeth, and probably molars. Thus, on the basis of one footprint, a zoologist could reconstruct a fairly accurate picture of the unseen animal simply by assigning the observed phenomenon to a class and then inferring other characteristics that all members of the class possessed.

The intelligence counterpart of this analogy can be seen in the analysis of a foreign aircraft's capabilities. For example, the Russian Sukhoi attack aircraft "Fencer," aside from its variable geometry, bears superficial resemblance to the Su-7BM "Fitter." Although close examination of both aircraft reveals distinguishing features, one can assume that the missions are probably comparable, and that the performance of the later "Fencer" would not be any lower than its predecessors, the Su-7 and the Su-17 aircraft. Similarly, the 11-18 medium-range transport is a civilian aircraft that is almost identical to the 11-38 ASW (anti-submarine warfare)/patrol aircraft. Since civilian aircraft are generally more easily observed than are military aircraft, a critical study of this aircraft would suggest characteristics of the less accessible military version.

To show further how classification can be used in intelligence research or analysis, the evolution of the periodic table will be discussed briefly. In 1869, Dmitri Ivanovich Mendeleev published a paper in which he classified the elements according to the properties the elements manifested. He wrote, "When I arranged the elements according to the magnitude of their atomic weights, beginning with the smallest, it became evident there exists a kind of periodicity in their properties . . . I designated the name "periodic law" to the mutual relations between the properties of the elements and their atomic weights. These relations are applicable to all the elements, and have the nature of a periodic function."[2]

Significant is the fact that in certain instances he found that his criterion for classification (the atomic weight) was inappropriate for ordering specific elements. For example, had Mendeleev adhered only to atomic weights, tellurium, with an atomic weight of 127.61, would have come after iodine (126.91). However, on the basis of its other properties, placing tellurium ahead of iodine on a periodic table put it under selenium, which it resembled closely, and iodine then fell under bromine, which it also resembled closely.

The value of this scheme became apparent when Mendeleev, not being able to complete his table, announced that the elements that should fit the empty spaces on his table "must be found." Furthermore, based on the properties of the elements that preceded and followed those spaces, Mendeleev *predicted* what the properties of those elements that still had to be discovered would be. (Within his lifetime, three of his predicted elements were discovered, and the elements had those properties predicted by Mendeleev.)

Creating an order of battle is an intelligence counterpart of constructing a periodic table. For example, based on knowledge of enemy doctrine and from past experience, it might be established that the enemy conventionally employed two units on line while holding one unit in reserve. Based on the identity of one unit on line and another unit, presumably in reserve, and on the basis of the composition of both known units, the composition and possibly the identity of the other unit on line could be inferred tentatively, even though contact with this unit had not yet been made. Of course, the intelligence analyst (just like Mendeleev) does not know for certain what the composition of the missing "element" will be. But he does have a plausible idea.

In another example of how classification permits analysts and researchers to make inferences, an analyst might know that the enemy conventionally deployed a certain weapon system, for example, a SAM complex, in a particular geometric pattern. If the analyst received partial information relating to an unknown weapon system that fitted the deployment pattern of the weapon system known previously to the analyst, the configuration of this pattern would permit the analyst to assign the weapon system to a particular group of weapons. From a knowledge of the group's characteristics, the analyst could infer the configuration of the remainder of the deployment pattern as well as the probable characteristics of that system.

Systematic propaganda analysis or content analysis (of foreign publications, mass media, or public announcements by key military or political figures) is another intelligence application of classification. In its most basic form, systematic content analysis involves the examination of public utterances, the identification of content elements of interest, the assignment of coded utterances (content elements) to predetermined categories, and the analysis of the results of the tabulations (e.g., correlations, interpretations, and so on). Although simply described, the implementation of the procedures may be considerably more difficult. For example, the content element (or better, the recording unit) may be a phrase, several words, or a single term. Thus, recording units must be defined precisely, and the classes or categories to which the recording units are to be assigned also must be defined unambiguously. Rules for assigning recording units to classes may require thesauri that are hundreds of pages long.[3]

WHY CLASSIFY?

Analysts and researchers classify for two main reasons: to understand their data, and for convenience. As an aid to understanding, classifications often reveal relationships that are not perceptible among unorganized data. As relationships are revealed, often additional bases for comparison and prediction can be established. To go back to two examples previously cited, it was by classifying and ordering his data that Mendeleev was able to predict the properties of the missing elements. Similarly, an analyst or a researcher might infer that two different aircraft may have the same performance characteristics if both can be classified in the same category on the basis of structural similarity.

Classifying data also helps the researcher to uncover gaps in his information. And discovering the existence of these gaps is the first step in generating future collection requirements. In addition, a classification system provides the researcher with a comprehensive overview of the structure of his data. It gives him a pattern or a gestalt of the territory with which he is working. But it is for convenience that most researchers classify their data. Having a system of classification permits one to communicate with others in generic or class names rather than having to refer to each specific entity within a class. For example, under most conditions "DO" or "destroyer" is considerably more convenient to use than "Destroyer Preston, No. 795, Later Fletcher Class." (Of course, there are other times when the complete identity must be known.)

Similarly, a classification system permits the researcher to free his mind of myriad details and to concentrate essentially on group characteristics or properties of the *class* of phenomena with which he is dealing. Since classified data are also indexed data, they can be retrieved easily. Consequently, the researcher with a classification system has a device for filtering detail when only class properties are important, as well as a device for recalling specifics when needed. In short, classifying permits the analyst to convert infinite amounts of data into finite manageable elements that can be stored and retrieved.

Another convenience a well-designed classification system provides is a method for accommodating new input without requiring extensive alteration of the files every time addition data are received. With an exhaustive classification system, a researcher can accommodate new data simply by expanding categories he had already established.

Finally, in terms of convenience to the user, classification systems permit any number of people to use the same system as long as the underlying rationale of the system is understood. The rationale of the system refers to the rules by which data are assigned to certain classes (or entered into the system) and the rules by which data can be retrieved. In fact, once the rules are spelled out explicitly, the actual classification, storage, and retrieval of data can be automated.

CODING: A BASIC TYPE OF CLASSIFICATION

The most basic type of classification process and, perhaps, the process most familiar to analysts and researchers, is the process of coding. Admittedly, coding is done primarily when large quantities of data are processed. But coding may also performed profitably when relatively small projects are undertaken. Coding involves two basic steps: (1) organizing the data into classes and (2) assigning a number or a symbol to the item according to the class in which it falls. This relatively simple process is required whenever computers are used. Every piece of data entered into a computer's database is a classified and coded piece of information. But coding and classifying data help the analyst in the manual analysis of data as well.

The summary sheets in figures 8.1 and 8.2 contain examples of personal data and responses to specific questions that might have been made during an interrogation of PWs. Initially, information would be

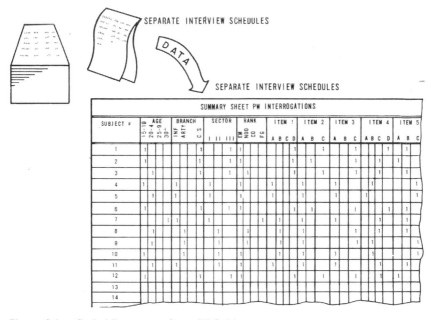

Figure 8.1.   Coded Responses from All Subjects

AGGREGATED RESPONSES OF PW INTERROGATIONS

	RESPONSES																
PERSONAL DATA	ITEM 1				ITEM 2			ITEM 3			ITEM 4				ITEM 5		
	A	B	C	D	A	B	C	A	B	C	A	B	C	D	A	B	C
AGE (N)																	
15-19 (41)	19	18		4	9	30	2	26	11	4		12	22	7	23	15	3
20-24 (44)	21	22		1	34		10	23	18	3	10	27	3	4	9	33	2
25-29 (3)		3			3			3					3			2	1
30 - (1)		1			1			1					1		1		
TOTALS (89)	40	44	0	5	47	30	12	53	29	7	10	39	29	11	32	51	6
BRANCH																	
INFANTRY (71)	30	41			39	26	6	43	27	1	9	36	23	3	28	41	2
ARTILLERY (13)	10	3			8	4	1	10	2	1	1	3	3	6	2	9	2
COM/SUPP (5)				5			5			5			3	2	2	1	2
TOTALS	40	44	0	5	47	30	12	53	29	7	10	39	29	11	32	51	6
SECTOR																	
I (67)	28	39			39	27	1	42	26	1	5	35	23	4	14	47	6
II (15)	12	3			6	3	5	9	3	1	3	3	3	6	11	4	0
III (7)		2		5	1		6	1		5	2	1	1	3	7	0	0
TOTALS	40	44	0	5	47	30	12	53	29	7	10	39	29	11	32	51	6
RANK																	
EM (78)	39	39			46	30	2	52	25	1	1	39	28	10	32	45	1
NCO (6)	1	4		1			6		4	2	5			1		5	1
CO/G (4)				4			4			4	4						4
FLD/G (1)		1			1			1					1		1		
TOTALS	40	44	0	5	47	30	12	53	29	7	10	39	29	11	32	51	6

Figure 8.2.　Responses Tabulated by Category

recorded on separate interview schedules or questionnaires. Obviously, data in this form is nearly impossible to handle. Furthermore, data on any single form would reveal information from and about a single subject, but it would not reveal any pattern of responses from the group of PWs as a whole. However, coding the responses on the basis of predetermined classes permits the analysis of group responses simply by tabulating categories of responses.

Figure 8.1 is a record of all individual responses. Figure 8.2 shows how the same data can be aggregated for additional analysis. It can be seen, for example, that the responses from all company grade officers were consistent, but were dissimilar to responses made by the other subjects, and that the responses made by infantry and artillery personnel tended to be similar, but unlike the responses made by support personnel. Admittedly, the sample size is relatively small, and the differences might not be significant statistically, but patterns of responses do emerge from tabulations of this nature. Should these data be entered into a computer, any number of runs could be made, which might reveal additional patterns of responses that are not perceptible on the aggregated response tabulation; for example, correlations between age and rank, correlations between branch and age, or correlations between sector and branch of service.

In the example just cited, the sample size (n) was only eighty-nine. If the sample size were considerably larger, data processing equipment should be used.[4] Of course, if any statistical analysis (other than counting) had to be performed on the data, a computer, or at least a hand calculator, would be needed.

TWO MEANINGS OF *CLASSIFY*

As a verb, *classify* has two meanings. In one sense, it refers to the act of assigning a specific datum to a predetermined position in a classification scheme. In another sense, *classify* relates to the act of breaking down data and organizing them according to related subclasses. Strictly speaking, this second operation is called division. To illustrate the first meaning of *classify*, that is, to assign a specific datum to a predetermined slot, the activities of an intercept receiver operator who detects a radar signal can be cited. The operator might identify a signal as originating from an early warning radar because the signal's parameters were all associated with a particular group of early warning radars. In this case, the predetermined upper and lower limits of each signal parameter would constitute the criteria for group assignment.[5]

To illustrate the second meaning of *classify*, that is, breaking down data and organizing them into classes, the activities of an analyst whose concern was military vehicles could be cited. Here, the analyst could divide the general class of military vehicles into any number of subclasses. For example, he might classify vehicles based on modes of propulsion, number of axles, general use, weight, and so on. The discussion that follows will relate essentially to this second meaning of the term (i.e., division).

THE STEPS IN CLASSIFICATION

The process of classification can be broken down into five steps. There are no hard and fast rules to follow, nor is there strict sequence, although it is difficult to see how an object can be assigned to a class before the class criteria are established. The steps are as follows.

1. *The purpose or purposes the classification system is intended to serve must be determined.* This is important because the purpose the system is to serve suggests the type of system that should be used.

Students of taxonomy (the science of classification) recognize two basic types of classification systems: *natural* systems and *artificial* systems. Natural classification systems are based upon the fundamental properties of the thing being classified, such as the number of parts, dimensions, color, or shape. Examples of natural systems would include the periodic table described previously, botanical classifications based on the floral parts of the plant, a classification of radars based on frequencies and other signal properties, or a classification of aircraft based on the mode of propulsion, number of engines, and so on.

An artificial classification, on the other hand, reflects primarily the user's needs. Examples of artificial systems would include a classification of radars on the basis of the country in which they were manufactured, a classification of aircraft as "bogey" or "friendly," a classification of coasts and landing beaches according to the extent to which they permit landing operations, and so on.

Halfway between completely natural and completely artificial classification systems are the *diagnostic* systems. Diagnostic systems reflect both natural properties of the objects or phenomena being classified as well as the needs of the classifier. Examples of diagnostic classifications would be classifications of roads and highways on the basis of their traffic-handling ability under varying climatic conditions, and classifications of radars based on the functions they perform.

Index classifications are entirely artificial systems. With index classifications, *accessibility* of data is the prime consideration. In this sense, the user's needs predominate in the selection of criteria for group assignment. Examples of index classifications would include the Dewey decimal system, the Library of Congress classification system, and the index of any book, as well as any alphabetical arrangement of data. More relevant to intelligence would be classifications of ships by pendant numbers, alphabetical listings of heads of state, and the classification of journal entries based on times of message arrivals.

To summarize, the purpose the classification scheme is intended to serve determines which type of classification system is most appropriate.

2. *When the purpose has been decided, the phenomena or data about the phenomena to be classified should be examined for those features or characteristics that could serve as possible criteria for classification.* Here the researcher should ask himself what the objects, events, or other phenomena have in common. What features do they have that are distinctive or unique? The researcher should extend his imagination to permit consideration of all of the parameters of that which he is classifying. Some of the characteristics that come to mind may appear superficial initially. However, this step is essentially an exploratory one for establishing all *possibilities* for classification.

3. *From the objects, events, or phenomena to be classified, those features that would satisfy the purpose the system is intended to serve should be identified.* The function the classification is intended to serve should point to those features of the phenomena that are relevant for classification purposes. Invariably, phenomena can be classified a number of different ways. The best way to classify is that way which satisfies a particular need of the user. For example, if a researcher is considering weapon systems with large-kill radii, he might find that a classification based on the weapon system's accuracy would be irrelevant since the kill radius would compensate for any lack of accuracy.

The variety of ways by which missiles can be classified according to different needs is shown below. When range is an important consideration, missiles can be classified as long-range missiles (over 5000 nautical miles); ICBMs, intermediate-range missiles (300–1500 nm); or IRBMs, short-range missiles (under 300 nm). When speed is an important consideration, missiles can be classified as subsonic, sonic, supersonic (air speeds ranging between Mach 1 and 5), and hypersonic (air speeds exceeding Mach 5). On the basis of control, missiles can be classified as either unguided or free-flight rockets, or as guided missiles. Guided missiles, in turn, can be classified according to the nature of their guidance systems, for example, command guidance, dead reckoning, position-fixing, and seeker or homing guidance systems.

There are other ways to classify missiles, but the point should be clear: phenomena invariably can be classified in a number of different ways depending upon the characteristics of the thing being classified, but most importantly, depending upon the needs of the classifier.

4. Relationships among and between classes must be identified. This step involves two operations. It involves, first, determining the qualitative criteria according to which two things may be said to be related. This step then involves considering the higher and lower categories to which something can be assigned. Essentially, this means that the researcher must determine (or establish) what entries would correspond to what rung on an imaginary ladder of abstraction. For instance, "Soviet Jet Fighter" is a class of airborne vehicles higher on an imaginary scale of abstraction than "MiG," but lower on the same scale than "fixed-wing aircraft."

The analyst and researcher will encounter instances that do not require the consideration of hierarchies. For example, radars might be classified based on frequency, PRF (pulse repetition frequency), pulse width, scan rate, and mode of polarization. In this case, those radars that had the same operating parameters would be grouped together. Radars operating on frequencies between 1550 MHz and 3900 MHz, for instance, would be grouped together and identified as S band radars, or all of the kinds of radars associated with a given geographic area might be grouped together and then further classified according to function, and so on. None of these classifications involves consideration of hierarchies.

5. Classification criteria should be applied to the "population," *and the entities should be assigned to specific groups.* When this step has been accomplished, a cycle has been completed. This step is identical to the first sense in which the term *classification* is used; namely, to assign an entity to a class.

TESTING THE CLASSIFICATION SYSTEM

Before a classification system is implemented on any large scale, it should be pilot tested. But even before testing, the system should be examined with respect to the following questions:

1. Are the rules for assigning phenomena to categories used consistently?

2. Are the categories or classes mutually exclusive, that is, do the categories overlap? (Phenomena may be classified many ways, but each mode requires a separate system.)
3. Is the system complete for the purposes for which it was designed (i.e., are there elements to be accounted for that do not fit into existing categories)?
4. Does every classification have *at least* two divisions? (Without two subdivisions, a class cannot be said to exist.)

CLASSIFICATIONS AS ABSTRACTS OF REALITY WITH PARTS DELETED

In the preceding discussion of classification, emphasis was placed upon the "either-or" logic of a dichotomous scheme of classification. It should be remembered that *all* classification schemes are arbitrary. Every classification system reflects the real world *more or less*. Although one can speak abstractly of an object or an event belonging to this category or to that, the real world seldom conforms to the niceties of a classification system. Often the classifier's decision on group assignment is a toss-up. When the purpose of the system is kept in mind, little damage is done in arbitrary decisions. However, it is important to be consistent in order that the same phenomenon will always be classified the same way by all system users. Finally, it must be remembered that even for professional taxonomists or "systematizers," the act of classification is not an end in itself. For intelligence research especially, it is only a beginning step in an analytic process.

SUMMARY

- Classification, or the process of assigning information to classes, is an essential step of nearly every type of research, many kinds of problem-solving activities, and all measurement.
- Classification is performed for two main reasons: to gain a better knowledge of the data, and for convenience in storing and retrieving data.
- The classification process typically involves five steps:
  - Establishing the purpose for which the classification will be performed
  - Examining the data about the phenomenon being classified in order to establish bases for assigning a datum to a category

- ° Selecting the bases for classification in light of the purpose for which the data were being classified
- ° Identifying relationships among and between classes of data, for example, hierarchies, subclasses, and the like
- ° Assigning data to specific groups or categories
- Rules of classification require that
  - ° phenomena (or data) be assigned to categories in a consistent manner,
  - ° all classes or categories be mutually exclusive,
  - ° the system must be complete in the sense that all elements of data can be assigned to a category and that there are no elements left over, and
  - ° every super class has at least two subclasses.

NOTES

1. In intelligence research and analysis, data are often classified, that is, assigned to specific categories, on the basis of the degree of danger to national security that would result from their unauthorized disclosure. This is perhaps the most familiar sense in which the term is used in intelligence.

2. Harold A. Larrabee, *Reliable Knowledge* (Boston: Houghton Mifflin, 1945), 239–248.

3. What really confounds the coding and classification process in propaganda analysis is that the statements being classified may themselves be ambiguous. For a discussion of additional problems in propaganda analysis see Jerome K. Clauser, *Propaganda Analysis: Techniques and Procedures for Analysts* (State College, PA: HRB-Singer, 1973).

4. The limit for convenient "hand processing" is about 150 subjects.

5. Another name for a category would be a nominal scale. Classification in the first sense of the term defined above is actually a form of measurement, albeit a crude form.

9

Basic Quantitative Techniques for Research and Analysis

When you can measure what you are speaking about, and express it in numbers, you know something about it; but when you cannot measure it, when you cannot express it in numbers, your knowledge is of a meager and unsatisfactory kind; it may be the beginning of knowledge, but you have scarcely advanced to the stage of science.

—Lord Kelvin

At some point in his career, practically every researcher or analyst will work with quantitative data. In some instances, the researcher personally may have to perform certain types of quantitative analyses. In more instances, the researcher will have to utilize the results of quantitative analyses performed by other researchers. This chapter reviews basic statistical and quantitative techniques that are relevant to intelligence research and analysis. In some cases, only a principle is addressed, and the application of that principle is left to the reader. In other cases, particularly where a clearly identifiable technique is discussed, the application of that technique to an intelligence problem is cited.

To the researcher unfamiliar with mathematical symbology, some of the equations used in this chapter might appear arcane and formidable. However, the operations required are usually quite simple, and anyone who has had some basic algebra should have no problems with the equations. The purpose of the chapter is to acquaint the researcher with basic fundamentals of statistics. It is not the intent of this chapter to train the reader to develop or apply a statistical technique to a specific problem. Entire texts are devoted to that objective.

STATISTICAL ANALYSIS

Statistics is the science of gathering, analyzing, and drawing inferences from masses of numerical data. There are three main types of statistics: descriptive statistics, sampling theory, and inferential statistics. Descriptive statistics indicate the magnitude and spread of a set of data. In the case of a suspected mobilization, for example, descriptive statistics could tell the researcher what the *average* number of flatcars carrying heavy equipment by train from, say, Volkovysk to Białystok had been, over the last several months. (The researcher could also compute a separate average number of flatcars returning empty.)

Sampling theory allows one to make inferences about many (or all) instances, occurrences, events, or conditions (the "population") on the basis of only a part of that population. The researcher who is concerned with the movement of material from the Soviet Union to Poland, for example, might know that four trains travel over a selected route daily in each direction (the entire population), but he might count the flatcars on the train only twice each week (his sample). Sampling theory permits him to plan the pattern of his observations and to decide how large his sample should be.

Inferential statistics perform several functions that concern drawing conclusions about a set or sets of data. Some inferential statistics allow a researcher to express quantitatively the degree of confidence he can place in his generalization of an entire population based on sampled data of that population. For example, the researcher might discover that the proportion of trains moving westward with loaded flatcars increased each successive week, and conversely, the number of trains moving eastward with empty flatcars also increased. Inferential statistics could indicate if the same trend would be evident whether observations were taken each day or once each week.

Statistical inference can also examine the *relationships* between two or more variables. If the number of loaded flatcars traveling west were no longer simply noted but were graphed according to time (figure 9.1), then time, as well as the number of flatcars would become an important variable. Using linear regression, a line could be drawn to indicate the trend toward increasing numbers of flatcars, over time. Statistical inference could also be used in the same example to explore the relationships among other variables; for example, the overall lengths of the trains and the number of passenger cars on each train.

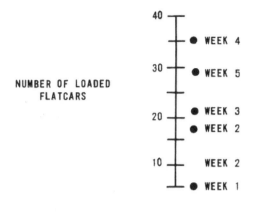

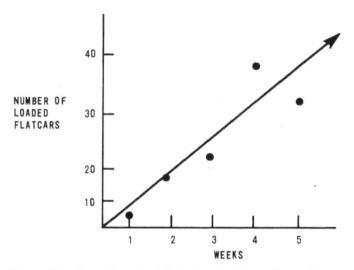

Figure 9.1.   Data Noted and Data Graphed According to Time

MATHEMATICAL ANALYSIS

Although statistical analysis is especially useful to intelligence research and analysis because conclusions must often be drawn from
partial data, there are times when it is better to use simple mathematical formulas. For example, if a commander determined that he
had engaged elements of two separate battalions, he could estimate
the size of the forces opposing him simply by multiplying the strength
of each unit times the number of units engaged. If he knew that the

two battalions with which he was engaged were part of a regiment, he could also estimate the size of the overall force with which he might be engaged in the near future by multiplying the total number of units in the regiment by the strength of each unit. In this case, simple arithmetic would suffice for making an estimate.

DESCRIPTIVE STATISTICS

Descriptive statistics are measures that are used to summarize large amounts of numerical information and to create profiles describing the information. Descriptive statistics can be expressed graphically, verbally, and mathematically. In the following section, methods and measures of descriptive statistics are introduced. They include frequency distributions, measures of central tendency, and measures of dispersion.

FREQUENCY DISTRIBUTIONS

Specific measures of traits or characteristics are called values. A trait or characteristic that assumes different values is called a variable. For example, a researcher might be interested in the heights, ages, wealth, educational levels, or years of military service of a group of people. The values of these traits *vary* among the individuals in the group; hence, they are called *variables*.

A tally might be made of the numbers of people of each category of height, age, or any other variable. For example, the heights of 292 American soldiers could be measured, and the tally might look like this:

Height (Inches)	Number of Soldiers of That Height
60–62	12
62–64	28
64–66	37
66–68	42
68–70	50
70–72	44
72–74	36
74–76	25
76–78	15
78–80	06

The heights of the soldiers are recorded according to two-inch intervals; thus, a soldier who is 68 inches tall cannot be distinguished from a soldier who is 69 inches tall by looking at the tally sheet. It is important for the researcher to choose the correct size of a class interval. The size of the interval is determined by the uses to which the data will be put. In this example, a one-eighth of an inch class interval would be a poor choice because an individual's height often varies more than one-eighth of an inch during a single day. On the other hand, a 20-inch class interval would not show the researcher any pattern at all. It is also advisable, for most purposes, to have all class intervals the same size (e.g., all two-inch intervals rather than some two-inch and some four-inch intervals).

The tally sheet indicates that many of the soldiers are 68 inches to 70 inches tall, whereas few are either very tall or very short. But the tally sheet does not give the reader a concise visual image of the pattern of heights. Graphing the data with heights recorded on a horizontal axis and the numbers of individuals recorded on a vertical axis (figure 9.2), however, does produce a visual image of the data.

A graph, which is a series of rectangles such as figure 9.2, is called a histogram. The image may be enhanced by joining the midpoints of the tops of each rectangle. The histogram shows the number of individuals constituting each class, the relative size of each class, and the distribution of the classes. The roughly symmetrical "curve" of the histogram indicates that there are about as many short soldiers as there are tall ones.

Figure 9.2. Height: American Soldiers (Inches)

MEASURES OF CENTRAL TENDENCY

Weapons are usually made in only one size. Weapons must be designed so that it is possible for the tallest soldier and the shortest soldier to use them. Therefore, a weapon is usually designed to suit the "typical" or "average" soldier.[1] The "typical" soldier's height is computed as one of three measures of central tendency: the mean, median, or mode. The mean is an average that may be computed by adding up all the individual values of a variable and then dividing that sum by the number of values. In the example of soldiers' heights cited earlier, there were many soldiers of the same height. Rather than adding each height individually, it is more efficient to calculate the mean in the manner shown below (table 9.1).

The middle height of each class interval, for example, 61 inches as the middle of the class 60–62 inches, is multiplied by the number of soldiers of that height to produce the third column, or the total number of "soldier-inches" in that class interval. To find the mean, columns (2) and (3) are each summed, and then the total of column (3) is divided by the total of column (2).

$$\frac{\text{Total soldier-inches} = 20421}{\text{Total soldiers} = 295} = 69.2 \text{ inches}$$

The median refers to the middle value of a variable. For example, if all of the soldiers were lined up in order of increasing height, the

Table 9.1. Soldiers' Heights and Total "Soldier-Inches"

(1)	(2)	(3)
Height (inches)	Number of Soldiers of That Height	Total Soldier-Inches
60–62	12	732
62–64	28	1764
64–66	37	2405
66–68	42	2814
68–70	50	3450
70–72	44	3124
72–74	36	2628
74–76	25	1875
76–78	15	1155
78–80	06	474
	295	20421

height of the soldier who was in the middle of the line would be the median. The median is found by arraying all the data again (table 9.2). In column (3), the number of soldiers in each class is accumulated with the number of soldiers in all previous classes, for example, 12 + 28 + 37 . . . . Since there are 295 soldiers, the soldier of *median* height would be the 148th soldier. Column (3) indicates that the 148th soldier would be somewhere between 68 and 70 inches tall. The mode is the class that occurs most frequently. In the current example, the mode is in the class 68–70 inches. (Fifty soldiers are in this class.)

If the United States were preparing to send weaponry or other military equipment to an ally, a comparative statistical analysis of the heights of American servicemen and their allied counterparts could aid planners in determining what sizes of uniforms or what types of weapons to provide. For example, a histogram of the heights of 225 allied soldiers (figure 9.3A) indicates that they are much shorter, in general, than their American counterparts. The mean of the distribution is 62.4 inches, whereas the median and mode both fall between 62 and 64 inches.[2] Therefore, to fit the typical allied serviceman, the uniforms issued would have to be designed for a man seven inches shorter than the typical American soldier.

MEASURES OF DISPERSION

The heights of the group of American soldiers are spread over 20 inches (60–80 inches). If a different-sized uniform were needed for the

Table 9.2.   Soldiers' Height Data Rank-Ordered

(1)	(2)	(3)
Height (inches)	Number of Soldiers of That Height	Cumulative Number of Soldiers
60–62	12	12
62–64	28	40
64–66	37	77
66–68	42	119
68–70	50	169
70–72	44	213
72–74	36	249
74–76	25	274
76–78	15	289
78–80	06	295
		295

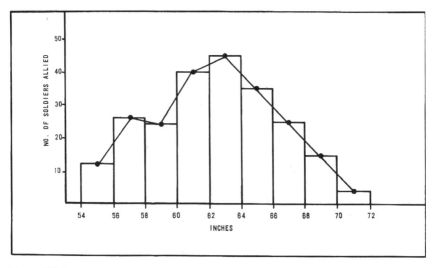

Figure 9.3A.

soldiers of every two-inch class of height, then ten different uniform sizes would be needed for the entire group. The difference in height between the tallest and the shortest allied soldier in the group (the *range* of heights) is only 18 inches. Using the same criterion as above, only nine uniform sizes would be needed for the entire group. Data that are spread widely about an average value are considered to be "dispersed." Histograms that are relatively tall and narrow show less dispersion than shorter, wider histograms. One of the more commonly used measures of dispersion is called the standard deviation. The standard deviation can express how close most of the soldiers are to the mean height of the group.

The formula for the standard deviation is shown below.

$$\sigma = \sqrt{\dfrac{\sum\limits_{i=1}^{n} (x_i - \bar{x})^2}{n}}$$

The formula involves the following steps: (1) the mean (x) must be subtracted from each individual value (x_i), (2) the results of each ($x_i - x$) must be squared, (3) all the ($x_i - x$)^2 are summed, (4) the result is divided by the total number of items, and (5) the square root of the result is taken.

The calculation of the standard deviation for the allied soldiers' heights is in figures 9.3A and 9.3B.

(1) MIDPOINT OF HEIGHT CLASS (x_i)	(2) $(x_i - \bar{x})$ $\bar{x} = 62.4$	(3) $(x_i - \bar{x})^2$	(4) NUMBER OF SOLDIERS OF THAT HEIGHT	(5) (3) X (4)
55	-7.4	54.76	12	657.12
57	-5.4	29.16	25	729.00
59	-3.4	11.56	24	277.44
61	-1.4	1.96	40	78.40
63	.6	.36	45	16.20
65	2.6	6.76	35	236.60
67	4.6	21.16	25	529.00
69	6.6	43.56	15	653.40
71	8.6	73.96	4	295.84
			= 225	= 3473.00

$$\sigma = \sqrt{\frac{\sum_{i=1}^{n} (x_i - \bar{x})^2}{n}} = \sqrt{\frac{3473.00}{225}} = 3.93$$

Figure 9.3B.

The midpoint of each class interval is used to represent the interval, as it was when the mean was calculated. Since there are many soldiers who are the same height, the $(x_i - x)^2$ are multiplied by the number of soldiers of a given height, and those results are summed in column (5). This is a shortcut similar to the one used in the calculation of the mean.

The standard deviation in height of the allied soldiers is 3.93 inches. This measure indicates that *most* of the soldiers are taller than 58.5 inches but shorter than 66.3 inches. If the distribution of heights formed a normal curve (figure 9.3A), then 68 percent of the heights would be included within one standard deviation of the mean and 95 percent of the heights would fall within ±1.96 standard deviations of the mean. In this example, the distribution of heights forms a curve similar enough to a normal, bell-shaped curve that it can be assumed that roughly two-thirds of the heights fall within one standard deviation of the mean.

The standard deviation of the distribution of American soldiers' heights is 4.07 inches. Therefore, most of the American soldiers are taller than 65.1 inches but shorter than 73.3 inches. In order to compare the dispersions of the two distributions, the standard deviations should be divided by the means. This standardizes the two measures of dispersion. The division is necessary because a difference of one inch from the mean for the shorter allied soldier is a greater *percentage* difference from the mean than in the case of the American soldier who is one inch taller or shorter than the mean.

The relative measure of dispersion is called the coefficient of variation and is equal to

$$\frac{\sigma}{x} = \frac{3.96}{62.4} = .063$$

for the allied group, and is equal to

$$\frac{\sigma}{x} = \frac{4.07}{69.2} = .059$$

for the American group.

This measure shows that the "allied" distribution is more dispersed than the "American" distribution. It should be noted that although the *range* and the *standard deviation* of the American soldiers' heights were greater, the *coefficient of variation* of the "allied" heights data was greater. The range and coefficient of variation measure different aspects of dispersion.

AN EXAMPLE OF THE USE OF DESCRIPTIVE STATISTICS

The United States and the Soviet Union constantly monitor the comparative strengths of their defense establishments. It is difficult to compare fleet strengths in the two nations' navies because the classes of ships are defined differently. As a preliminary part of the analysis of the two fleets, the number and size (displacement) of frigates in the two navies might be compared (figure 9.4). The histogram representing the ships indicates that the definition of frigates differs greatly. The Soviet frigates are much smaller than the American *frigates*, and there are also many more Soviet frigates.

A "typical" frigate for each navy is described utilizing the figures below (table 9.3).

The mean size of the U.S. frigates is 6379 tons, the median size is 5670 tons, and the mode is 4700 tons. In this distribution, which does not conform to a bell-shaped curve, values of the mean, median, and

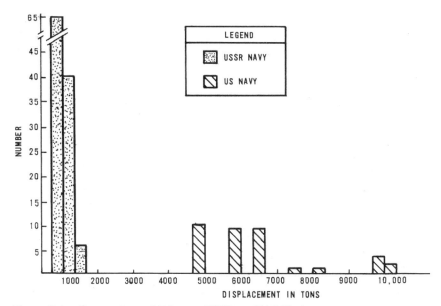

Figure 9.4.   Comparison of Frigates, USSR and U.S Navies

Table 9.3.   Frigates of the U.S. and USSR Navies

FRIGATES OF THE UNITED STATES NAVY		
(1) DISPLACEMENT (TONS)	(2) NUMBER OF SHIPS	(3) (1) X (2)
10,150	2	20300
10,000	3	30000
8,200	1	8200
7,600	1	7600
6,570	9	59130
5,670	9	51030
4,700	10	47000
	35	223260
FRIGATES OF THE U.S.S.R. NAVY		
(1) DISPLACEMENT (TONS)	(2) NUMBER OF SHIPS	(3) (1) X (2)
1500	6	9000
1200	40	48000
950	20	19000
950	45	42750
	111	118750

mode are quite different. The mean size of the Soviet ships is 1070 tons, and the median and mode are both 950 tons. The coefficients of variation are .2723 for the U.S. ships and .1463 for the Soviet ships. Therefore, the class of U.S. ships called frigates is a relatively broader class than Soviet frigates.

The American ships known as ocean escorts are more comparable to Soviet frigates than are American "frigates." A histogram of ocean escorts would show that there are some ocean escorts about the same size as Soviet frigates, although the U.S. class of escort ships is generally somewhat larger. The mean, median, and mode sizes of American escort ships are 3494, 4100, and 4100 tons, respectively. Similar analyses might be undertaken for all the types of ships and various characteristics of those ships in both navies. The resultant profile of fleet strengths would then be a concise method of comparing the fleets on the basis of displacement and class.

SAMPLING THEORY

There are many times when an analyst or a researcher would want to develop a profile of the "other side's" activities. Profiles are essential for detecting deviations from the norm. Without profiles (or other baseline data), it is impossible to determine whether a certain event or condition is typical or atypical. For example, an intelligence analyst might want to develop a profile that described the types of information transmitted by the wire services of a specific country. He would want the profile to be representative of a "typical" day, so he would try to review wire service releases transmitted over a period of time. If the analyst could not read every story that was transmitted by the wire services, he would choose only a portion of the stories for careful review.

All of the items of interest to the researcher might include every release transmitted by the wire services during a specific month. This entire body of data is known as the population or universe. The part of the entire population that is selected for analysis is called a sample. If a sample is selected carefully, it is possible to make inferences about characteristics of the overall population based upon characteristics of the sample. There are several methods for selecting samples, and the method that is chosen depends upon the purpose for which the sampling is being conducted.

RANDOM SAMPLING

A random sample gives each member of the population an equal chance of being chosen. Often a random number table is utilized for selecting a random sample. Other procedures include drawing numbered slips of paper out of a hat or tossing dice. In the current example, a random number table could be used to help choose when wire service releases would be reviewed at length. It might be predetermined that ten releases would be reviewed on a given day. The ten releases would be chosen by consulting the random number table and noting the last two digits of ten five-digit blocks of numbers. Reading across the first row, the ten two-digit numbers might be 56, 57, 42, 22, 06, 45, 55, 05, 30, and 80. For the given day, then, the releases to be reviewed would be the fifth item, sixth item, and so on through the eightieth item transmitted after 2400 hours.

An even simpler sampling scheme for this example might utilize the time/date group in the header data of each article, for example, the release transmitted each hour on or about 37 minutes after the hour might be selected. Although acceptable, this type of sampling sometimes introduces bias. For example, if radio broadcasts were monitored, and if the analyst examined the transmissions at fifty-five minutes after every hour, he might discover that sports or weather were always reported at that time. A profile based on this biased sample of radio broadcasts would suggest that sporting events and weather information were reported 100 percent of the time that the station was on the air.

A major advantage of random sampling is that it allows the analyst to assess the accuracy of the measures of central tendency of dispersion derived from the sampling. Thus, an analyst is able to answer the question, "How *confident* am I that the mean I calculated from sampling is within a certain range of the mean of the population?"

The example of the heights of allied soldiers may serve to show the usefulness of establishing confidence levels. The 225 allied soldiers whose heights were measured were a random sample taken from a population of, perhaps, millions of soldiers. The mean of their heights was 62.42 inches. This mean height may be the same as the mean height of the population. On the other hand, the analyst may be challenged by someone who states that the average allied soldier was 64 inches tall. The analyst could establish a confidence level for his calculation of the mean height in the following way.

He knows his sample size, sample mean, and sample standard deviation, as shown below.

$$n = 225$$
$$x = 62.42''$$
$$\sigma = 3.93''$$

From the mathematical theory associated with random sampling, he also knows that there is a chance that his sample mean may be either higher or lower than the true mean for the population. If several samples are taken from a population, most sample means will be too large or small by a small amount, but some samples will be a great deal too large or too small (figure 9.5).

In figure 9.5, if ^{x} pop. is the true mean of the population, many sample means will be nearly equal to the true mean (there are 33 samples with a mean of x_2, just slightly larger than the true mean). Only a few sample means will be very inaccurate (there are only eight samples with a mean of x_1, much smaller than the true mean). The distribution of errors of sample means around the true mean forms a normal or bell-shaped curve (figure 9.5).

The standard error (σx) of the sample mean must be computed to determine how likely it is that the estimated average height of 62.42 inches falls within a certain range of the true mean height. The formula for the standard error is shown below.

$$\frac{\sigma}{x} = \frac{O}{n}$$

If the σ of the sample is used as the estimate of the standard deviation of the population, this formula becomes as follows.

$$\frac{\sigma}{x} = \frac{3.93''}{225} = \frac{3.93''}{15} = .262''$$

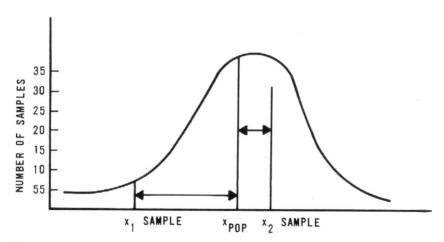

Figure 9.5. Distance of the Sample Means from the True Mean of a Population (A Normal Curve)

To establish confidence levels for the estimated average height of 62.42 inches, a table of areas under the normal distribution must be consulted. The table tells the analyst how likely it is that his estimated mean is within a range of the true mean. For example, if the analyst specifies that the range of heights is to be

$$62.42'' - 1\ \sigma_{\overline{x}}\ \text{or}\ 62.42'' - .262'' = 62.158''$$

to

$$62.42'' + 1\ \sigma_{\overline{x}}\ \text{or}\ 62.42'' + .262 = 62.682''$$

the table tells him that the likelihood that the true mean falls within this range is 68 percent.

Alternatively, an analyst can specify that he wants to find the range of heights so that there is a 95 percent likelihood that the true mean falls within an interval. The analyst would consult the table and find that the 95 percent confidence level would be 1.96 standard deviations above and below the sample mean. The boundaries of the range are then set.

$$62.42'' - 1.96\sigma_{\overline{x}}\ \text{or}\ 62.42'' - .514'' = 61.906''$$

$$62.42'' + 1.96\sigma_{\overline{x}}\ \text{or}\ 62.42'' + .514'' = 62.934''$$

As the confidence level *increases*, in this case from 68 percent to 95 percent, the *size of the range* also increases. Random sampling schemes also allow the researcher to determine how many data points (value of n) must be included in the sample in order to be certain of a specific level of confidence in his results.

STRATIFIED SAMPLING

The object of stratified sampling is to choose a cross section of the population. Stratified sampling is accomplished in two steps. Initially, the population would be classified into subgroups that tended to share similar values for the characteristics under study, and the size of each subgroup would be recorded. A random sample would then be taken within each subgroup, with the sample size determined by that subgroup's percentage of the total population.

For example, it might be necessary to assess the opinions of villagers toward a military civic-action program—the construction of a bridge, perhaps. If it were not possible (or desirable) to interview every individual in the village, the number and type of subjects to be interviewed could be established by first classifying groups of villagers according to age, sex, and occupation (in this example) and then determining how many subjects constituted each group. The percentage of the total village population that each group constituted would be calculated. Then, for each 5 percent of the population contained in each group, one subject would be selected to be interviewed. Thus, in the example in table 9.4, children constituted 30 percent of the total village population. Therefore, six children would be selected randomly as being representative of all of the children in the village. In this example, choosing one subject for each 5 percent of the total population would yield a sample size of about twenty. (Controlling the sample size helps the analyst to estimate his total interviewing time.)

In order for at least one person to be interviewed from each group, at least one man in the category "other" would have to be interviewed. Since the category "other" represents only 3 percent of the population, the category is slightly overrepresented in the sample.

If the division of the population into subgroups (classification) is done wisely, this type of stratified sampling will yield a better cross section of the population than most random samples. However, confidence levels cannot be assessed for the values yielded from stratified samples. Also, much must be known about the population in order to define the subgroups, and in instances where demographic data are lacking, this may be a problem.

Table 9.4. Stratified Sampling Scheme, Village Population

Groups of Individuals in The Village Classified by Sex, Age, and Occupation	Number of People	Percent of Population (%)	Number in Sample
Children (under Age 15)	64	30	6
Women (Ages 15–50)	60	28	6
Men (Ages 15–50)	50	24	5
Farmers	33	16	3
Small Businessmen	11	5	1
Other	6	3	1
Elderly (50 or Older)	39	18	4
Total	213	100	21

INTRODUCTION TO PROBABILITY

Probability theory provides the mathematical foundation for inferential statistics. Probability theory generates "idealized" distributions of the frequency of occurrence of chance events. The normal curve is one example of such a distribution (figure 9.6, example A). In an "ideal" case, the relative frequency of specific values of x_i could be plotted accurately so that the six selected values of x_i lie on the normal curve (figure 9.6, curve A). Real-world data rarely fit ideal mathematical models exactly. Events occur too frequently or not frequently enough with respect to the ideal model. For example, in figure 9.6, curves B and C, the six selected values lie above or below the curve. However, the two sets of data represented by B and C approximate the normal curve closely enough that the curve can serve as a basis for analyzing the data.

Probabilities range from impossibility (a probability of 0) to absolute certainty (a probability of 1). With probability theory, an event must be considered as occurring or not occurring. Given that p is the probability of the occurrence of event E, the probability that E will not occur is equal to equation 1.

$$q = 1 - p \qquad (1)$$

For example, the Democrats, Republicans, Liberals, and Conservatives each have a candidate running for the U.S. Senate. Assuming that the two former candidates each have about twice as great a chance of winning the election as each of the two latter candidates,

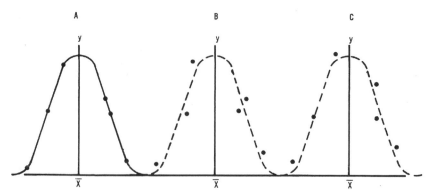

Figure 9.6.   The Normal Distribution (Curve A); Approximations of the Normal Distribution (Curves B and C)

and assuming that the election is certain to be held, then the probability of each candidate winning can be expressed as in equation 2.

$$Pr[D] + Pr[R] + Pr[L] + Pr[C] = 1, \text{ or } \frac{2}{6} + \frac{2}{6} + \frac{1}{6} + \frac{1}{6} = 1 \quad (2)$$

The probability of the Liberal candidate's *not* winning is shown in equation 3.

$$Pr[\text{not } L] = \frac{2}{6} + \frac{2}{6} + \frac{1}{6} = \frac{5}{6} \quad (3)$$

Equation 3 is an example of the *additive* law of probability, which states that the probability of any one of several mutually exclusive events occurring equals the sum of the separate probabilities of the events.

Another law of probability, the *multiplicative* law, states that the probability of all of several independent events occurring in succession equals the *product* of the separate probabilities of the events. In the election example, the multiplicative law could be applied to the probability of two Liberal candidates winning the senatorial race in two states.

Assuming the probability that the Liberal will win each state is 1/6, the probability can be expressed by equation 4.

$$Pr[L \text{ in both}] \frac{1}{6} \times \frac{1}{6} = \frac{1}{36} \quad (4)$$

PROBABILITY DISTRIBUTIONS

Data that can be counted, like the number of people in a city, are called *discrete* data. Data that can occur anywhere within a range, like the speed of a car, are called *continuous* data. Intelligence researchers must sometimes measure both discrete and continuous phenomena. There are several important probability distributions for each type of phenomena, but only three will be discussed at length: the normal distribution, the binomial distribution, and the exponential distribution.

All probability distributions can be illustrated graphically by plotting the number of events on one axis and the probability of occurrence of these events on the other axis. The relationship between a histogram showing the frequency of certain data values and the probability distribution associated with the same set of data is explained below using the example of intelligence quotient (IQ) test results.

A histogram showing intelligence test results (figure 9.7) illustrates the distribution of intelligence quotients for a given sample group. It shows that there is a large group of people with average IQs. The histogram is also *nearly* symmetrical; there are nearly equal numbers of people with high IQs and with low IQs.

NORMAL DISTRIBUTION

The appearance of the histogram tells the experienced researcher that the distribution can be approximated by a normal distribution. When the normal distribution is used as the model for the data, further analysis is based upon the normal distribution rather than upon the original histogram of data. The fitting of real-world data to ideal probability distributions is often associated with taking a sample from a large population. For example, the normal distribution (figure 9.7) is used to describe intelligence test results from a sample of 230 people out of a population of 10,000 people. The researcher is assuming that the distribution of IQs in the entire population is normal. The slightly

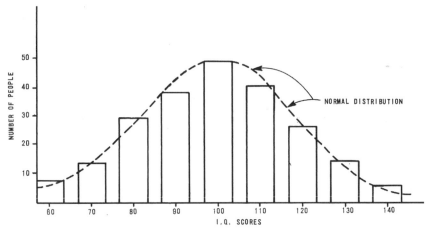

Figure 9.7.   Distribution of IQs

irregular distribution of IQs in the sample arises only because the sample is not quite representative of the population. The normal distribution is a continuous distribution. It describes many types of data well, including abilities, heights of people, and the slight irregularities in the sizes of a product produced by machine.

BINOMIAL DISTRIBUTION

The binomial distribution describes *discrete* data. It arises when events depend upon a fixed probability of occurrence, p, and when the number of trials, n, is limited. For example, planners might be concerned with resupplying insurgents in a hostile area by an airdrop. They might know that the insurgents constitute only one-third of the total population ($p = 1$). They would be interested in the likelihood of reaching at least five insurgent groups if ten bundles of supplies were dropped. Figure 9.8 shows the binomial distribution when $n = 10$ and $p = 1/3$.

   In order to find the probability of reaching at least five groups of the target population when ten bundles are dropped, the additive law of probability must be applied to the binomial distribution.

1. $Pr[\text{at least } 5] = Pr[5] + Pr[6] + Pr[7] + Pr[8] + Pr[9] + Pr[10]$
2. $Pr[\text{at least } 5] = .136 + .057 + .016 + .003 + .0003 + .00002 = .21232$

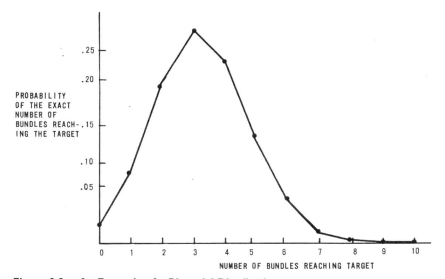

Figure 9.8.   An Example of a Binomial Distribution

The probability of reaching at least five groups of the target population is only .21 or about one chance out of five. Such a simple analysis does not take into account the size of either the *total* population or the *target* population. The population size would become important if, for instance, the objective of the mission were to reach at least 50 percent of the target population.

EXPONENTIAL DISTRIBUTION

The exponential curve provides an accurate description of the likelihood of occurrence of an unlimited number of events. For example, the length of time between the arrivals of aircraft on a carrier may be called an event. If two aircraft arrive simultaneously, the length of time between their arrivals is zero (0). Therefore,

Event 1 (time between arrivals) = 0.

If the next aircraft arrives 2 minutes later, then

Event 2 (time between arrivals) = 2.

In certain situations—for example, after an air strike—it would be common for several aircraft to arrive at the carrier almost simultaneously. Therefore, the most common value for the event (time between arrivals) is zero (0). So, in a probability distribution describing aircraft arrivals, the value zero (0) has the highest probability. It is less probable for there to be one minute between arrivals and even less probable for there to be five minutes between arrivals. The duration of a message transmission might also be called an event. It is most likely that a message will be of a very short duration, less likely that a message will last three minutes, and even less likely that a message will last six minutes. The duration of message transmissions is very well described by the exponential distribution.

Another common use of the exponential distribution is the description of the life span of pieces of equipment. For example (figure 9.9), all radio transmitters in a lot are checked before leaving the factory, and all work properly. One year later, most of them still work, but at the end of four years, very few work (without having been repaired).

The choice of a particular distribution depends upon the nature of the phenomenon to be described. A duration of time, for example, is often described by the exponential distribution, whereas the apportion-

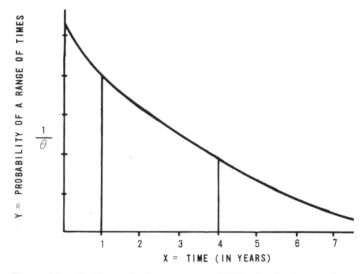

Figure 9.9.   An Example of an Exponential Distribution: Transmitter Lifespan

ment of abilities is described by the normal curve. Probability distributions are powerful tools for prediction because they tell a researcher which values of an event are most likely to occur. The intent of these brief descriptions is not to teach how to create or develop the distributions, but rather to describe types of distributions that might be highly relevant to a problem.

SUMMARY

- Statistics is the science of collecting, analyzing, and drawing inferences from masses of numerical data.
- Quantitative data do not always require statistical analysis. At times, a simple mathematical formula suffices for an analysis of quantitative data.
- Descriptive statistics permit a researcher to create an image of the data distribution. Descriptive statistics include:
  - Frequency distributions (or profiles of data values),
  - Histograms (frequency distributions in the form of bar graphs),
  - Measures of central tendency: mean, mode, and median, and
  - Measures of dispersion or spread of data: standard deviation, coefficient of variation, and others.

- Sampling theory allows one to generalize about population characteristics on the basis of an analysis of only a small part of the population.
  - Two common sampling types are random sampling and stratified sampling.
  - An advantage of random sampling is that it permits one to ascertain how likely it is that the sample has similar characteristics to the whole population.
- Probability theory provides the mathematical foundation of inferential statistics.
  - Probability theory makes it possible to generate "ideal" distributions of data for purposes of comparison with actual distributions of data.
  - Three common distributions are illustrated by the normal, binomial, and exponential curves.

NOTES

1. This is no trivial matter. One reason for the popularity of the M1 carbine in Asia was its small size and light weight.
2. In normally distributed data, the mean, median, and mode are roughly equivalent.

10

Descriptive Analysis Methodologies

Descriptive and predictive research constitute the major types of intelligence analysis and research activities, as pointed out earlier. Just as the distinction between description and prediction is somewhat tenuous, so are distinctions between descriptive and predictive methodologies tenuous. It will be recalled that, strictly speaking, the term *predictive research* should be limited to those activities relating to developing and validating conceptual models that could be applied to a variety of future-oriented problems. But in order to develop models, the phenomenon being modeled first must be described. In short, description is the basis of all intelligence research.

This chapter and the next discuss various methodologies that are or can be used in strategic intelligence production. This chapter addresses methodologies that are used for descriptive or analytic purposes. The next chapter will address methodologies that are used more commonly for *predictive* purposes even though they may be essentially descriptive. Some of the methodologies described in the next chapter relate to developing conceptual models. Developing, validating, and applying these conceptual models to a variety of different problems qualifies as predictive research in the most rigorous sense. Other methodologies described in the next chapter may be equally suitable for descriptive *or* predictive research but tend to be used more commonly for predictive purposes.[1]

Specific instructions on how to apply the techniques to numerous types of intelligence problems are beyond the purview of this chapter and the next one, because an entire volume might be required to describe adequately any one technique. As such, this chapter and the next should be considered overviews of representative methodologies. For specific information on how to apply any given technique, the references cited should be consulted.

ANALOGY: THE PERENNIAL ANALYTIC MODEL

One of the most widely used tools in intelligence analysis is the analogy. Analogies serve as the basis for constructing many predictive models, are the basis for most hypotheses, and rightly or wrongly, underlie many generalizations about what the other side will do and how they will go about doing it. Very briefly, analogies relate to the real or presumed *similarities* between two things. In an example cited earlier, analysts or researchers might reason that because two aircraft have many features in common, they may have been designed to perform similar missions. The form of this reasoning looks like figure 10.1.

Some analogies are better than others depending upon what is known about the properties that two objects, events, or conditions have in common. Aside from superficial external similarities, if it were known that two aircraft were powered by similar engines and if the performance characteristics of one engine were known, then the performance of the "unknown" aircraft could be inferred fairly reliably. The strength of this argument derives from the fact that the performance of the aircraft is logically connected to the quality of its engine. It is the ability to establish the cause-and-effect relationships or the invariant relationships between qualities and capabilities that ultimately determines the strength of analogies.

In the case of inferring the capabilities of an unknown aircraft on the basis of associated qualities, the argument would look like figure 10.2. The key to reasoning from analogy revolves around the bases that are used to establish similarities. The "force" of an argument from analogy is a function of how well connections (or "linking generalizations") can be established. If the connection between a given condition

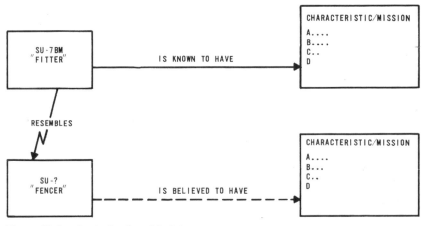

Figure 10.1.   Basic Analogy Model

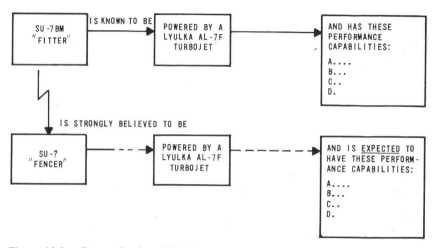

Figure 10.2.   Strong Analogy Model

and a specified result is a strong one, then a good case can be made for a generalization drawn by analogy. But an important part of reasoning by analogy is to consider also those conditions, qualities, characteristics, and so on that are *dissimilar* between two phenomena. It may well be the case that the dissimilarities are so great that the similarities that do exist are negligible.

Analogies are used in many different kinds of intelligence analyses from military and political intelligence to industrial intelligence. For example, major U.S. automakers purchase their competitors' models as soon as they appear in the showrooms. The new cars are taken to laboratories where they are completely and methodically disassembled. Each component, regardless of how seemingly insignificant it might be, is priced. The aggregate price for all of the parts collectively represents the material costs of producing one unit. To these costs would be added overhead, labor, and profit rates—rates that are generally similar throughout the industry. Reasoning by analogy, that is, assuming that it would cost one producer the same amount to produce or purchase the same components used by another, the major auto producers can estimate their competitors per-unit production costs, any cost-saving measures taken, and how much profit is earned by the sale of a single unit.

The strategic intelligence counterpart of this example (which is also an analogy) is not hard to envision. What confounds the problem in intelligence production, however, is establishing currency equivalences. General Motors, Ford Motor Company, and Chrysler all use the same currency. However, determining the rate of exchange between the *yuan* or the ruble and the U.S. dollar is a different matter.

Analogies may be economic (as in the example just described), physical (as was the case in the comparison of aircraft), or historical (as will be shown in the next chapter, as when Max von Hoffman predicted the behavior of two Russian generals on the basis of previous behaviors). Reasoning by analogy is fairly common in economic intelligence, in scientific and technical intelligence, and, to a lesser degree, in political, biographic, and armed forces intelligence. The technique is useful, but it must be used guardedly. In the excitement of discovering superficial similarities between phenomena, it is very easy to overlook the significant differences that may exist as well.

LINK ANALYSIS

Link analysis is an analytic technique for making relationships explicit. The technique was first used in human factors research but has since been applied to problems of social analysis as well. The technique requires the preparation of an association matrix and a link diagram based on the matrix. For example, based on a variety of intelligence reports, a matrix showing the confirmed and suspected associations of a number of individuals might be prepared as shown in figure 10.3. A solid dot rep-

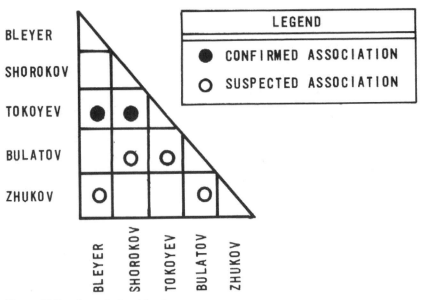

Figure 10.3.   Association Matrix

resents a strong link (a confirmed association), and an open dot represents a suspected association. (No dot represents no known or suspected association.)

Based on the matrix, a link diagram can be prepared (figure 10.4). The solid lines represent strong (or confirmed) links; the broken lines indicate weak (or suspected) links. No lines, of course, indicates that no association had yet been established. The link diagram can be enhanced further by superimposing organizational structures on the personnel linkages as shown in figure 10.4.

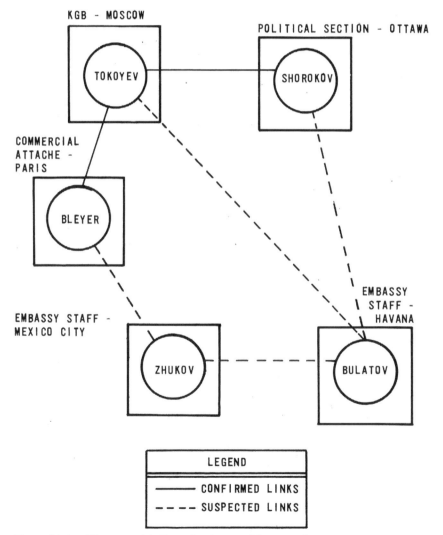

Figure 10.4.   Diagram with Organizations and Personnel

Link analysis can be used to construct inferential structures of organizations or interactions, which can be tested later. It is very well suited for hypothesis construction and can be applied to a variety of problems in armed forces intelligence (e.g., orders of battle), in political intelligence, and in sociological intelligence research and analysis.

SOCIOMETRY

In its applications to problems in social psychology, sociometry relates to techniques for depicting graphically the structure of relationships within a group. An organizational chart may depict formal relationships among elements within an organization; however, organizational charts do not reveal who actually talks to whom. Sociometric depictions—sociograms—do reveal the actual patterns of lines of communication and interaction. Given access to a group, interactions can be measured directly by observational techniques, or they can be measured by use of scaling devices such as questionnaires, which would be administered to members of a group. However, the types of groups that are of primary interest to the intelligence analyst or researcher are generally groups to which the researcher has only limited access. Consequently, the more conventional measuring techniques cannot be used.

One crude sociometric technique, however, might involve counting the number of instances in which a government official interacted with other officials at a formal reception. (But preparing a sociogram of this behavior would be of questionable value because a formal reception is an artificial situation and important people may talk to unimportant people as a matter of courtesy.) Another crude sociometric procedure would be to count the number of times certain names appeared in state-controlled mass media. Of course, the manner in which names are treated, that is, positively or negatively, must also be taken into account. The assumption in this type of analysis is that there is a direct correlation between the number of times a name appears or is mentioned and its importance.

In instances in which behavior can be observed—a researcher analyzing communication traffic, for example—records could be made of who interacts with whom and who initiates the interaction. Observations could be recorded as shown below in figure 10.5.

In figure 10.5, the observations are recorded initially as checkmarks placed at the matrix intersection of the sender and receiver. The checkmarks are converted to ones and zeroes in the second matrix.

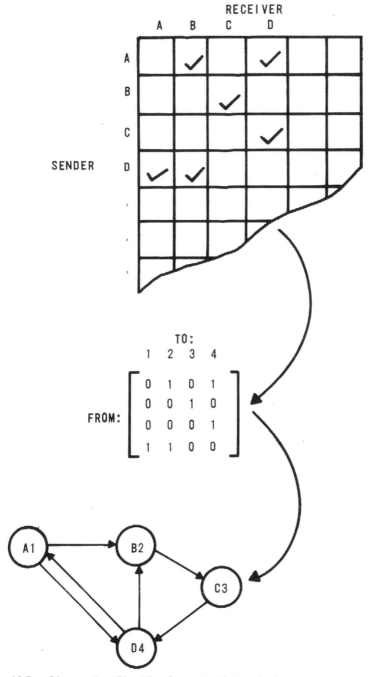

Figure 10.5. Observation Checklist Converted into a Sociogram

This representation is necessary if matrix multiplication is to be used to determine the number of indirect connections between various senders and receivers. In the example above, for instance, if the matrix were squared, then the link element of the new matrix (a'_{ik}) would be:

$$a'_{ik} = \sum_{j=1}^{n} a_{ij} a_{jk}$$

In the example above, the element $a_{i'2} = 0 \times 1 + 1 \times 0 + 0 \times 0 + 1 \times 1 = 1$. In other words, there is only one indirect connection between elements 1 and 2. (Element 4 is the link, e.g., $1 \rightarrow 4 \rightarrow 2$. Inspection shows, however, that there is also one *direct* connection between elements 1 and 2.)

This example, of course, is simple, and the linkages could be determined directly from the sociogram without too much difficulty. However, if the number of elements were great or if the analyst were concerned with determining various degrees of connectivity, then matrix multiplication would be necessary.

Another crude sociometric technique is to assess the significance of an individual on the basis of his proximity to the leader. For example, for years Lin Biao, the former heir apparent to Mao Zedong, could be seen standing next to Mao on reviewing stands, and the vicissitudes of Zhou Enlai could be observed (if not measured) by the number of other Chinese officials who would stand between Chou and Mao. The rank ordering of Soviet and Chinese officials at affairs-of-state parades, funerals, reception lines, and so on has been used widely as a crude sociometric device for establishing the relative prestige and importance of the individuals. Literally and figuratively, in the Soviet Union and in the People's Republic of China, people who fall from power fade out of the picture.

Sociometric techniques can be used in political intelligence, sociological intelligence, military intelligence (e.g., orders of battle, traffic analysis), and, conceivably, in biographic intelligence.

GAME THEORY

Game theory is basically a theory of decision-making participants in a *conflict* or *competitive* situation. In a competitive situation, each participant attempts to "influence in the action" in such a manner that the outcome is optimal for him. Game theory permits the decision maker to select an optimal course of action in light of the number of options available to each player and in light of the "rules" within which the options can be exercised. An optimal course of action is one that maximizes the player's probability of success and minimizes his probability of failure or loss.

Games can be classified according to the number of plays and according to the nature of the payoff. With respect to payoff, games are classified as either zero-sum games or non-zero-sum games. A zero-sum game is one in which the outcome of the game is a "win" for one participant and a "loss" (equal value) for the other. Translating game theory terminology to a real-world conflict situation, an unconditional surrender would be an example of a zero-sum conclusion, and a "negotiated settlement" would be an example of a non-zero-sum outcome.

Policy makers, disarmament negotiators, planners, and field commanders all use game theory in one form or another. For example, when a field commander makes his estimate of the situation and then chooses an appropriate course of action, he is using game theory. Although it is seldom done in the field, an estimate of the situation can be expressed mathematically in a series of matrices. The advantage of the mathematical depiction is that sometimes an optimal strategy becomes apparent that otherwise might be overlooked.

A very basic example of strategies and payoffs is shown in the matrix below (figure 10.6). Blue's strategies and payoffs are shown in the

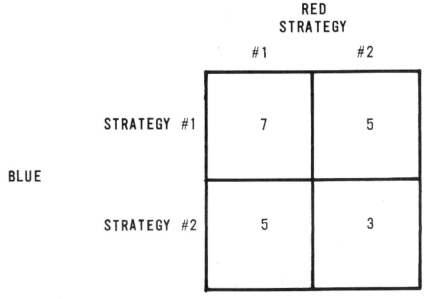

Figure 10.6.   An Example of a Two-Person Game Matrix

rows; Red's strategies and losses are shown in the columns. In figure 10.6, strategy 1 for Blue could pay off 7 or 5, whereas strategy 2 would yield 5 or only 3. From the standpoint of maximum gain, strategy 1 would be better for Blue. But Red can influence the outcome as well. For example, if Red would select strategy 1, Red could lose 7 or 5. However, by selecting strategy 2, Red could lose 5 or only 3. Obviously, strategy 2 would be better for Red. In strategy 2, Red's losses would never exceed 5, and they might be as low as 3.

In this example, the optimal choice for *both* sides would be a combination of Blue's strategy 1 and Red's strategy 2. This combination will guarantee that Blue's payoff will be *at least* 5, and it guarantees that Red's losses *will never exceed* 5. When a single value exists that is at the same time the minimum value in a row, and the maximum value in a column, the value is called a saddle point. In conflict situations, saddle points are usually the places where negotiations would prove most profitable to both sides. If the payoff matrix in the example just cited contained other values (as in figure 10.7), no saddle point would exist. In a case such as this, each player should adopt a mixed strategy by using each strategy a certain percentage of the time in order to maximize his gains and minimize his losses.

The percentage of the time a strategy should be used by a player is derived in the following manner. (1) Each player takes the absolute difference between the payoffs associated with each strategy. For Blue, | 7 − 3 | = 4, and | 5 − 6 | = 1. For Red, | 7 − 5 | = 2, and | 3 − 6 | = 3. (2) The differences between payoffs are summed for each player. (3) Each player calculates a proportion derived from each strategy and assigns that proportion to the alternate strategy. Therefore, Blue should play strategy 1 one-fifth of the time and strategy 2 four-fifths of the time. Red, on the other hand, should play strategy 1 three-fifths of the time, and strategy 2 two-fifths of the time (figure 10.8).

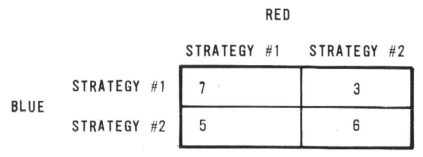

Figure 10.7.   An Example of a Two-Person Game Matrix with No Saddle Point

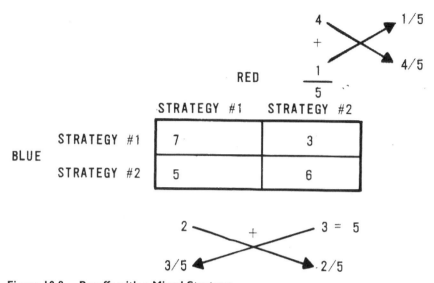

Figure 10.8.   Payoffs with a Mixed Strategy

Assuming that Blue always wishes to maximize his gains and that Red always wishes to minimize his losses, the expected payoff for Blue would be obtained by multiplying the values in column 1 by the proportion of the time Blue played each strategy, or the following equation.

$$\frac{(7 \times 1)}{5} + \frac{(5 \times 4)}{5} = \frac{27}{5}$$

Column 2 gives the same result, for example, as follows.

$$\frac{(3 \times 1)}{5} + \frac{(6 \times 4)}{5} = \frac{27}{5}$$

Likewise, for Red, the expected loss would be obtained similarly, for example, the following two equations.

$$\frac{(7 \times 3)}{5} + \frac{(3 \times 2)}{5} = \frac{27}{5}$$

and

$$\frac{(5 \times 3)}{5} + \frac{(6 \times 2)}{5} = \frac{27}{5}$$

Since this is a zero-sum game, Red's losses always equal Blue's gains in the long run. In a mixed-strategy solution, each strategy must be chosen randomly if the calculated payoff is to result.

To the reader who is unfamiliar with game theory, it may come as a surprise to discover how complex a seemingly simple game may become. For example, in the game of "Morra," in which each of two players shows one, two, or three fingers and at the same time guesses the number of fingers his opponent will show, each player has nine choices of strategy, and the possible combinations of payoffs for both players is eighty-one.[2] In "gaming," a situation in which an aircraft loaded with a certain mix of electronic devices would be flown (symbolically) against a target with another mix of electronic detectors and fire-control devices, the combination of choices and payoffs (i.e., combinations that would optimize the chances of the aircraft reaching the target undetected) could be of such magnitude that a computer would be necessary in order to identify the optimal mix. It is for this reason that computers are usually used in major war-gaming exercises.

Game theory, as developed by John von Neumann and Oskar Morgenstern, tends to be highly mathematical and addresses conflict primarily in the economic sense. Since the publication of their *Theory of Games and Economic Behavior*,[3] however, game theory has been applied to military and political conflicts as well. Perhaps the most popular and essentially nonmathematical treatment of game theory related to political and military problems can be found in Thomas C. Schelling's *The Strategy of Conflict*.[4] Game theory is basic to simulations involving conflict, for example, war games. Although game theory is not a predictive technique per se, its application does permit the researcher to anticipate appropriate strategies for all players. Assuming that all players of the game were rational and that the players would opt for the minimax solution—the solution that minimizes the chances for loss and maximizes the chances for success—game theory can be used as a basis for predicting outcomes given certain conditions of conflict.

WAR GAMING

War games are experiments with alternative tactics and strategies in a conflict situation.[5] Participants in war games often use game theory, but *game theory* and *war gaming* are not synonymous. Game theory relates to techniques of selecting optimum strategies. War gaming involves the applications of various strategies under various constraints in conflict situations. Game theory, in short, provides the theoretical basis for war gaming. One can utilize game theory apart from war games, and war games can be played without a mathematical analysis of payoffs.

Three terms are used typically in the discussion of war games: *games*, *models*, and *simulations*. Very briefly, a game is a contest played according to rules and decided by skill, strength, or chance. Games are essentially symbolic conflicts. No one gets hurt in the symbolic conflicts, but lessons can be learned from these conflicts nevertheless. A model, on the other hand, is a representation of an object or a process. For example, a mock-up is a model of a real piece of equipment, and a flowchart is a model of a process. Simulations, finally, are dynamic imitations of processes. To put it another way, a simulation is a dynamic model.

War games can be classified according to the extent to which they are abstract. Army-wide games in which units actually maneuver on the terrain and engage each other represent one end of a continuum. Computer simulations of conflict represent the other end. In the middle of this continuum are any number of combinations of realistic and symbolic analogs. A command post exercise (CPX) may be considered a war game, but other than the command posts, no subordinate units move physically. The "enemy" in a war game may consist of human "aggressor force" personnel, or the enemy may consist simply of unit designators and numerical indications of strength given to the players in writing or displayed electronically on a screen. The outcome of a game may be determined by the umpires on the ground, who observe the action and ostensibly make objective judgments, or the outcome may be determined by the mathematical manipulation of variables according to some theoretical and, ideally, validated model.

The nature of the game to be played determines the nature of the steps involved in the design of the game. For example, a game could be a man-to-man game, which would involve the actual movement of forces, or it could be a computer-assisted game, probably played on maps, in which a computer performed the clerical duties associated with games—duties such as scoring, determining kills, and keeping time. Or the game could be a man-machine game in which the machine made all of the evaluations and determined outcomes on the basis of the values submitted, tactics or strategies used, and the rules of play that were programmed into the computer.

In the first type of game, a scenario could be prepared and given to the players. The scenario would describe the general situation, perhaps a general order of battle, the respective missions of the two (or more) sides, and the rules of play. Upon receipt of the general plan, the forces would move to the field. Umpires who accompanied the opposing sides would do the scoring, make kill determinations, and perform other bookkeeping functions manually. The computer-assisted and man-machine games, on the other hand, would require the preparation of a series of mathematical or logical models that would represent certain subelements of the conflict; for example, a model of a surface-to-air missile engaging an aircraft, or an antisubmarine warfare model, and so on. Developing these kinds of games requires a sequence of steps, which include (1) defining the action to be gained; (2) identifying and classifying variables in terms of significance; (3) identifying and quantifying relations among variables; (4) designing the model (initially in flowchart form) and translating the model into computer instructions; (5) specifying trade-offs for the models and programming the computer accordingly; and (6) collecting real-world data for the purposes of obtaining realistic values for variables and for validation purposes (i.e., for determining if the simulated conflict did in fact yield outcomes that a genuine conflict situation would yield).

War games involving international conflict may require months, if not years, of preparation in order to develop models that would address the numerous subelements involved in such a conflict; for example, the military, political, and economic factors and their major interactions. Typically, as war games become more global, they also tend to become more general simply because the costs in modeling anything less than a major element of the conflict in fairly general terms would become prohibitively expensive. Furthermore, the nature of the game play also tends to become more complex when numerous subelements are addressed.

With respect to the predictive value of war games, the point made earlier in the discussion of game theory applies: a war game can only determine the statistical probability of an event occurring given certain variables and rules for manipulating these variables. In a weeklong war game played at the Naval War College in which the outcome of an engagement depended upon Green's forces detecting Red's surface units, a reconnaissance flight failed to detect the presence of Red's forces, and in the ensuing battle, Green was "defeated." By those who had access to both the Red and the Green side as well as to the master display (which the players did not), it was observed that the success of that single, critical flight was determined by one run of an analog computer. That single computer run (or toss of the dice) would hardly permit anyone to state unequivocally that Red's deployment and tactics were necessarily better than Green's, but it did drive home dramatically the importance of that single reconnaissance mission.

However, games serve an excellent diagnostic purpose by identifying which variables have the greatest effects on the outcomes. Aside from their value as training mechanisms and as a research vehicle, games are usually used to evaluate various courses of action in order to arrive at conclusions with respect to plans and policies.[6]

LINEAR PROGRAMMING

Goals can sometimes be expressed in terms of achieving a maximum payoff for a minimum investment or risk. For example, an investor might want to receive the maximum number of dollars of return on his investment, a manufacturer might want to produce the maximum number of units with a minimum amount of material, and a purchaser might want to buy the most or the best of a commodity for the least amount of money. Linear programming is a method that allows one to find a maximum or a minimum point (optimum point) to satisfy a goal (objective).

In nearly every type of operation (or organization), there are limitations or constraints upon the use of time and resources. If the limitations can each be expressed by the equation of a line, or equation 1, then linear programming may be used to find an optimum solution.

$$y = ax + b \qquad (1)$$

For example, the operations officer of a PSYOP unit that was operating a strategic radio broadcasting facility could use linear programming to maximize the number of potential listeners in light of certain operational constraints. His basic objective would be to maximize the size of the target audience that would hear spoken commentary, since the PSYOP "message" would be transmitted in this commentary. However, he realizes that the best way to gain and to hold his target audience's attention is to play traditional and popular music. Commentary, therefore, would have to be interspersed between musical selections.

If the broadcast day were defined as a mixture of time devoted to music and commentary, the proper proportions of each type of broadcasting can be discovered by solving a simple linear programming problem. Initially, the operations officer notes that his broadcast day is twelve hours long and that it will be divided into two types of broadcasts. The broadcast day is described by equation 2, where x equals the number of hours per day devoted to commentary, and y equals the hours devoted to music (figure 10.9).

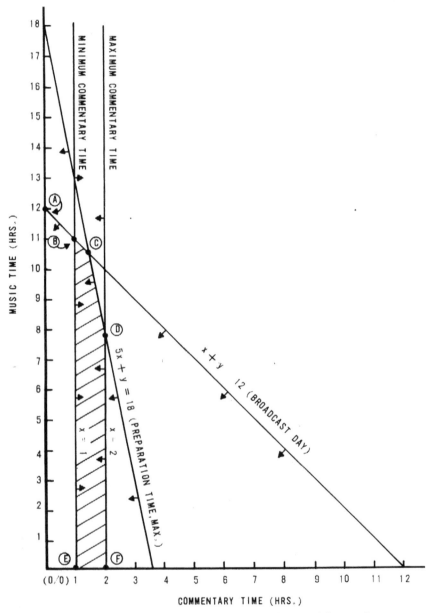

Figure 10.9. Graph of Optimal Programming with Imposed Constraints

$$12 \geq x + y \qquad (2)$$

The next limitations placed upon the program day are that there must be no fewer than five but no more than ten minutes per hour reserved for commentary. These limitations must be converted to the same units (hours) in order to be graphed. Two equations to describe these limitations are equations 3 and 4, since five minutes per hour equals one hour per twelve-hour day, and ten minutes per hour equals two hours per twelve-hour day.

$$x \geq 1 \qquad (3)$$

$$y \leq 2 \qquad (4)$$

Finally, the number of man-hours available to prepare broadcasts is limited. There are eighteen hours of labor available each day. It only takes one hour to prepare one hour of music, but it takes five hours to prepare one hour of commentary. (Actually, preparation of commentary consumes about fifteen hours for each hour of broadcast time, but it can be assumed that each message is repeated three times.) The equation to describe the constraint is equation 5.

$$18 \geq 5x + y \qquad (5)$$

After all of the important constraints are specified, the original objective must be expressed in terms of the common units (hours, in this case). Since the objective is to maximize the number of listeners to the station, something must be included about how different kinds of programs attract listeners. In the current example, it is assumed that music is twenty times as likely to attract and hold listeners as commentary.[7] Therefore, the total number of listeners would be a function of the number of commentary hours, plus twenty times the number of music hours, times a constant, or

$$N = k(x + 20y) \qquad (6)$$

The only points that are permissible solutions for the objective function are those that fall within the boundaries of all the constraints. For example, points B, C, and D as well as all the points in the shaded polygon (figure 10.9) are allowable mixtures of music and commentary programming. Point C is on the line $x + y = 12$, which means it uses up all 12 hours of programming. It is also on the line $5x + y = 18$, which means it uses up all 18 hours of labor. Point C also falls between the limits of 5 and 10 minutes of commentary per hour.

Point A, on the other hand, is not a valid solution because it allows no time for commentary and, therefore, violates the constraint of $x \geq 1$. It does satisfy the other two constraints and would be a valid solution if the $x \geq 1$ constraint were abandoned.

Linear programming theory also states that optimal solutions for the objective function are found at a *corner* of the polygon of acceptable solutions. The five corners of the polygon in the current example are B, C, D, E, and F. The only way to determine *which* corner is the optimal solution is to solve equation 6 at each corner (table 10.1).

Clearly, the value of N is maximized at point B $(N = 221K)$. Therefore, the maximum number of listeners would be achieved when the program consisted of 1 hour of commentary, or 5 minutes per hour, and 11 hours of music. The point B solution, although it uses the entire 12-hour broadcast day, does not require the 18 hours of preparation time. In fact, it requires (equation 7) only 16 hours of labor.

$$5(1) + 11 = 16 \tag{7}$$

The example of radio broadcasting contained in this explanation is much simpler than most real-world linear programming problems, but it contains all the necessary elements. In summary, the following factors must be present if linear programming is to be applied to a problem.

1. The researcher must be trying to optimize (maximize or minimize) something.
2. There must be more than one type of product, commodity, or output under consideration. In this case, the product was the composition of a broadcast day.
3. There must be constraints or limitations upon the resources that must be used to produce the commodity or product. (In the example cited, there were labor constraints, a limit on the broadcast day, and the constraint that between one and two hours must be used for commentary during a broadcast day.)
4. All constraints must be able to be described by linear equations.

Table 10.1.   x and y Values of Five Points

Point	x Value	y Value	K(x + 20y) = N
B	1	11	221K
C	1.5	10.5	211.5K
D	2	8	162K
E	1	0	1K
F	2	0	2K

The current example involved only two products. But linear programming may be applied to solve for any number of products. Most linear programming problems are complicated and time-consuming; consequently, they are best solved by use of computers. The General Electric System of the Defense Intelligence School has computer programs for solving linear programming problems.

There are some optimization problems that have constraints that cannot be expressed by lines, but that should be described instead by curves.

REGRESSION AND CORRELATION

The ability to identify a relationship is an important asset in solving problems, and regression analysis and correlation analysis are two invaluable techniques for studying relationships. Regression analysis, the first technique that will be described, enables a researcher to answer the question, "How much does one variable (a phenomenon, such as a condition, a number of events, and so on) increase or decrease when another variable increases or decreases?" For example, regression analysis could be used to determine how much the amount of supplies transported along a given road system would vary with increases or decreases in the amount of precipitation.

Correlation analysis (as discussed earlier in the book) enables the researcher to answer the question, "How strong is the relationship between two variables?" Correlation analysis, for example, would enable the researcher or analyst to determine how much confidence he could place in his estimate of the number of loads of supplies transported along a certain road network predicted on the basis of the amount of rainfall. Although regression analysis and correlation analysis often go hand in hand, they do not measure the same thing.

To illustrate the application of regression analysis and correlation analysis to a typical intelligence problem, the relationship between the monthly rate of inflation in a country and the number of acts of violence per month directed toward the government in that country will be analyzed. The data for both variables (table 10.2) are measures taken each month for ten successive months. The data are recorded in chronological order, but it should be noted that the timing of a particular violent act or of a particular inflation rate does not enter into calculations. Although the timing of these variables may be important, the timing would have to be explained by another type of analysis.

Table 10.2.   Number of Acts of Violence and Monthly Rates of Inflation

MONTH	MONTHLY RATE OF INFLATION (x_i)	NUMBER OF ACTS OF VIOLENCE/MONTH (y_i)	RATE X ACTS $(x_i \cdot y_i)$	RATE SQUARED $(x_i \; y_i)$	ACTS SQUARED $(y_i)2$
1	.4	2	.8	.16	4
2	1.6	6	9.6	2.56	36
3	2.4	14	33.6	5.76	196
4	1.6	17	27.2	2.56	289
5	3.2	14	44.8	10.24	196
6	3.6	26	93.6	12.96	676
7	3.2	22	70.4	10.24	484
8	4.4	29	127.6	19.36	841
9	4.0	21	84.0	16.00	441
10	1.2	7	8.4	1.44	49
	$\Sigma x_i = 25.6$	$\Sigma y_i = 158$	$\Sigma x_i y_i = 500$	$\Sigma x_i^2 = 81.28$	$\Sigma y_i^2 = 3212$
	$\mu u x_i = 2.56$	$\mu u y_i = 15.8$			

Once the data had been plotted on a graph (figure 10.10), the analyst would draw a single line to represent the relationship between the data. He could do this in several ways. The simplest way would be to take a straightedge and draw a straight line between the points so that the line would be as close as possible to each point on the graph. However, there are disadvantages with this technique: it is subjective and unreliable. Different analysts will obtain different results using this method, and, therefore, it provides a poor foundation for further analysis of the strength of a relationship.

The most common mathematical method for drawing a regression line is called the least-squares method. The method is so named because it specifies the line that makes the total of the squared distances from actual y values to the line as small as possible. The actual y_i minus the predicted y ($y_i - \hat{y}_i$, figure 10.10) is measured parallel to the y axis. The final form of the equation is the same as the equation of any line, namely equation 1, where y is a predicted y value, x is an actual x value, a is the slope (or rate of increase in y divided by the rate of increase in x), and b is the intercept point (or where the line crosses the y axis).

$$y = ax + b \tag{1}$$

The equations necessary to solve for the values of a and b are equations 2 and 3.

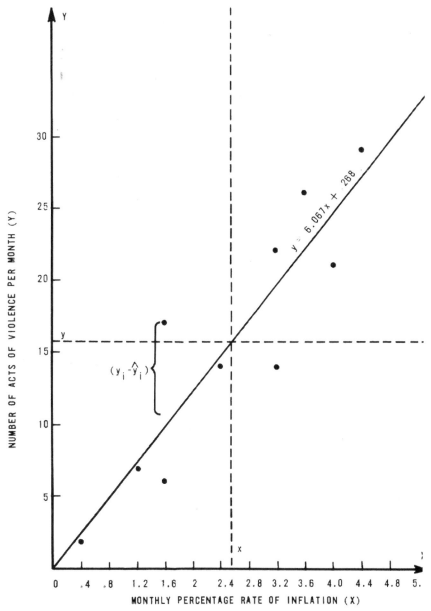

Figure 10.10. Regression and Correlation Analysis of Acts of Violence and Monthly Rates of Inflation in Country X

$$\sum_{i=1}^{10} y_i = a \sum_{i=1}^{10} x_i + b \cdot n \tag{2}$$

$$\sum_{i=1}^{10} x_i y_i = a \sum_{i=1}^{10} x_i^2 + b \sum_{i=1}^{10} x_i \tag{3}$$

Although equations 2 and 3 may appear involved, they are easy to solve. The analyst knows all the x_i values and y_i values, and he knows that n equals 10 (that is, ten months, in this example). He can compute the necessary sums and products (which appear in table 10.2). Therefore, 2 and 3 become two simultaneous equations containing two unknowns, which can be solved by elementary algebra. Making the necessary substitutions, equations 2 and 3 become equations 4 and 5.

$$158 = 25.6a + 10b \tag{4}$$

and

$$500 = 81.28a + 25.6b \tag{5}$$

The value for a equals 6.067. The value for b equals .268. The equation for the regression line is equation 6.

$$y = 6.067x + .268 \tag{6}$$

When the analyst has an x value, he then uses this equation to *predict* a corresponding y value. If he were told, for example, that next month's inflation rate would be about 2.8, he would compute equations 7 and 8.

$$y = (6.067 \times 2.8) + .268 \tag{7}$$

$$y = 17.2556 \tag{8}$$

When the analyst uses the equation $y = ax + b$, the purpose is to predict y from a given x value. If it were desired to predict x from a given y value, the proper equation would be $x = ay + b$. The a and b values in this equation would be different from the a and b values in $y = ax + b$.

Throughout this discussion, the prediction of y values from x values has been stressed. The prediction of one variable from another is very different from saying that one variable *causes* another. Usually several analyses of the relationships among variables would be necessary before the cause of a variable could be established.

After the relationship described by the equation of a line is established, the analyst may wish to determine *how well* the line describes the set of data points. If the line contained all of the actual data points, the points are said to be correlated perfectly, and the correlation coefficient for the data would equal ± 1.0. At the opposite extreme is a set of points that would appear as a fat cloud when plotted. Such a set of data points would have a correlation coefficient of 0.0. A correlation coefficient is positive if one variable increases while the other variable increases. A correlation coefficient is negative if one variable increases while the other decreases. Either correlation may be important.

The correlation coefficient is calculated using the following formula:

$$ r = \frac{n\Sigma xy - \Sigma x\Sigma y}{\sqrt{[n(\Sigma x^2) - (\Sigma x)^2]\,[n(\Sigma y^2) - (\Sigma y)^2]}} \tag{9} $$

Again, equation 9 looks complicated. But it is easy to substitute the various products and sums computed earlier. For the current example,

$$ r = \frac{5000 - 4044.8}{\sqrt{(157.44)\,(7156)}} \tag{10} $$

$$ .8999 \text{ or approximately } .90 \tag{11} $$

A correlation coefficient of .90 is very high, as indicated by the fact that none of the points is very far from the regression line (figure 10.10).

If the analyst wished to establish a confidence level for an estimated value of y, he must then compute the *standard error of the estimate* $(\sigma y \bullet x)$. Since there is a normal distribution of data points around the regression line, it can be said that 68 percent of the actual y values fall within 1 $\sigma_{y \bullet x}$ above or below the regression line.

The formula for the $\sigma_{y \bullet x}$ is shown in equations 12 through 15.

$$ \sigma_{y \bullet x} \quad \frac{\sqrt{\Sigma y^2 - b\Sigma y - a\Sigma xy}}{n - 2} \tag{12} $$

Therefore, in the current example:

$$\sigma_{y \bullet x} = \frac{\sqrt{3212 - 42.344 - 3033.5}}{8} \tag{13}$$

$$= \frac{\sqrt{136.156}}{8} \tag{14}$$

$$= 4.125 \tag{15}$$

If the analyst were asked to predict the likely number of acts of violence, given that next month's inflation rate would be about 2.8 percent, he would first compute equation 6 and determine that there will be 17 acts of violence. Finally, using the $\sigma_{y \bullet x}$, he could report that there is a 68 percent likelihood that there will be (equations 16 and 17) 13 to 21 acts of violence in the next month, and a 95 percent likelihood that there will be (equations 18 and 19) between 9 and 25 acts of violence in the next month.

$$17.2556 - 1_{y \bullet x} = 13.1306 \tag{16}$$

$$17.2556 - 1_{y \bullet x} = 21.3806 \tag{17}$$

$$17.2556 - 1.96_{y \bullet x} = 9.1706 \tag{18}$$

$$17.2556 - 1.96_{y \bullet x} = 25.3406 \tag{19}$$

History has shown that citizen unrest is often correlated with economic instability, so the current example probably shows a meaningful correlation between sets of data. However, sometimes one discovers high values of correlation that are spurious.[8] The analyst's best defense against placing too much importance upon the value of the correlation coefficient is his own knowledge of the variables.

Although a line was fitted to the data sets in the current regression example, sometimes a curve rather than a straight line better describes a relationship. The mathematical expressions necessary to create these curves are, for the most part, much more complicated than the equations for the linear relationship.

The current example used only two variables, but regression and correlation analysis may also be completed for three or more variables. For example, the monthly rate of inflation, the number of acts of violence per month, and the margin of profit for large industries could all be subjected to correlation analysis. Regression analysis and correlation analysis are described in nearly every book on statistics.

GRAPHIC DEPICTIONS AS AIDS TO ANALYSIS

The value of graphics in printed reports or as briefing aids is obvious. What may not be apparent, however, is the value that graphics may have in the *analysis* of data. Graphic depictions do more than transform numerical data or words into pictures. Very often graphic depictions reveal relationships that might not be apparent otherwise. Described below are four examples of the uses of graphics in various types of analyses.

UTILITY CURVES

One example of a graphic depiction that directly aids analysis is the utility curve. Utility curves are often used in business and industry to determine "break-even" points—points where, for example, a return could be realized on an investment, or the point in time when the per-unit cost of manufacturing a certain commodity would be lowest. In mass production, the first item produced is the most expensive. As more items are produced, the per-unit cost decreases until a certain point is reached. Utility curves help the analyst to determine these points (figure 10.11).

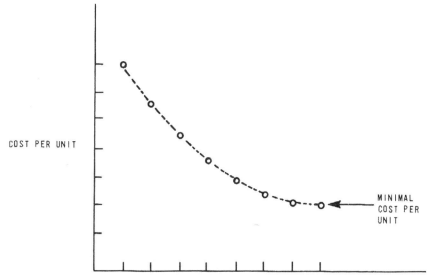

Figure 10.11.   A Utility Curve Showing the Decreasing Costs per Unit over Time

Utility curves might be employed in analyzing geopolitical problems as well. For example, the United States, over the years, may have been providing a fixed amount of assistance annually to a country in exchange for base privileges. It may be the case, however, that the recipient country would begin restricting privileges granted earlier. A graph such as the one shown in figure 10.12 would depict the value (or worth) of the privileges received for a fixed amount of dollars paid out over a number of years. The worth or value of the privileges received would have to be expressed in a unit that would permit comparisons with expenditures. In

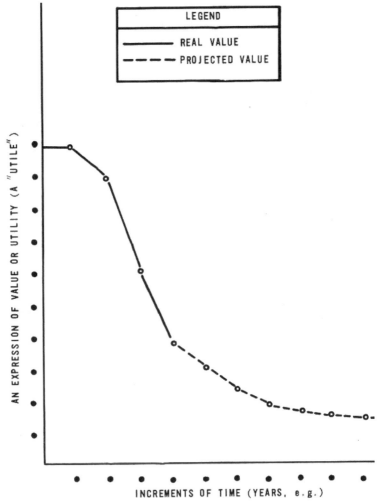

LEGEND

REAL VALUE

PROJECTED VALUE

AN EXPRESSION OF VALUE OR UTILITY (A "UTILE")

INCREMENTS OF TIME (YEARS, e.g.)

Figure 10.12.   A Graph of the Actual and Projected Worth of a U.S. Expenditure in Country X over Time

short, it might require the researcher or analyst to place a dollar figure, for example, on intangibles such as "international goodwill," or on the worth of a country participating in an alliance—admittedly, no easy matter in some cases.

The graph would indicate that the value of the privileges gained versus the funds expended fell off sharply after the second year, and that the projected return on investment was estimated to continue to decline but at a slower rate. The graphic depiction, in this case, makes the presentation of data more dramatic than, say, a column of figures. But the graph may serve another purpose as well.

If the political or military objectives of the host country were known, a similar type of curve could be plotted for that country. For example, the host country might need a certain quantity of material to equip a specified number of units of its armed forces. If the major source of financial aid used for the purchase of this equipment were credits or payments made by the United States for base privileges, then the degree to which that country was progressing toward its immediate objective could be plotted (figure 10.13.)

The graph shows that the point where the two lines cross over is about the point in time where the host country's returns (returns in the form of some capability that was translated into dollars or into some other expression of utility) begin to accelerate. The crossover point might also represent a point beyond which the United States might no longer consider its investment to be cost-effective. At the minimum, however, this crossover point would indicate a point in time when negotiations might prove most fruitful.[9]

In this example, only one "utile" value was expressed. Presumably, this single value represented a composite of many separate elements. Generally, it would be easier and perhaps more valid to plot the utilities of each component value separately rather than expressing all values as one single value.

BAR GRAPHS FOR COMPARISON

As mentioned earlier, sometimes depicting data graphically reveals information that would not be too apparent otherwise. An actual example of this is shown below. The thematic output of North Korea's international and domestic broadcast facilities was tabulated over a two-week period in 1971. The tabulated data, categorized by themes, are shown in figure 10.14A. Graphing the same data, however, made readily apparent the differences in the amount of time devoted to certain themes in domestic broadcasts versus the amount of time devoted

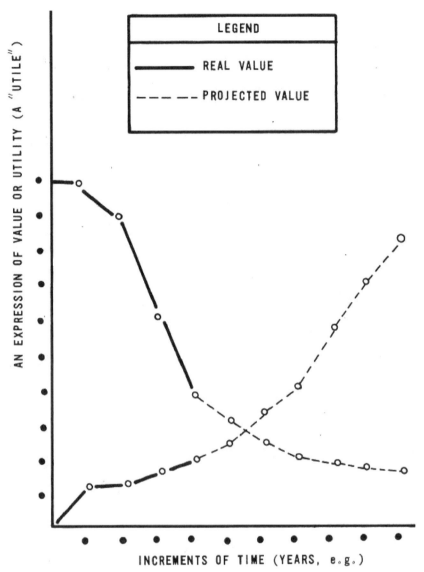

Figure 10.13.   A Graph of the Actual and Projected Worth of a U.S. Expenditure for Country X and for the United States

to the same themes in international broadcasts. For example, the theme "propagation of ideology" constituted 34 percent of the output for international audiences, but only 14 percent for domestic audiences. On the other hand, the theme "present success of socialism" constituted 49 percent of the output for domestic audiences, but only 18 percent for the international audience (figures 10.14 A and B).

THEME	INTERNATIONAL BROADCASTS		DOMESTIC BROADCASTS	
	MINUTES	PERCENT	MINUTES	PERCENT
PRAISE OF THE LEADER	35	3	45	3
PROPAGATION OF IDEOLOGY	349	34	177	14
GLORIFICATION OF THE REVOLUTION	22	2	1	1
PRESENT SUCCESS OF SOCIALISM	180	18	640	49
GUIDANCE FOR FUTURE SUCCESS	12	1	41	3
INTERNATIONAL PRESTIGE	210	20	191	15
SUPPORT FOR PEOPLE'S STRUGGLE	8	1	32	2
NEGATIVE TREATMENT: U.S.	32	3	12	1
NEGATIVE TREATMENT: ROK	136	13	140	11
NEGATIVE TREATMENT: JAPAN	46	5	16	1

Figure 10.14A.   Comparison of North Korea's International and Domestic Thematic Coverage for a Two-Week Period

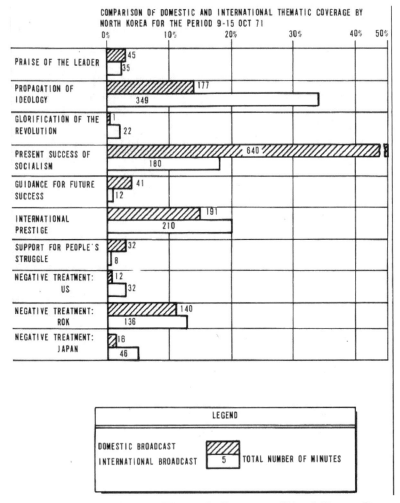

Figure 10.14B. A Bar Graph of Thematic Coverage of North Korean Domestic and International Broadcast Facilities for a Two-Week Period

TERRAIN PROFILING

Terrain profiling is often used to determine areas that could not be reached by direct-fire weapons. But it can be used for other purposes whenever line of sight is critical. For example, a telecommunications analyst might want to determine how many microwave relay towers would have to be constructed in order to permit microwave transmissions to and from two cities. In the example shown in figure 10.15, for instance, the analyst could determine that seven relay towers would

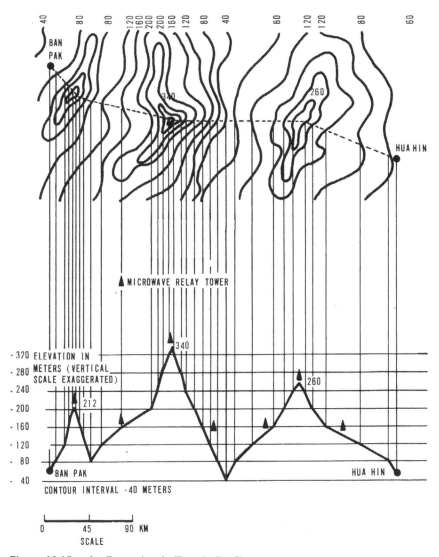

Figure 10.15.   An Example of a Terrain Profile

be required between Ban Pak and Hua Hin. His determination would be based upon a maximum transmission range of approximately 90 kilometers between towers and a direct line-of-sight requirement. The exaggerated terrain profile was prepared by extending vertical lines from the most plausible route for the location of towers—the route that would utilize the highest terrain elevations and that would have the minimum "masking."

TREND ANALYSIS

Graphs are especially useful in trend analysis. For example, the graph in figure 10.16 shows the number of anti–United States statements appearing in a foreign country's official newspaper for an eight-month period. The graph reveals peak periods in May and June, and plausible reasons for these peaks would have to be established, possibly from a chronology of past events. However, the analyst or researcher might be called upon to determine if the plotted data indicated anything unusual or significant. If prior data for similar periods in the past were available, separate graphs would be overlaid (or a combined graph prepared) as shown in figure 10.17, and a comparison could be made directly. In the example cited, for instance, it would appear that the current "trend" represented no dramatic departure from prior "trends."

Graphs can be used to plot likely times to completion. For example, if the rate of progress had been established for constructing the rail line from Maoming (21º 41'N, 110º 51'E) to Hsinhsing (22º42'N, 112º13'E), then the estimated distances to be completed within certain time periods could be graphed (figure 10.18). Another way of depicting progress would be to make the estimated time plots on a quasi-map graph, as shown in figure 10.19.

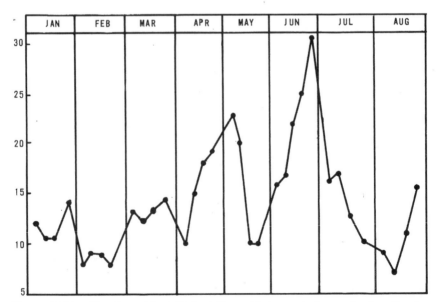

Figure 10.16.   Number of Anti–United States Statements Appearing in a Foreign Medium for an Eight-Month Period

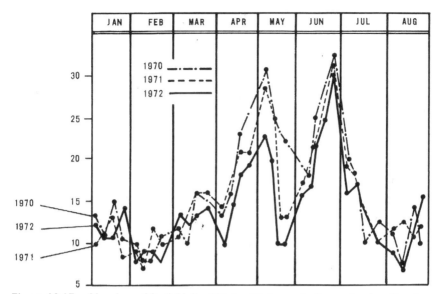

Figure 10.17. Number of Anti–United States Statements Appearing in a Foreign Medium for an Eight-Month Period (Three Years)

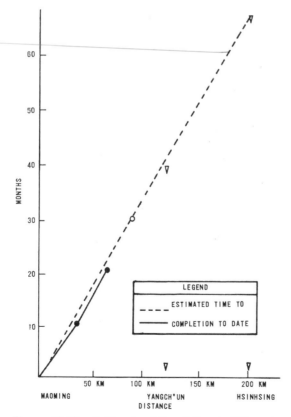

Figure 10.18. A Graph of the Estimated Time to Complete a Rail Line

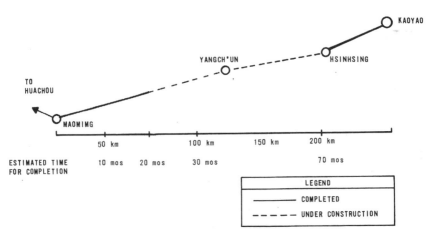

Figure 10.19.   Estimated and Real Time to Complete a Rail Line Plotted on a Map

SUMMARY

- Descriptive methodologies are basic to descriptive as well as to predictive research. Very often it is necessary to describe what exists at the present time in order to be able to predict what will exist or occur in the future.
- The construction of analogies is a basic analytical procedure used most universally in intelligence research. War games, simulations, and models are all analogies of different aspects of reality. Analogies are used as guides to reasoning in all of the components of strategic intelligence.
- Graphic depictions are not so much specific analytical techniques as they are methods for transforming data. Consequently, they are relevant to descriptive as well as to predictive research and analysis activities.

NOTES

1. The methodology referred to as "The Generation of Alternative Futures" in the next chapter is a case in point. There is nothing in the methodology that involves developing and validating conceptual models, and the products of the methodology are scenarios (descriptions) of future conditions that might exist if certain events were to occur. However, this methodology is employed in future-oriented problems, and not for description of current situations.

2. There are nine strategies for each player, hence, a square matrix with nine rows, nine columns, and eighty-one payoff squares.

3. John von Neumann and Oskar Morgenstern, *Theory of Games and Economic Behavior* (Princeton: Princeton University Press, 1947).

4. Thomas C. Schelling, *The Strategy of Conflict* (Cambridge, MA: Harvard University Press, 1963).

5. As the term is used in this context, war games would include any type of *conflict* simulation. By this definition, simulations of political, economic, and technological conflict would be considered variations of war games along with the more familiar military conflict simulations or *Kriegspiele*.

6. Clark C. Abt, "War Gaming," *International Science and Technology*, August 1964, 29–37.

7. This ratio is not unrealistic. In countries where listening to foreign broadcasts is prohibited, radio programming that utilizes the maximum amount of music for the minimum amount of spoken commentary poses the least risk of detection for the surreptitious listener.

8. For example, for many years the number of graduates in theology from Oxford University was nearly perfectly correlated with the number of arrests made for prostitution in an Australian city.

9. In game theory terminology, this crossover point would be roughly analogous to a saddle point.

11

Prediction, Forecasting, and Haruspicy

With the intelligence community's overriding concern for reducing uncertainty, it is not surprising that techniques for anticipating future events or conditions would have a special attraction for the intelligence researcher or analyst. This chapter discusses selected techniques for anticipating future events or conditions that have been (or can be) used in intelligence research and analysis. The first part of this chapter discusses the nature of prediction and forecasting, discusses assumptions underlying predictions, and describes the relationship of a technique to the nature of the phenomenon being considered.

Although this chapter is concerned with methodologies for forecasting, there is nothing sacrosanct about the methodology that limits its application to predicting or anticipating future events. Simulations, for example, can be used for diagnostic purposes as well as for predictive purposes. That accurate predictions have been made on the basis of nonpredictive techniques thus is not only possible, but is also highly probable.

TYPES OF PHENOMENA AND THEIR RELATIONSHIP TO FORECASTING

At the outset, it should be apparent that some types of phenomena are easier to forecast than others. At one end of a continuum, for example, are short-term, unique events that occur at specific points in time. These are the most difficult types of phenomena to predict because they may not have any precedents. Very often, unfortunately, these are the types of events that are of most concern to the intelligence community. An example of this type of phenomenon would be an unexpected coup that toppled a government overnight, or the defection of a key scientist on a highly classified defense-related project, or a discovery of large deposits of a strategic commodity.

In the middle of the continuum are events that occur over a period of time. There may be little doubt about the outcome, but the concern may be to establish when the outcome will occur or what the effects may be. Admittedly, the point in time at which a phenomenon started may be considered a unique event, but the event is nevertheless continuous for a given period of time. An example of a continuous event would be a country's construction of its first aircraft carrier. The precise time that the carrier was started (e.g., the specific point in time when the first line was drawn on a plan) was a unique event. But, for the sake of this discussion, the time events and occurrences that would take place until the carrier completed its sea trials and became fully operational could be considered as a continuous sequence of events. At the other end of the continuum of phenomena are cyclical events or conditions whose occurrences are just short of inevitable; for example, phases of the moon, tides, seasons, and, of course, the diurnal cycle itself.

PROBABILISTIC STATEMENTS AND THEIR RELATIONSHIP TO TYPES OF PHENOMENA

Predictions in intelligence are nearly always couched in some probabilistic terms. (Even this statement is translatable into probabilistic terms.) Not surprisingly, the highest probabilities of occurrence can be associated with cyclic phenomena. Not only is the probability of a cyclical event occurring high, but the confidence that an analyst or a researcher may have in his prediction is also high.[1] With respect to continuous phenomena, once they have been detected, subsequent events or effects can often be predicted with a fairly high degree of accuracy. In many cases, precedents exist for continuous phenomena, and researchers can infer future events on the basis of analogous antecedents. Furthermore, by monitoring development of continuous phenomena, analysts and researchers can revise their estimates and change their probabilities.

Unique events, however, pose the most difficult problems in forecasting. And it is in the realm of forecasting unique events that the more esoteric prediction methodologies are employed. Interestingly, as will be pointed out later, these methodologies for addressing unique events are essentially techniques for employing subjective judgments of experts. However, even these more esoteric techniques deal more often with *possibilities* relating to *classes* of events rather than *probabilities* relating to a *specific and unique* event.

ASSUMPTIONS—PRAGMATIC AND PROBLEMATIC

Every prediction (or predictive model) is based on assumptions. And it is usually the validity of the assumption that determines the accuracy of the prediction.[2] Perhaps one of the most fundamental assumptions is that events which occurred in the past will occur again in the future. The causal factors for an event's occurrence may not be known, but predictions based on the assumption that previous events will occur again are usually based on large numbers of observations. For example, it is not necessary to understand how or why lunar eclipses occur in order to predict that they will occur and when they will occur.

Higher on an imaginary ladder of abstraction are assumptions that the same collective factors that brought about (or caused) an event in the past will bring about a similar result in the future. The most familiar expressions of this assumption are weather forecasts. Having established and tested cause-and-effect relationships and having classified and coded all of the factors that determine meteorological conditions, meteorologists can make very accurate predictions for different time periods.[3] Predictions based on the identification of causal factors are generally highly reliable, and in laboratory situations, they are practically infallible. The identification of causal factors permits researchers to construct deterministic models—models that will unerringly predict accurate outcomes *if* the data provided to the model are correct. Again, this is relatively easy to do in laboratory situations, but very difficult to do in unstructured situations involving human behavior.

Another common assumption, and one that manifests itself especially in the behavior of investors in stocks, is that a trend that exists now will continue—at least for the immediate future. Thus, upward surges of the market are stimulated in part by their own momentum, and downward plunges are exacerbated by the expectation that the downward trend will continue. A drop in the market generates pessimism, which stimulates more selling. Aside from "technical adjustments" due to profit taking, trends continue until some potentially significant event brings about a change in buyers' expectations. The assumption that trends continue (or will continue for some specified period of time) is the assumption that underlies all extrapolations, one of the more common techniques for predicting trends.

In the realm of social behavior, assumptions are made about how the other side will behave. In fact, interpersonal relations would be impossible without minimal expectations (assumptions) of how humans will behave under certain circumstances.

Expectations of human behavior are also based on observations of past behavior, and again the prevailing assumption is that behaviors which existed in the past will persist in the future.

This assumption paid off well in the decisive battle of Tannenberg in 1914. Very briefly, Colonel General Max von Prittwitz und Graffon's Eighth German Army under Hindenburg faced two Russian armies in East Prussia whose combined forces greatly outnumbered their own. However, Lieutenant Colonel Max von Hoffman, a German staff officer, recalled that the two Russian generals, Pavel Rennenkampf and Aleksandr Samsonov, were bitter enemies. (They were seen fighting in a railway station in Mukden during the Russo-Japanese War.) On the basis of their past behavior, von Hoffman predicted that neither would make any special effort to come to the aid of the other if he were hard-pressed. On the basis of this prediction, Hindenburg ordered Prittwitz und Graffon to expose his flank and to engage the Russian Second Army commanded by Samsonov. Rennenkampf, true to his predicted behavior, did little to relieve the pressure on Samsonov, who was subsequently defeated. Shortly thereafter, Rennenkampf's First Army was also defeated at the Battle of the Masurian Lakes. Von Hoffman's prediction of behavior based on past observation proved accurate.[4]

A fundamental assumption that is typically made about other humans, for example, the "other side," is that they are rational—rational in the sense that certain acts would be perceived by *all* participants or observers as being beneficial or detrimental, either with respect to cost for benefit gained or with respect to survival. And admittedly, assumptions of this nature are necessary starting points. But they have their weaknesses.

For example, from a rational standpoint of cost-effectiveness, the procedures used by the scientists and engineers on the Manhattan Project to develop the atomic bomb were fantastically expensive. Not knowing which of two methods would work, General Leslie Groves ordered the construction of two production facilities, one using the gaseous diffusion method and the other using a centrifugal method for producing fissionable material. Both methods had only a theoretical chance of success, and both procedures were very costly. But the stakes were high, and the fear that Germany would develop fissionable material first made the risk of wasting millions of dollars an acceptable one. In light of the monumental technical difficulties that had to be overcome, and in light of the tremendous costs in time, manpower, and facilities, it is little wonder that the highly rational German scientist Werner Heisenberg refused to believe that the Americans had in fact detonated successfully three atomic devices.

Heisenberg's incredulity about American atomic capabilities reflects a host of other assumptions that prevail when behavior is anticipated. For example, Heisenberg assumed that because the highly touted German physicists could not devise methods for producing large amounts of fissionable material, neither could any other group of physicists. For years, American planners assumed that the Japanese would never surrender in battle and, if they were captured, would refuse to cooperate with their interrogators. Both assumptions initially had a degree of face validity, but subsequently proved invalid.

Success in battle is often a function of risks, and risks are not rational in the conventional sense of the word. Assumptions are a necessary part of every predictive technique. Assumptions serve a pragmatic function in the sense that they provide a basic framework on which a predictive model can be constructed. In addition, assumptions are necessary for planners to choose an optimum course of action. As T. C. Schelling stated, "In any analysis that leads to a choice of a particular strategy or weapon system from among several alternatives, there is typically some assumption about the behavior of the enemy. If it is not explicitly stated, it is embedded somewhere in the analysis."[5] But in the realm of anticipating behavior, the unvalidated assumption can debase the whole predictive exercise.

DELPHI TECHNIQUES

The simplistic solution to the problem of predicting what will happen in the year 19— would be to ask the experts. And decision makers have been "asking the experts" for centuries (with varying degrees of success).[6] On the assumption that the collective judgment and wisdom of several experts is better than the estimates or predictions of one, a technique for eliciting and combining judgments systematically from a group of experts has been developed. Appropriately, the technique is referred to as the Delphi technique.

This is how the technique is applied. A series of questions is asked of each expert. The experts submit their judgments individually. The results of all of the judgments are tabulated, and these results are sent back to the experts for modification. In essence, the experts are asked to reevaluate their original estimates in light of the estimates and the rationales for the estimates submitted by other experts. The results of the second iteration are tabulated, and the new results are again sent back to the experts for revision. The process continues until a fairly high degree of consensus is reached, or until the experts would no longer modify their previous estimates.

Typically, the technique has been used in technological forecasting. But the technique could be used in any type of problem-solving situation for which there was no answer, but only varying opinion. For example, in an early study conducted by RAND, the technique was used to address issues such as predictions of scientific breakthroughs, predictions of the impact of automation, predictions on progress in space, and predictions of weapon systems of the future.

The technique can be employed in a number of different ways. For example, questionnaires can be administered anonymously so that one expert would not know the identities of other experts, and the results of these questionnaires could be processed manually. Another procedure would be to have the experts interact directly with each other, either in a face-to-face meeting or by use of teleconferencing techniques. Still another method would be to employ teletype devices connected to computers' memory devices. Although expensive and restrictive (in the sense that the expert must be near a terminal), this method permits the computers to perform the relatively simple statistical operations (e.g., calculating means, medians, and quartiles), to store and retrieve earlier responses, and to present new data in real time.

The major advantage of the technique is that it permits analysts to obtain an objective consensus of expert judgment. Another advantage of the technique is that it makes the rationale underlying a specific estimate or prediction explicit for everyone.

The weakness of the technique is that a truly perspicacious expert's judgment might be lost when a consensus that actually represents a *range* of judgments is produced. In face-to-face situations, for example, one expert might be swayed more by the rhetoric than by the validity of another expert's argument. But the potential for this problem exists whenever humans interact, and is not necessarily a weakness of the Delphi technique per se. Administering the technique remotely and anonymously is one way of reducing the impact of "rhetorical intimidation."

The Delphi technique would be applicable to a range of estimative or predictive-type problems encountered in economic, political, scientific and technical, and, possibly, military intelligence research and analysis.

GENERATION OF ALTERNATIVE FUTURES

Although similar to the Delphi technique, the generation of alternative futures does not require the systematic eliciting of experts' judgments until a consensus is reached. Instead, the generation of alternative futures uses the creative powers of a single person or of a group of experts working together to produce a number of scenarios.

Basically, the generation of alternative futures involves specifying certain assumptions about a people, a country, an international situation, or a technological development, and then inferring the various outcomes that might result under the stated conditions. Alternative futures are usually cast in the form of scenarios—narratives that describe conditions, behaviors, and acts of people and their impacts on a future environment.

Alternative futures are not predictions in their own right. They are simply descriptions of possibilities. Alternative futures can be ranked in terms of possible, plausible, and most likely outcomes, but they are not predictive in the sense that what is forecast must necessarily come to be.

Herman Kahn developed a number of alternative futures for the 1970s in which he attempted to describe the results of United States-Soviet detente, the effects of political and military realignments on NATO, and the effects of evolving military technology. In developing his alternative futures, Kahn used game theory, systems analysis, and cost-benefit ratios to create a set of realistic, plausible futures. In a less detailed fashion, Morton H. Halperin, in his short book *China and the Bomb*,[7] also generated a series of alternative futures pertaining to the People's Republic of China's acquisition of a nuclear capability and delivery system.

Alternative futures are often used in policy formulation. Although one cannot necessarily predict which of several "futures" will result, one can usually anticipate what the results of certain futures will be. Alternative futures, in a more limited sense, are also generated when scenarios of war games are prepared. Interestingly, one of the purposes for which a game may be played is to determine (quasi-empirically) what the implications of certain futures may be.[8]

There is no single technique that comprises the methodology for generating alternative futures. In certain cases, the Delphi technique has been used, and in other cases, simple, straight-line extrapolations of present conditions into the future have been used. Experts familiar with the problems being addressed can identify limiting factors and modify the straight-line extrapolations accordingly. Like in every other technique that utilizes judgment, expert knowledge of the subject matter is essential if the alternative futures are to have any validity.[9]

EXTRAPOLATION

One of the more common methods of forecasting future conditions or trends involves projecting into the future the trends or conditions that have existed in the past and exist at the present. In its simplest form, this "extrapolation" technique involves extending a line of a graph to depict the anticipated changes in the future on the basis of the information known to date (figure 11.1).

In the first example of extrapolation (figure 11.2), a constant number of items was added each year. In other words, N items $(y_2 - y_1)$ were added during time T $(x_2 - x_1)$, and the numerical change, or N/T, was constant. The increase in many phenomena through time is constant, so the figure that describes those phenomena through time is a straight line.

Some types of phenomena are not described well by straight lines, however. Population growth is a case in point. Plotting population growth is like compounding interest. As the number of people in a population increases, so does the base, which produces subsequent generations, increase.

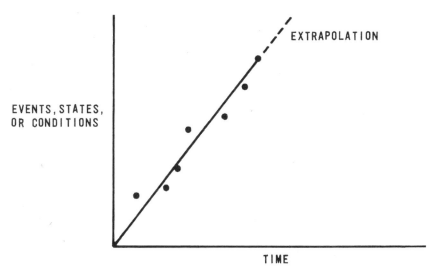

Figure 11.1.   Simple "Straight-Line" Extrapolation

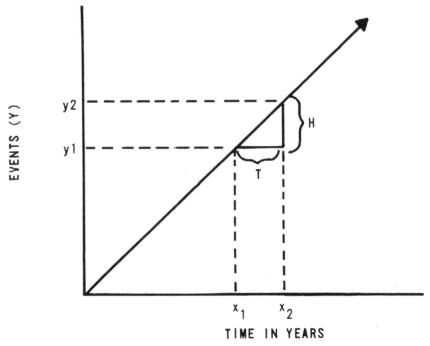

Figure 11.2.   Extrapolation with a Constant Change

The number of people in a population that is growing by a constant *percentage* can be illustrated by an exponential curve (figure 11.3). The curve can be drawn by hand, or a formula can be applied to the known data. The simplest form for the equation that describes a constant percentage growth rate is

$$y_2 = y_1 (1 + r)^N$$

where y_1 equals the current population, r equals the yearly percentage increase in population, N equals the number of years between the present (x_1) and the year for which the population projection is being made (x_2), and y equals the projected population in year x_2.

When this formula is employed, r, the yearly percentage increase in population, is computed by using the known population levels in the past few years. Most of the points that represent the known population levels do *not* lie on the curve. When the formula is used, however, the projected populations for future years do lie on the curve. This characteristic is common to all extrapolation techniques. It is not

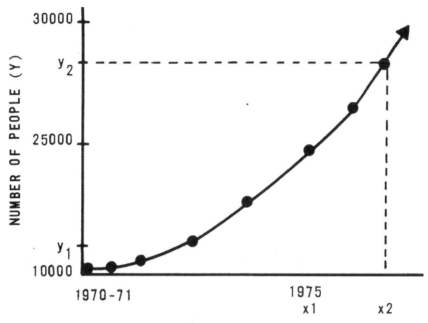

Figure 11.3.   Extrapolation with a Constant Percentage Change

uncommon for percentage rates of change to vary slightly so that a projected population may be slightly higher or lower than the actual population. Seemingly simplistic, extrapolations based on the known dynamics of a system are not at all trivial. And although it takes little skill simply to extend a line on a graph, it does take considerable insight and judgment to know how to alter that line.

Short-range projections are relatively simple to make, and simply extending a line of a graph that represents current conditions usually suffices for predicting the immediate future. But long-range projections—the projections that are usually of greater interest to forecasters—are made up not of single continuities, but rather of a series of continuities (figure 11.4). The factors that affect or determine the overall series of continuities must be analyzed before a researcher is able to determine when, how much, and in what direction that extrapolated line on a graph should be bent.

(Lines with arrows would be short-range projections based on the immediate past and current information.)

Knowledge of plans, knowledge of the ways certain variables behave characteristically, and knowledge of special conditions provide

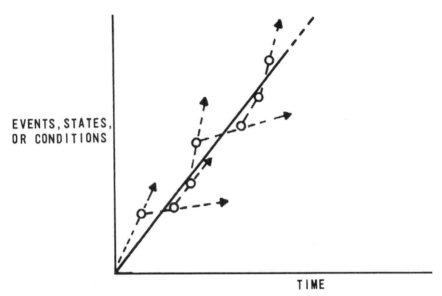

Figure 11.4.   Long-Range Projection Based on a Series of Continuities

clues in predicting trends and making projections. For example, precise knowledge of a government's budget for the current and forth-
coming fiscal years provides some indications as to the extent that a
current program will continue into the next fiscal year. And this information, coupled with information pertaining to the previous fiscal
year, would give a fairly strong indication of the continuity of a trend
at least for a short-range period.

In other cases, certain variables may tend to behave in fairly predictable modes, and these modes provide some basis for projecting and
interpreting series. For example, depletions of inventories generally her-
ald an increase in production, and the introduction of new models usually brings about increased sales. Knowledge of special conditions can
also be used as a basis for prediction. For example, foreknowledge that interest rates will increase can be used to anticipate a decrease in new
housing construction. And a major technological advance in a nuclear delivery system can be expected to bring about a new series of arms races.

Extrapolations can also be refined by knowledge of limiting conditions. For example, a country could increase its military manpower annually, but only until, theoretically, every individual in that country
would be in uniform. Clearly, this projection should be refined to exclude the aged, the very young, and those engaged in critical activities
such as government, agriculture, and industry. One could have pro-

jected the increase in size in U.S. naval ships, but until the World War II era, a limiting factor on the size of a naval ship was the size of the locks on the Panama Canal. Limiting factors may be physical constraints, cultural constraints, "laws of nature" (e.g., gravity, speed of light), or economic constraints.

Obviously, there are dangers to "blind" extrapolation, dangers such as concentrating on short-range trends to the exclusion of long-range trends. However, one way of minimizing the errors in extrapolation is to limit the span of future projections to the span of time for which historical data exist. Another way of minimizing error is to avoid predicting specific details. For example, in technological forecasting, attempts are sometimes made to project technological developments based on an analysis of each component of a system. The assumption is that the performance limits of the components will, collectively, determine the performance limits of the system or device. Historically, however, extrapolations based on this type of analysis have proved too conservative because major inventions ("breakthroughs") typically changed the very nature and basic configuration of the system or device.[10]

Another way of minimizing error is to express forecasts in terms of envelope curves, which express the upper and lower limits of expectations and which are broad enough to accommodate normal contingencies and a normal rate of innovation (figure 11.5).

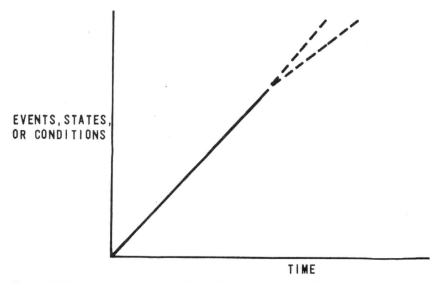

Figure 11.5.   An Extrapolation with an "Envelope Curve" Showing the Upper and Lower Limits of Expectations

Extrapolation techniques are often discussed in works related to technological forecasting. The references suggested in the section dealing with morphological analysis discuss extrapolation techniques as well. Extrapolation techniques might be applied to armed forces intelligence, scientific and technical intelligence, and sociological and economic intelligence research and analysis.

BAYESIAN ANALYSIS

Intelligence analysts are often asked to make a quick assessment of the likelihood of the occurrence of an event. The initial assessment must often be made off the cuff, on the basis of information already known about the problem. Bayesian analysis allows the analyst to update his probabilities systematically as new information becomes available. For example, an analyst might be asked to assess the probability that a certain developing nation will produce a nuclear device. He formulates two hypotheses:

H_1: The nation will develop a nuclear device
H_2: The nation will not develop a nuclear device

and he assesses the prior probability that H_1 will occur as .2 and the prior probability that H_2 will occur as .8. Stated another way, the odds are .2 to .8 (or 1 to 4) that H_1 will occur.[11]
The analyst now seeks new information that might influence the likelihood of H_1. His analysis differs from probability diagram analysis (which will be described later) in that initially he does not try to outline all of the major conditions upon which H_1 depends. Instead, he revises the probability of H_1 every time he receives a new piece of information.
After making his initial assessment, the researcher might note that a cadre of nuclear physicists and engineers trained in the Soviet Union has returned to the country in question. The analyst decides that this fact (D) influences the probability of H_1. He is now ready to apply Bayes's theorem.
Bayes's theorem is usually expressed as:

$$P(H_1|D) = \frac{P(D|H_1)\,P(H_1)}{P(D)} \tag{1}$$

where

$P(D)$ = probability of the datum occurring
$P(H_1)$ = prior probability of hypothesis H_1.
$P(D|H_1)$ = probability of the datum occurring given that the hypothesis
is true
$P(H_1|D)$ = posterior, or revised, probability that the hypothesis is true
given that the datum has occurred.

It is often easier for many analysts to think in terms of *odds* than in *probabilities*. The odds that assess the relative likelihood of occurrence of H_1 and H_2 may be expressed by repeating Bayes's theorem for both hypotheses:

$$P(H_1|D) = \frac{P(D|H_1)\, P(H_1)}{P(D)} \qquad (2)$$

and

$$P(H_2|D) = \frac{P(D|H_2)\, P(H_2)}{P(D)} \qquad (3)$$

When equation 2 is divided by equation 3, the $P(D)$s cancel out and the following remains:

$$\frac{P(H_1|D)}{P(H_2|D)} = \frac{P(D|H_1)\, P(H_1)}{P(D|H_2)\, P(H_2)} \qquad (4)$$

or, using the most common verbal definitions,

$$\text{Posterior Odds} = \text{Likelihood Ratio} \times \text{Prior Odds.} \qquad (5)$$

Equation 4 can now be used to revise the prior odds to posterior odds as a function of the information in the observed datum. To go from prior odds to posterior odds, one must assume first that H_1 is true and then assume that H_2 is true. The analyst then asks himself how likely it is that the datum would be observed under each assumption. If $P(D|H_1)$ is greater than $P(D|H_2)$, the posterior odds are greater than the prior odds. If $P(D|H_2)$ is greater than $P(D|H_1)$, the prior odds are greater than the posterior odds.

In the example of the nation that may or may not be developing a nuclear device, $P(H_1)$ was already assessed as .2. The analyst estimates that it is three times more likely that a large number of people would be educated in nuclear physics and related fields if the nation *were* proceeding toward a nuclear capability than if the nation *were not* working toward such a capability. The equation to compute posterior odds for this example is shown in equation 6.

$$\frac{P(H_1|D)}{P(H_2|D)} = \frac{3 \times .20}{1 \times .80} = \frac{.60}{.80} = \frac{1.00}{1.33} \tag{6}$$

Therefore, the odds concerning the nation's progress toward a nuclear capability have increased from 1:4 to 1:1.33.

The analyst assigns a 2:1 likelihood ratio in favor of the purchase of fuel if H_1, nuclear device development, is true. Using the posterior odds computed in equation 6 as the new prior odds, he calculates as shown in equation 7.

$$\frac{P(H_1|D)}{P(H_2|D)} = \frac{2 \times 1.00}{1 \times 1.33} = \frac{2.00}{1.33} = \frac{1.50}{1.00} \tag{7}$$

For the first time during the current analysis, the odds have increased so that they are greater than 50:50. It now seems that it is more likely than not that the nation will develop or is developing a nuclear device. This procedure could continue indefinitely. The analysis could be used by the researcher as a method to monitor a situation. It could also be used to determine when to begin to make policies relating to a situation. In the current example, it might be decided to try to seek information more directly once the odds were 5:1 in favor of H_1.

Bayesian analysis may be extended to a many-valued case when more than two hypotheses are under consideration. The following formulas address the many-valued case where H_1 is each possible hypothesis.

$$P(H_1|D)P = \frac{(D|H_1)P(H_1)}{P(D)} \tag{8}$$

All the $P(H_1)$ must sum to one.

In the two-valued case, the initial formula was converted to equation 4 so that the analysis could proceed by the assessment of odds rather than probabilities. In a many-valued case, it is more difficult to keep track of all the likelihood ratios. Although the basic mathematical operations are the same, the short cut for assessing posterior odds appears different in the many-valued case.

The analyst begins by listing all prior hypotheses and associated probabilities (table 11.1, columns (1) and (2)). Next, he assigns likelihoods to $P(D|H_1)$ (table 11.1, column (3)). He multiplies column (1) values by column (2) values, which gives him the numerator of equation 8, or $P(D|H_1)P(H_1)$. The sum of all posterior probabilities must be 1 (equations 9 and 10).

$$\sum_{i=1}^{n} P(H_i|D) = 1 = \frac{\sum_{i=1}^{n} P(H_i)P(D|H_i)}{P(D)} \tag{9}$$

or

$$P(D) = \sum_{i=1}^{n} P(H_i)P(D|H_i) \tag{10}$$

Therefore, column (4) is summed to obtain $P(D)$. Finally, each $P(H_1) P(D|H_1)$ is divided by $P(D)$ to obtain $P(H_1|D)$—column (5).

Bayesian analysis is appropriate for assessing the probability of occurrence of an event that might be influenced by many other events. The intermediate events should be used as data (D) when it seems more helpful to apply Bayes's theorem than to assess probabilities directly.

Table 11.1.   A Three-Valued Bayesian Analysis

(1)	(2)	(3)	(4)	(5)
Hypothesis	Prior Probability	Likelihood	Joint Probability	Posterior Probability
H_1	$P(H_1)$	$P(D|H_1)$	$P(H_1)P(D|H_1)$	$P(H_1|D)$
Nuclear Club	.2	.9	.18	.29
Power Plants	.5	.7	.35	.56
No Nuclear Interest	.3	.3	.09	.15
			$P(D)= .62$	1.00

PROBABILITY DIAGRAMS

Probability diagrams are tools for assessing the likelihood of occurrence of events that depend upon a large number of conditions. A probability diagram allows one to separate a problem into its component parts. The construction of such a diagram is explained here by use of an example problem: the concern of U.S. policy makers about the possible withdrawal of Country P from a military alliance.

If an analysis is to be complete, all possible outcomes of the event must be included. For example, if the event of interest is the status of Country P's membership in a military alliance, the possible outcomes include:

P remains in alliance.
P drops out of alliance.

The detailed outcomes need not be made explicit, although all outcomes are accounted for. "P drops out of alliance" can include P dropping out of all its alliances, dropping out of one and joining another, and so on. "P drops out of alliance" accounts for all of these outcomes. When one particular outcome is of special interest, such as "P remains in alliance," it is convenient to account for all other outcomes by using the negative of that statement. This simplifies the analysis by requiring only two choices at each branch. However, there are many instances when more choices at each level are appropriate. Diagrams of various choice combinations relating to the roll of a die, for example, are shown in figure 11.6.

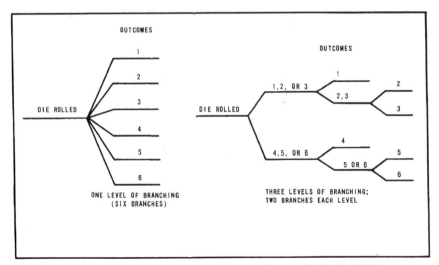

Figure 11.6.   Various Choice Combinations Relating to the Roll of a Die

Outcomes must be mutually exclusive (non-overlapping). For example, "P remains in alliance" and "P remains in alliance but files a formal protest" overlap, so both may not be included in the diagram as final outcomes. According to probability theory, if all mutually exclusive outcomes are included, the addition of their probabilities must equal 1. Therefore, at any one level of branching in a probability diagram, the fractional probabilities of two mutually exclusive branches must sum to 1.

An expert estimates the probability of Country P dropping out of the alliance as .7 *before* he begins an in-depth analysis. He is not basing this probability on any assumptions or branches in the probability diagram, so it is an *unconditional* probability estimate. On the other hand, when the expert begins to study the problem in depth, he decides that the outcome of a future election for national assemblies is the major condition upon which Country P's alliance status would depend. Similarly, the outcome of the election depends upon the value of Country P's currency, and the value of the currency depends upon whether or not Country P experiences a trade deficit this year. Once the analyst identifies all the major conditions upon which the status of Country P's military alliance depends, he can build a probability diagram (figure 11.7). It is critical that the analyst diagram the events in the proper order. For example, if the value of currency depends upon the balance of trade, the value of currency must branch from the outcomes of the balance of trade, not the other way around.

Numerical probabilities are assigned to each branch, beginning with the first level of branching (trade deficit or no trade deficit, in this case). The trade deficit and no trade deficit probabilities must sum to 1.0. The expert decides, based on all his past experience, to assign a .7 probability to trade deficit, and a .3 probability to no trade deficit. In order to assess probabilities at the next level of branching, it is assumed, for the time being, that a given outcome has occurred. Given that a trade deficit has occurred, either there will be a devaluation of currency or there will not be a devaluation of currency.

A path probability can be traced for each unique set of conditions and outcomes. In the alliance example, a path probability is traced for the uppermost branches (figure 11.8). The conditional probability that P will remain in the alliance given a Communist majority in the national assembly, devaluation of currency, and a trade deficit is obtained by multiplying all the individual probabilities of these branches.

$$P_1 \times P_2 \times P_3 \times P_4 = .7 \times .7 \times .8 \times .1 = .0392$$

At the last level of branching, all of the outcomes based on all paths sum to one. One of the more important outcomes of the example

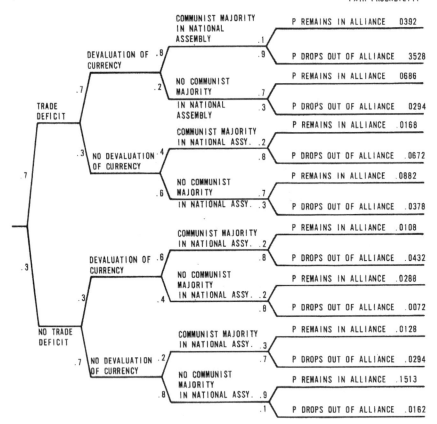

Figure 11.7.   A Probability Branching Tree

problem would be to determine the total probability of P dropping out of the alliance *regardless* of the conditions causing this outcome. Addition of all path probabilities for the given final outcome solves such a problem. In the example (figure 11.7), .3528 + .0294 + .0672 + .0378 + .0432 + .0072 + .0294 + .0162 = .5832.

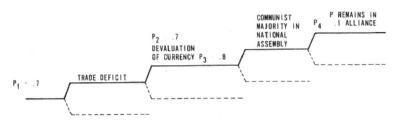

Figure 11.8.   Probabilities Assigned to Branches

The expert can now compare the computed probability of about .6 with his estimated probability of about .7, and he may decide to revise his estimate on this basis. Sensitivity analysis allows a person to assign a range of probabilities rather than a single probability to a condition. Final outcomes are computed based on the upper and lower limits of the range, and the effect of the range on the final outcome may be determined. Sensitivity analysis can indicate conditions that should be studied in greater depth.

Probability diagrams are tools for identifying the conditions that lead to certain outcomes. But it must be remembered that the assigned probabilities are subjective and are usually based upon the opinions of a few people. The final results of a probability diagram analysis should be considered only as approximations, and the values should be rounded off.

PSYCHOHISTORICAL AND PSYCHOLINGUISTIC ANALYSIS

Behavior patterns as manifested in speech (oral or written) have been used for purposes of analysis (description) and prediction. The predictions are based on established associations between the words and deeds of a principal actor, a head of state for example. In World War II, British propaganda analysts established that German propagandists, particularly Joseph Goebbels, would not boast of capabilities that Germany did not have because the expectations of the German population would soar and then plunge precipitously when anticipated results did not come about. Conversely, when the German propaganda machine did begin to allude to new terror weapons, the analysts inferred correctly that a new weapon was nearing operational status. (The weapons were the V-1 and V-2 rockets.)

Numerous other studies have attempted to correlate threatening statements of leaders with subsequent activities that their countries carried out. More conventional attempts to establish these associations have usually involved interdisciplinary teams—teams composed of, say, political scientists, historians, sociologists, and anthropologists. In recent years, psychologists and psychoanalysts have also participated in these types of analyses. Embracing in part sociology and anthropology, psychoanalytic theory attempts to establish the psychological as well as the cultural determinants of a principal actor's behavior. Linguistics, a branch of anthropology, attempts to define the role that language plays in determining a member of a certain culture's perception of the world and consequently, his behavior patterns.

In intelligence, for the greater part, psycholinguistic analyses would address contemporary figures. But psycholinguistic analysis (or psychohistorical analysis) has been performed on historical figures as well. For example, Jean Leclerq, presently Abbaye of Clervaux, made a psycholinguistic analysis of the writings of William of Saint-Thierry, a twelfth-century abbot. William's writings were compared to writings of his contemporaries, his accounts of events were compared to other historical and economic data, and the consistency of his perceptions throughout his writings was analyzed. On the basis of this analysis, a psychoanalytic "profile" was made, which revealed, for example, that William tended to project pessimism onto the subjects he wrote about, notably St. Bernard.

Similar types of analyses have been performed on public pronouncements by contemporary heads of state, and tentative hypotheses pertaining to the relationship between words and deeds have been established. Given a notably vociferous head of state, Fidel Castro, for example, numerous opportunities for testing the hypotheses may exist. Psycholinguistic (as well as many psychoanalytic) analyses may be very tenuous. For example, the analysts are usually addressing figures of a culture different from theirs. As anyone who has done any cross-cultural analysis knows, interpretation of behavior such as speech, which carries connotative as well as denotative meaning, is subject to numerous failings and error. In many cases, the validity of the basic psychoanalytic theory itself is in question.

Psycholinguistic and psychohistorical analyses are not without their detractors. Kenneth M. Colby, a psychoanalyst himself, says:

> Psychoanalytic studies of Moses, Leonardo, Poe, and Shakespeare are fascinating and entertaining. But they are not science; they belong to art, literature, or history. . . . Science is interested in useful generalizations about a class. An individual biography may illustrate some generalizations arrived at through other evidence . . . . These ideographic, rather than nomothetic, efforts may result in literature, but not in science. When art and science accost the same questions they have quite different criteria for acceptable answers.[12]

Although almost any careful researcher can establish relationships between words and deeds (if they exist), attempting to postulate reasons for the behavior (interpret behavior) requires highly specialized knowledge and skill. As such, psychoanalytic techniques are better left to the experts. Psycholinguistic analyses would be appropriate for political intelligence research and analysis, as well as for sociological and biographical intelligence.

MORPHOLOGICAL ANALYSIS

Morphological analysis is a technique that was originally devised for technological forecasting. Since its introduction in the 1940s, the technique has been applied to exploratory studies of future geopolitical environments and situations as well. At its most general level, morphological analysis is a method of multidimensional classification. Fritz Zwicky, the astrophysicist and engineer who pioneered the use of morphological analysis, classified the totality of all jet engines operating in a pure medium (e.g., vacuum, air, water, earth) that contained only simple elements and that was activated by chemical energy. His classification looked like table 11.2 (the number of variations of each class is shown in parentheses.)

Excepting the instances in which certain classes were self-contradictory (e.g., internal or external thrust generation would not apply in conditions of zero-thrust augmentation), 25,344 possible jet engine combinations were generated. By examining various combinations, Zwicky was able to propose radically new inventions—inventions that were later developed successfully.[13]

Zwicky states four rules for performing morphological analysis:

1. The problem to be addressed must be stated with great precision. (This is a fundamental rule for all types of analyses or problem-solving activities, including intelligence research.)
2. The parameters or characteristics of that which is being analyzed must be identified. (This identification should be complete—a requirement that is more easily stated than accomplished.)
3. Each parameter or characteristic must be subdivided into specific cases or "states," sometimes called extensional characteristics. (This step may be difficult to perform when continuous phenomena are involved. For example, in classifying objects on the basis of speed, the division between supersonic and hypersonic is a tenuous one.)
4. The implications of the various combinations of extensional characteristics must be analyzed for possibility, plausibility, feasibility, practicality, and so on, depending upon the nature of the phenomenon analyzed; for example, a technological process, a device, or a military or political condition.

In the example below (table 11.3), researchers were concerned about possible new technological developments of missiles. On the basis of combinations of extensional and intensional characteristics of missiles

Table 11.2. Zwicky's Classification of Jet Engines

$p_1 1, 2$	INTRINSIC OR EXTRINSIC CHEMICALLY ACTIVE MASS	(2)
$p_2 1, 2$	INTERNAL OR EXTERNAL THRUST GENERATION	(2)
$p_3 1, 2, 3$	INTRINSIC, EXTRINSIC, OR ZERO THRUST AUGMENTATION	(3)
$p_4 1, 2$	INTERNAL OR EXTERNAL THRUST AUGMENTATION	(2)
$p_5 1, 2$	POSITIVE OR NEGATIVE JET	(2)
$p_6 1, \ldots, 4$	POSSIBLE THERMAL CYCLES (ADIABATIC, ISOTHERMAL, ETC.)	(4)
$p_7 1, \ldots, 4$	MEDIUM (VACUUM, AIR, WATER, EARTH)	(4)
$p_8 1, \ldots, 4$	MOTION (TRANSLATORY, ROTATORY, OSCILLATORY, NONE)	(4)

that exist today, a matrix showing actual and possible combinations of missile characteristics could be generated. In a morphological analysis of possible future conflicts, the intensional and extensional parameters might look like table 11.4. Matrices of the type shown here have been used to generate conflict situations for gaming exercises.

Table 11.3. Intensional and Extensional Characteristics of Missiles

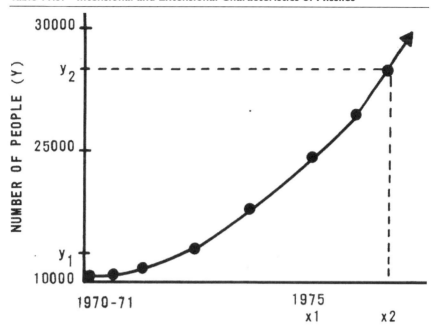

Table 11.4. Intensional and Extensional Parameters of a Conflict Situation (After Ayres)

INTENSIONAL CHARACTERISTIC		EXTENSIONAL CHARACTERISTIC
$p_1 1, 2, \ldots, n_1$	REGIONS	EUROPE, MIDDLE EAST, ETC.
$p_2 1, 2, \ldots, n_2$	LEVEL OF CONFLICT	SUBCRISIS MANEUVERS, INTENSE CRISIS, INSURGENCY WAR, NUCLEAR WAR, ETC.
$p_3 1, 2, \ldots, n_3$	REASON FOR UNITED STATES INVOLVEMENT	TREATY PARTNER OF ONE BOTH SIDES, TRADITIONAL FRIEND OF ONE BOTH PARTIES, IDEOLOGICAL COMMITMENT TO ONE SIDE, UNITED STATES MILITARY BASES THREATENED, RAW MATERIAL SUPPLY THREATENED, ETC.
$p_4 1, 2, \ldots, n_4$	STRATEGIC OBJECTIVE	ENGINEER A COUP D'ETAT, STALEMATE, ENCOURAGE NEGOTIATION TO SOLVE PROBLEMS, PUNISH ONE SIDE, MILITARY VICTORY...
$p_5 1, 2, \ldots, n_5$	TYPE OF INTERVENTION	DIPLOMATIC, TAKE TO UNITED NATIONS, TRADE BOYCOTT, TRADE EMBARGO, BLOCKADE, SEND ADVISORS, SUPPLY WEAPONS, AIR/SEA INTERDICTION, GROUND FORCES, TACTICAL NUCLEAR WEAPONS, ETC.

Morphological analysis shows only the possibilities that may result given the combination of various elements: it says nothing about the likelihood that certain combinations would ever be realized. Despite this, the technique is a useful one for examining possibilities or for suggesting alternatives to what exists at the present time.

The potential value of the output of the matrices is a function of the quality of the extensional and intensional analysis. Again, the thoroughness and creativity of the researchers play a critical role. Morphological analysis would be an appropriate methodology for scientific and technical intelligence, and, to a lesser degree, to economic and political intelligence research and analysis.

MODELS AND MODEL BUILDING

Models, as mentioned earlier, are abstractions or representations of reality. Stated another way, models are gross simplifications of reality. Only those critical portions of reality that are essential to decision making (or to any other purpose for which the modeling is performed) are represented in models. For example, in a model for calculating a missile system's cost, reliability of the missile would have to be represented by the model since it is a critical characteristic of the system, but color and shape of the missile would be inconsequential and would not be taken into account by the model.

Models, as discussed earlier, can be used to represent objects, processes, or functions. Very often models of objects take the form of a physical mock-up. Physical objects can also be modeled symbolically by expressing the object in terms of its dimensions and weight. Processes can be modeled statically by portraying the sequence of steps or events involved in that process. Flowcharts, for instance, are static models of processes. Processes can also be modeled dynamically. Simulations are dynamic models of processes. Models are sometimes theoretical constructs of processes and organizations, for example, Graham Allison's behavioral models of decision making under three different conditions of government.[14]

Although models are sometimes expressed in physical form, and often in verbal form, for the greater part, models are expressed mathematically. The advantage of mathematical models is that once they are constructed and validated, any number of different coefficients can be substituted in an equation. Hence, one basic model permits the researcher to determine any number of outcomes, given any changes of values provided to the model. For the greater part, large war games are composed of numerous mathematical models that were designed to address specific subelements of a situation; for example, an economic model, a conflict model, a political model, and so on.

An example of a portion of a model—a mathematical model that was developed to compare missile systems' costs—is shown below:

$$C = C_L m - RC_M Nm - C_M(1 - R)m$$

In this equation, C is the output of the model, that is, the dollar cost of a system that would be capable of destroying a specified number of enemy targets; and

C_M, C_L = cost coefficients (i.e., the cost per missile fired and the cost of maintaining a missile in a ready state),
$\quad R$ = ground reliability,
$\quad m$ = the number of missiles ready for firing on each salvo, and
$\quad N$ = the number of salvos in the campaign.

In this specific example, inputs to portions of the equation above would be outputs of other equations that were also models. One advantage of models is that they sometimes permit decisions to be made even though actual values for all elements may not be available.

Since models and games are so closely related, it is not surprising to find that the steps in developing models are similar to the steps involved in developing games. R. D. Specht identified four steps in model building: (1) identifying the factors that are relevant to the question being addressed; (2) selecting the quantifiable factors—factors that can be expressed numerically; (3) aggregating ("lumping together") the relevant, quantifiable factors in order to reduce the complexity of the problem; and (4) spelling out in quantitative terms the relationships between and among elements.[15] In instances in which a real-world counterpart to a model exists, a researcher would employ a fifth step: he would attempt to validate his model by comparing the model's output with the output (or characteristics) of the real-world system.

Employment of the model for calculating the cost of a missile system described above would require only a pocket calculator, paper, and pencil. But obviously, the most complex models would require the use of a computer. When computers are used and when programs are not available for performing certain functions, then specific programs must be developed. Although this step does not add to the complexity of the model, it does add to the cost of implementing the model.

Practically every academic discipline has an array of models, and models are used extensively in intelligence analysis and research. For example, there are models of transportation systems, models for predicting grain yield, models of missile systems, and models of various types of conflict, for example, electronic warfare, air battles, and so on. Before attempting to construct a model, the researcher is advised to determine what models already exist. Model building and model implementation are time-consuming and expensive tasks, particularly when long runs on a computer are required.

CYBERNETIC MODELS AND SYSTEM DYNAMICS AS AIDS IN FORECASTING

In instances where elements that constitute a system can be defined and where the functions the system performs are understood (and, ideally, can be expressed in quantitative terms), cybernetic (feedback) models can be used as a basis for forecasting. Very briefly, a system is an interacting organization of people or objects that is united by some common purpose, objective, mission, or function. Models used to represent systems must account for certain system characteristics; for example, they must define the boundary of the system. A system boundary specifies the components of the system that will be analyzed. The boundary includes all of the elements within the system that define or determine the system's behavior.

Models must also account for the control mechanism or the feedback of the system. Feedback mechanisms are means by which the functions of a system are regulated. In a closed system, the past behavior of a system, or feedback, is used to control its present and future behavior. In an open system, there is no feedback. Outputs result from inputs, but inputs are not affected by outputs in an open system. In simple systems there may only be one feedback loop. In highly complex systems, there may be numerous feedback loops.

Feedback loops are either positive or negative. A positive feedback loop is one in which an activity or function continues and, in effect, gains momentum as it progresses. An example of a positive feedback phenomenon in an ecological system would be a geometric increase in the population of a species when its predators had been eliminated. A negative feedback loop, on the other hand, is one that constantly limits a function. A thermostat that turns off a furnace when a certain temperature level has been reached is an example of a negative feedback loop. In an ecological system, a finite food supply that limits the size of a grazing herd would be an example of negative feedback.

In a military supply line, an automated system that constantly monitored the numbers and types of replacement parts on hand, automatically ordered replacements when a certain level of depletion had been reached, and automatically "logged in" new parts as they were received would be another example of a negative feedback loop. In simple form, this system would look like figure 11.9. This inventory system, of course, would interface with other systems—a transportation system and a production system—and these systems could also be modeled similarly.

Simple systems can be represented simply at gross levels. But systems become complex very quickly. Furthermore, by their very nature, social systems in which values of the human components of the system must be taken into account are usually very complex. For example, Jay W. Forrester, a pioneer in system dynamics, modeled a "cybernetic" town that contained three types of organizations, three types of dwellings, and three types of industries. In order to show the interconnections between the eighty-one possible combinations, more than 150 equations had to be used.

Interesting analogs can be seen among systems, and one reason for studying system dynamics is to uncover generalizations that would apply to a variety of systems. Karl Deutsch, in examining the

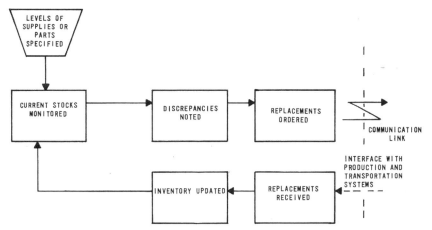

Figure 11.9.   An Automated Supply System Exhibiting a Negative Feedback Loop

relationship of cybernetic models to the political sciences, pointed out that the capabilities of a feedback system can be assessed in terms of the nature of the corrections that a system must make to achieve a certain output and the likelihood that the system will achieve the corrections within a finite period. These capabilities, in turn, are determined by (1) the system's information load with respect to goal-seeking operations; (2) the lag in the system's reaction (the greater the lag, the lower the probability of achieving an objective); (3) the gain expressed as a ratio of the intensity of the reaction and the basic information (dangers of under control or over control, e.g., a thermostat adjusted so finely that a furnace is constantly started and stopped); and (4) the lead in the system's reactive behavior. (An example would be attacking an incipient problem and taking appropriate action before the need became real).

These observations, although theoretical, appear as relevant to hardware analogs as they do to real-world command and control systems. For example, system dynamics models could be constructed to describe the United States's behavior in two similar incidents, North Korea's seizure of the USS *Pueblo* and the Khmer Rouge's seizure of the *Mayaquez*.

In both instances, the objective-seeking behavior related to the recovery of a ship and the crew. In the case of the *Pueblo*, there was a notable lag in the response of the system, and, as Deutsch pointed out, the probability of attaining an objective (i.e., recovering the ship) lessened as the lag increased. In the case of the *Mayaquez*, the gain, that is, the ratio of the intensity of the system's reaction and the information (the facts of the seizure) seemed appropriate to the situation. Hostilities were confined essentially to the area in which the ship and its crew were detained. Whether or not the lead in the system's reaction was appropriate cannot yet be determined.

System dynamics modeling requires the same sequence of steps required for gaming and simulations described earlier: (1) defining the problem, (2) defining the relevant factors and the cause-and-effect relationships, (3) expressing the factors and relationships in a symbolic form that can be manipulated (e.g., a mathematical model), (4) obtaining values for the variables either empirically or from experts' judgments, and (5) comparing outputs of the model with real-world counterparts and revising the model accordingly.

Although the steps in dynamic modeling are simply stated, their implementation may be considerably more difficult. It is fairly easy to depict closed hardware systems' analogs such as industrial control and regulatory systems or certain self-regulating ecological systems, but defining what constitutes the boundary of an economic or social system is another matter.

The predictive value of system dynamics modeling, like all models, depends upon the validity of the model and the correctness of the values that are manipulated in the model. In addition to the predictive value of system dynamics models, however, modelers gain insights into the system that is being analyzed. The methodology of system dynamics modeling is itself a dynamic and ongoing process of refinement that starts at a top level of generality and progresses downward through levels of greater detail (and complexity) as data become available. Consequently, the models can be refined and revised until their outputs correlate with the real-world counterparts. System dynamics modeling is one of the many techniques that falls under the rubric of systems analysis. Its uniqueness lies in the emphasis that is placed on the regulatory and control mechanisms in the systems.

SUMMARY

- The quality of any prediction is a function of the nature of the phenomenon about which the prediction is made as well as the underlying assumptions about the phenomenon.
- The quality of a prediction is also a function of the validity of the model as well as of the validity of the assumptions reflected in the model.
- Some so-called predictive techniques provide the researcher with insights into systemic or organizational behaviors that may be more valuable than the predicted outcome the technique provides.
- Listed below are various methodologies described in the last two chapters and elsewhere in the text. The components of strategic intelligence in which the methodologies are or can be employed are indicated; however, no attempt has been made to indicate the degree or extent to which a methodology might be employed within any component. Clearly, some methodologies are much more relevant to one component than to another. The predictive or descriptive uses of the methodologies are indicated, and the chapters in which the methodologies are described are shown in Table 11.5.

Table 11.5. Methodologies and Components of Strategic Intelligence

METHODOLOGY	COMPONENT OF STRATEGIC INTELLIGENCE									PURPOSE FOR WHICH METHODOLOGY IS NORMALLY USED	
	BIOGRAPHIC	ECONOMIC	SOCIOLOGICAL	TRANSPORTATION & TELECOMM.	MILITARY GEOGGRAPHIC	ARMED FORCES	POLITICAL	SCIENTIFIC & TECHNICAL		DESCRIPTIVE	PREDICTIVE
ANALOGY	X	X	X	X	X	X	X	X		X	X
GAME THEORY		X				X	X			X	X
WAR GAMING		X				X	X			X	X
LINK ANALYSIS	X		X	X		X	X			X	X
PSYCHO-HISTORICAL PSYCHO-LINGUISTIC	X						X			X	
SOCIOMETRY	X		X			X	X			X	
CODING & CLASSIFICATION	X	X	X	X	X	X	X	X		X	X
LINEAR PROGRAMMING		X		X		X		X		X	
STATISTICAL ANALYSIS (VARIED)	X	X	X	X	X	X	X	X		X	X
DELPHI TECHNIQUE		X					X	X			X
GENERATION OF ALTERNATIVE FUTURES		X	X			X	X	X			X
MODELS AND MODEL BUILDING		X	X	X	X	X	X	X		X	X
MORPHOLOGICAL ANALYSIS				X				X			X
CYBERNETIC MODELS SYSTEM DYNAMICS		X	X	X		X	X	X		X	X
EXTRAPOLATION		X	X	X				X			X
BAYESIAN ANALYSIS		X		X		X	X	X			X
REGRESSION & CORRELATION		X	X	X			X	X		X	X
PROBABILITY DIAGRAMS		X		X			X	X			X
GRAPHIC DEPICTIONS		X	X	X	X	X	X	X		X	X
CONTENT ANALYSIS	X	X	X	X	X	X	X	X		X	X

NOTES

1. As anyone who has worked with subjective probabilities can point out, the two expressions of likelihood are not the same. For every flip of a coin, the probability of tossing a "tail" remains .5 (50/50), but a gambler who has tossed ten consecutive tails may feel very strongly that the next toss will be a "head."

2. Sometimes the assumptions are valid, but the facts are wrong. For example, the assumption that the Japanese Manchurian Army would fight tenaciously was a valid one. But for years, the Japanese Manchurian Army existed only in the minds of U.S. military planners.

3. That the predictions are sometimes inaccurate is due to a lack of the most recent information, not to a fallacy of the predictive models.

4. One of the more ambitious undertakings in identifying, coding, and analyzing patterns of national behavior for the purpose of predicting future behaviors of nations as they interact with other nations is the DON (Dimensionality of Nations) project. Employing factor analysis and linear algebra, the project attempts to identify major attribute patterns in terms that would permit the analysis of cross-national data. The attribute patterns include size, economic development, political orientation, density, Catholic culture, foreign conflict, and domestic conflict. The project analyzed over 100 behavioral variables for about 400 two-nation combinations. The focus of the project is to identify regularities in the relationship of attributes, and behavioral variable regularities that would serve as the basis for predicting future behavior. The research was performed by the Department of Political Science and the Social Science Research Institute of the University of Hawaii under a grant provided by the National Science Foundation.

5. T. C. Schelling in E. S. Quade, *Analysis for Military Decisions* (Chicago: Rand McNally and Company, 1964), 199.

6. Prophets, augurs, soothsayers, and haruspices provided this service in the past. Delphi technique derives from the Greek oracle who lived in Delphi.

7. Morton H. Halperin, *China and the Bomb* (New York: Frederick A. Praeger, 1965).

8. Herman Kahn, "Alternative World Futures," paper Hi-342-B IV, (New York: Hudson Institute, April, 1964).

9. Alvin Toffler, *Future Shock* (New York: Random House, 1970).

10. The advent of the pocket electronic calculators might be cited as a case in point. Any forecaster who, forty years ago, would have projected the extent to which calculators would be in common use, probably would have made a very conservative estimate had he based the estimate on the current state of the art. Vacuum tubes, size, and weight of the electronic calculating devices of the 1940s, to say nothing of costs, made these devices impractical for general use. But the development of printed circuitry and solid-state components reduced the size, weight, and costs of the devices and increased the speed and reliability. Solid-state components were not mere extensions of technology: they were revolutionary developments.

11. Stated still another way, the analyst feels that the likelihood that a certain nation *will not* develop a nuclear device is four times greater than the likelihood that the nation *will* develop a nuclear device.

12. Kenneth Mark Colby, *An Introduction to Psycho-analytic Research* (New York: Basic Books, 1960), 74. That different types of research (description and prediction, for example) have different criteria for acceptance is a point that needs to be stressed.

13. This incident is similar to the one in which Dmitri Mendeleev predicted the properties of elements that had not yet been discovered. The procedures involved in constructing the periodic table were nearly identical to the procedures of morphological analysis.

14. Graham T. Allison, *Essence of Decision: Explaining the Cuban Missile Crisis* (Boston: Little, Brown, 1971).

15. The example appears in R. D. Specht, "The Why and How of Model Building," *Analysis for Military Decisions*, 66–67.

12

Preparing the Report

This chapter discusses the last of the four phases of a research project, report preparation. In well-planned and well-executed research projects, report preparation begins as soon as data become available for analysis. In fact, report preparation may begin even in the data collection phase as bibliographies are compiled. As was the case in every other phase of the research project, planning is essential to ensure that enough time remains to prepare the report properly and to ensure that assistance is available when it is needed—assistance in the form of typists, technical art production specialists, editors, and reviewers. Invariably, report preparation requires more time than is anticipated. Unfortunately, by the time the researcher has reached the report preparation phase, he typically has little flexibility in time and costs. Again, this makes prior planning all the more critical.

Report preparation connotes writing, and writing consumes a large portion of the report preparation phase. But checking footnotes, compiling bibliographies, reviewing, revising, and proofreading may require nearly as much time as the writing requires. Failing to take these tasks into account during the planning phase invariably results in frenetic activity in the days and hours prior to the time the report must be submitted. This chapter discusses the mechanics of preparing the report, considers expository writing and canons of format, and describes basic tools that can assist the writer.

FORMAT[1]

In self-initiated research projects, the researcher has more flexibility in selecting the format most appropriate to the research he is conducting.

If the report will be submitted in fulfillment of an academic requirement, then policies of the institution must be followed. If the writer
intends to publish his report in a professional journal, then the format
required by the journal must be adhered to. Academic theses are rarely
suitable for publication in professional journals without major revision and condensation. Theses invariably read like theses and even
major publishing houses shun them in the form in which they were
prepared originally. Supervisors or faculty advisers can recommend appropriate formats, and ultimately, these people will pass judgment on
the product. Assigned research projects and self-initiated projects often
serve different purposes, and it follows that formats may differ considerably. For example, research projects are assigned in order to obtain
answers to specific questions. The competency of the researcher is
taken for granted when the assignment is made. The product will be
judged on its completeness and accuracy, of course, but the researcher
will be evaluated only indirectly, if at all.

With self-initiated research projects, and particularly with research projects conducted as a part of an academic requirement, the research report is used as a means for evaluating the technical competency of the researcher. Consequently, content that would rarely
appear in an assigned report may be very important in a self-initiated
project. A review of the literature would be a case in point. In an assigned research project, the reviewers of the report will assume that all
relevant and pertinent materials had been reviewed; thus, large sections of a report devoted to this review would rarely be required. In academic research, however, advisers want demonstrable proof that the
researcher had examined the basic works in his area and that his conclusions were based on reliable source data. Therefore, reviews of the
literature might constitute an important part of the research product.

Another big difference between formats of assigned intelligence research projects and formats of self-initiated projects is the manner in
which the findings are presented. In assigned projects, reports generally start with a statement of the problem, followed very closely by the
conclusions or recommendations, and end with the justification. In
most scholarly reports, on the other hand, the report first identifies the
problem, then discusses the factors bearing on the issue, and ends with
conclusions.

For the greater part, most research reports prepared as part of an
academic requirement comprise three sections: (1) a preliminary section containing the title page, approval sheet, preface and acknowl-
edgements, a table of contents, and a list of tables and figures; (2) the
text of the report, including sections devoted to a statement of the

problem, review of literature, findings, and conclusions; and (3) the reference materials in the form of bibliographies and appendices (if any).

A standard work in preparing theses and reports is William Giles Campbell's *Form and Style in Thesis Writing.*[2] In addition to sections on footnotes and bibliographic entries, the manual also contains sections on forms and format. Especially helpful are the numerous specimen forms. Another work that might be consulted is George Shelton Hubbell's *Writing Term Papers and Reports.*[3] This latter work is more comprehensive in the sense that it discusses steps in collecting and evaluating information as well as in preparing the report. However, it lacks the detail of Campbell's manual.

The writer who intends to submit his work for general publication by other than U.S. government agencies should consult *A Manual of Style.*[4] This is considered to be the basic work relating to typographical and other rules for authors, printers, and publishers. If a particular organization does not have its own style manual and if a report is to be published as an official U.S. government document, then the *U.S. Government Style Manual* should be followed.[5] A word of caution: manuals differ in subtle ways and later editions of the same manual may have important changes. Regardless of the manual used as a guide for form and format, one manual should be used *consistently and exclusively.*[6]

USE OUTLINES APPROPRIATELY

It is inconceivable that a research report could be prepared without some kind of an outline. In fact, very often an outline is submitted at the point when the research project is assigned or approved. But the outline is a guide, not a mold, and as content is prepared, the writer may find that the original outline is no longer adequate for his purposes. Consequently, outlines should be adapted to the requirements of the writer and modified when necessary. There are limits to these modifications, of course, and major changes would require approval from either the supervisor or the faculty adviser. Outlines are often used as "delaying tactics" by those who procrastinate. One can always claim that the outline needs more detail, and one can arrange and rearrange topics interminably. But this tactic does not get the report written. When deadlines approach, it is imperative that the outline be put to rest and that the writer get on with his major task, preparing the content.

SCHEDULE WORK SESSIONS

Starting up and winding down are, for the greater part, time-wasting activities. Efforts should be made to keep this wasted time to a minimum. One method is to schedule relatively large blocks of time for writing. An hour might suffice to record notes, but it hardly suffices to resurrect the continuity of thought of the previous day's efforts. Starting-up activities consume the same amount of time regardless of how little content is written; therefore, the more time one can spend writing at any one sitting, the greater the efficiency realized.

Another method for shortening the starting-up time is to end one day's effort in the middle of a section—in the middle of a paragraph, for example. Then, when writing resumes the following day, the writer has a framework in which to continue. Getting over the initial step of putting the first word to paper is the hardest part of writing. Invariably, words flow after a bit of preliminary pump priming, and this priming should be done at the conclusion of each work session.

AVOID INTERRUPTIONS

Interruptions are not only annoying, they may be destructive to a writer who is attempting to translate elusive concepts into written words. Some writers become "monastic" when they work. For example, they may retire to solitary work spaces, they may take telephones off the receiver, they may keep their office doors closed, or, in a crowded office, they may arrange their desks so that they face a wall. These acts are not idiosyncrasies; they are methods that keep distractions to a minimum and thus increase efficiency.

Efficiency can also be achieved by working at the same place as much as possible. This ensures that most of the necessary materials will be available when and where they are needed. Furthermore, distractions of new environments are eliminated. Goal setting is another method for increasing efficiency. For example, some writers set a daily goal of a specified number of words or a certain number of typewritten pages. Whatever technique is used is a technique for self-discipline, and discipline is essential for preparing an acceptable research product on time.

Adherence to standards of grammatical usage is basic to effective style. But style—an almost indefinable quality of good writing—requires more than correctness. If written material "reads well," if it communicates clearly, unambiguously, effortlessly, and concisely, then it has "good" style. In formal writing, the best style is usually the least obvious style. Good writing communicates concepts; it does not call the reader's attention to syntax. Listed below are suggestions for writing effectively.

USE THE ACTIVE RATHER THAN PASSIVE VOICE

For example, "we conclude that" is stronger, more forceful, and more direct than "it is believed that." Or "data support the conclusion that" is preferred to "conclusions are supported by the following data." The active voice is rigorous, less ambiguous, and invariably shorter. For years, a canon of scholarly writing required that it be written in the third person. For example, with the exception of the "rules" described in this section, which are written in the second person, this entire text is written in third person. For certain types of writing, however, adherence to third person usage requires more words. For instance, it is more direct and shorter to write "we believe that" in place of "it is believed that" or "now collate the data" in place of "the data should be collated now." Although canons of writing (to say nothing of taste) require that the writer be kept in the background and that personal pronouns (*I*, *we*, *you*, *me*, *my*, *our*, and *us*) should not appear in the text of a scholarly paper, there are times when this rule should be bent for clarity, directness, and conciseness. Knowing when and how to deviate from the third-person rule is a skill that must be acquired. For the sake of uniformity, however, the writer should use the same combination of person, voice, or mode consistently regardless of the combination chosen.

USE SIMPLE SENTENCES

Nothing communicates so well as a simple sentence. Admittedly, excessive use of simple sentences may interfere with the "flow" of the discourse. But simple sentences are usually unambiguous, direct, and short. It is indeed strange that simple sentences are not used more often. Adverbs weaken sentences. Most of the time adverbs need not be used. Adjectives also tend to weaken sentences, but they are necessary at times. When subtle shades of distinction must be made, adverbs and adjectives should be used. At the risk of suppressing individual creativity, it is recommended that only accepted spellings, terminology, and abbreviations be used. Unorthodox spellings, obscure abbreviations, and excessive use of highly technical terminology reflect poorly on the writer. Worse yet, they obscure the message.[7]

WRITE AT A LEVEL APPROPRIATE FOR THE READERS

In order to write at a level suitable for the reader, the researcher must analyze his target audience. He must consider the audience's level of education, background, and familiarity with the subject matter. Then he must adapt his writing accordingly. If decisions are to be made on the basis of what is written, then the material must be organized and structured in a manner that facilitates decision making by people who are usually very busy. On the other hand, if the purpose of a report is simply to present new information, the style may be more discursive. In any formal writing, clichés, colloquialisms, and most idiomatic expressions have no place, regardless of the audience.

FOOTNOTES AND BIBLIOGRAPHIES

There are two kinds of footnotes. The first kind of footnote expands or clarifies the main text. This kind of footnote is used when its inclusion in the main body of the text would break the continuity of the discourse or distract the reader. The second type of footnote cites the source reference. This type of footnote indicates the writer's authority for making an assertion in the main body of the text. It would be used if a writer were paraphrasing or quoting another authority. In certain types of official reports, footnotes are also used to indicate nonconcurrence by a dissenting member of the group submitting the report.

Footnotes provide a service to the reader. They indicate where additional information can be found, they identify the authorities whose observations and conclusions were cited, and they indicate that an assertion in the main body of the text reflects more than the writer's personal opinions. In the latter sense, footnotes also increase the writer's credibility. Notes are placed at the bottom of the page, at the end of a chapter, or at the end of the text (but before the bibliography). Different organizations have different requirements for placing footnotes. For reader convenience, however, it is best to place notes at the bottom of the page. Constantly requiring the reader to turn to the back of the text is annoying. Not surprisingly, notes at the end of chapters or at the end of texts are rarely read except by diligent scholars.

Although the form of a reference footnote may vary somewhat among different publishers and organizations, all reference footnotes contain essentially the same information: information relating to the author(s), title, facts of publication (place, name of publisher, and date), and volume and page numbers. For periodicals, the same information is required except that the place of publication is seldom mentioned. For specific information relating to the various forms of footnotes, Kate L. Turabian's or William G. Campbell's manuals should be consulted. These manuals have been basic reference guides for students for decades.

Bibliographies usually list the sources that were consulted in preparing the report. In most cases, many more works are used in preparing a report than are cited in a bibliography—works that every reader would assume were consulted by the author. Consequently, bibliographies typically list only the more relevant works bearing on the report. Any work that was quoted or cited in a footnote, however, should be included in the bibliography. Bibliographies may also list books that the author recommends for additional information. Rarely do intelligence reports contain this type of bibliography, however.

Like footnotes, bibliographic entries may take several forms, depending upon the requirements of the publisher or sponsoring organization. The appropriate stylebook should be consulted before the bibliographies are prepared.

Bibliographic entries, unlike footnotes, must be organized or classified in some manner. One common method is to organize bibliographic entries as books, periodicals, and special reports. Within each group, specific entries might be arranged alphabetically by author, chronologically, or topically. Footnotes and bibliographies are services provided to the reader. They indicate where specific information can be found and how the reference can be located. Forms that footnotes and bibliographies take are of secondary importance: the critical point is that the entries be correct, complete, and that the forms are used consistently. It is for this reason that only one style manual should be used for any single report.

REVIEW AND REVISION

Before a report is submitted, it should have undergone numerous readings and probably revisions as well. The writer typically reviews and revises as he composes. After setting aside a section of draft copy for several days (or weeks, if time permits), the writer may review the copy again. The writer who has any aesthetic sensitivity to prose typically is dismayed to find that the words he so carefully articulated earlier may now be incomprehensible. Thoughts may no longer hang together, the syntax may be garbled, assumptions may not have been stated, and all of the mechanical errors in the draft that were overlooked may become embarrassingly evident. The only solution, of course, is to wield the blue grease pencil, cut and paste vigorously, and review again.

One of the more difficult things for a writer to do is to submit his draft to a jury of peers. It takes courage to reveal one's foibles to one's colleagues. But as unpleasant as it may be, the step is absolutely necessary. Perspectives other than the writer's are essential for uncovering hidden biases, unsupported assertions, and faulty logic. Few writers can uncover these things in their own material. How much should be reviewed and revised at one time depends upon the size of the work. If a book is being prepared, separate chapters would be logical portions to review and revise. If shorter reports are prepared, then an entire section of the report should be reviewed and revised at one time. Ideally, drafts should be reviewed as sections are completed. This precludes having to scrap the entire effort and start over at a stage when time and funds may no longer be available.

If the writer is able to employ or use the services of an editor, he is indeed lucky. Good editors can uncover errors and weaknesses that are not apparent to the writer. Good editors can improve a text immeasurably, provided that the writer heeds the advice they give. In the absence of editors, colleagues may suffice, but rarely do the researcher's colleagues have the technical skills of a trained editor. Reviews often result in revisions, and revisions are time-consuming and exasperating. But they are essential for removing the inevitable errors—errors of commission and errors of omission. For example, spelling errors have an insidious way of occurring. "Difficult" words are usually checked by the writer and misspellings of these words rarely appear in finished texts. More common are misspelled familiar words, words that the writer may have assumed were correct and never bothered checking. A draft may be fairly clean until it is submitted for final preparation, and then "mechanical" errors may be introduced—typographical errors, for example. Fast readers who are reading familiar text are often unable to detect these mechanical errors. So, again, it is important for someone unfamiliar with the text to proofread the copy.

Rarely does a major report, thesis, or book make it through the entire publication cycle without some error remaining. Nevertheless, an error-free product should be the goal of every writer. The trivial flaw that escapes the writer's and reviewer's attention seemingly takes on greater significance when it is seen in its final printed form, and it remains a source of embarrassment as long as the work is read.

SUMMARY

- Although the report preparation phase is the last phase in the sequence of activities in a typical research project, it need not be the last phase started. In fact, report preparation can begin as soon as data are available.
- As was the case in every preceding phase, prior planning is important to ensure that sufficient time will be available to produce a quality product.
- The form and content of a report should be tailored to the needs of the reader. If the report is a product of an assigned research project, then the formats prescribed by the agency or the assigning authority should be followed. If the report is a product of a self-initiated research effort, then the format should comply with established rules set forth in standard reference works.
- Format and content apart, the manner in which a report is assembled is largely a matter of personal preference. The writer must determine what techniques and procedures work best for him, and then consistently and routinely adhere to his own standing operating procedures.
- Styles of writing vary widely. The best style for expository writing, however, is that which is least pretentious. Statements made clearly, concisely, and unequivocally characterize the better style for reports. Accepted standards of grammatical use, a minimal use of modifiers, use of the active rather than passive voice, and use of orthodox terminology are recommended for scholarly, technical writing.
- Footnotes and bibliographies are usually present in formal research reports. Footnotes either cite the source or the authority for an assertion made in the text, or they provide additional information to the reader. Footnotes and bibliographies are aids to the reader and should contain sufficient information to enable the reader to locate the works for his own examination. Regardless of the form or format used in footnoting, it should be used consistently.
- Review and revision are continuous processes that occur during the entire time that a report is being prepared. However, prior to the submission of the draft for final publication, the draft should be reviewed critically by an editor (ideally), or by the writer's peers as an alternative. Revisions should be made as sections are reviewed in order to preclude the writer's having to rewrite the entire document when time may be extremely limited.

- The written report is often the only tangible evidence of months or sometimes years of concentrated effort. The quality of the report reflects the quality of the research. Therefore, every attempt should be made to produce a high-quality product.

NOTES

1. A word of caution: format specifications change periodically, so it is important that the latest documents be used as guides.
2. William Giles Campbell, *Form and Style in Thesis Writing* (Boston: Houghton Mifflin, 1954).
3. George Shelton Hubbell, *Writing Term Papers and Reports* (New York: Barnes and Noble, 1962).
4. The University of Chicago Press, *A Manual of Style* (Chicago: The University of Chicago Press, 1969).
5. United States Government Printing Office, *U.S. Government Style Manual* (Washington, DC: Government Printing Office, 1978).
6. For example, the "correct" bibliographic form for a book with more than one author, according to Campbell's *Form and Style in Thesis Writing*, is to invert the order of the first author's name and then list the other authors' names in the normal fashion of first name, middle initial, and last name. Turabian, on the other hand, in *A Manual for Writers*, uses the inverted form for all of the authors' names. Kate L. Turabian, *A Manual for Writers of Term Papers, Theses, and Dissertations* (Chicago: The University of Chicago Press, 1973).
7. Theodore M. Bernstein, *The Careful Writer: A Modern Guide to English Usage* (New York: Atheneum, 1965).

13

An Example of a Small-Scale Intelligence Study

Earlier chapters described the sequence of phases through which an intelligence research program typically passes and described various methodologies that were appropriate for intelligence research. This chapter describes a short research study conducted by one of the authors in the Republic of Korea (ROK) in 1972. Not all of the steps described in earlier portions of the text were performed in this study. Because of constraints of time and resources and because the study was essentially self-initiated, the researchers had considerable freedom in defining the scope of the problem and in delineating terms of reference. Again, since the study was self-initiated, no review cycles were required. Unfortunately, nor was there any opportunity to influence the manner in which data were collected, as will be discussed later.

The purpose of this brief example is *not* to cite an ideal example of how an intelligence research problem should be approached, but rather to describe how an actual study was conducted in light of operational constraints that intelligence researchers typically encounter.

BACKGROUND AND ORIGIN OF THE PROBLEM

Ever since the cessation of hostilities in the Korean War, a state of low-intensity conflict has existed between North Korea and the Republic of Korea. The intensity of the conflict varied over the years and hit a peak during the 1968–1969 period when North Korea dispatched a team to assassinate President Park Chung-hee, when a force of over a hundred armed North Koreans raided and terrorized the Samchok-Ulchin region of the Republic of Korea, when the *Pueblo* was captured, and when the EC-121 aircraft was downed.

From 1969 to 1971, hostile acts committed by North Korean forces continued, but the intensity and number of acts decreased. In the winter of 1971 and spring of 1972, North Korean diplomatic activities appeared to take on a new complexion. Although North Korean mass media still made vituperative attacks against the United States, certain observers detected what appeared to be a conciliatory tone toward the ROK. On January 16, 1972, for example, an analyst of the 24th PSYOP Detachment in Seoul noted what appeared to be a departure from North Korea's previous position on the subject of unification.

Very briefly, the traditional stand of North Korea had been that a peace treaty between the North and South could be concluded only *after* the withdrawal of all U.S. forces from Korea. However, in mid January, Korean Central News Agency (KCNA) wire service reports describing an interview that Premier Kim Il-sung had with a Japanese Socialist Party official suggested that this position had been reversed and that now a peace agreement between the North and South could be concluded without the precondition of U.S. forces actually being withdrawn.

The implications of this reversal in policy—if it were true—were significant for not only North Korean-ROK relations but also for U.S. foreign policy vis-à-vis the ROK and North Korea. The perennial problem, of course, was determining whether or not the appearance of reality had any further substance in fact. In its broadest terms, the research problem was defined as one of determining whether or not North Korea was changing (or had changed) its previous position with regard to concluding a peace treaty with the Republic of Korea.

PLANNING THE RESEARCH PROGRAM: PROBLEM DEFINITION

The small-scale research program that ensued was essentially self-initiated, as stated earlier. Working closely with the 24th PSYOP Detachment on a larger basic research program contracted by the Department of Army, the researchers had neither the time nor the resources to launch a thoroughly exhaustive study. Furthermore, the researchers were constrained to work with the materials that were available or that could be provided or obtained without necessitating an extensive data collection effort.

The problem definition phase ultimately resulted in the formulation of three hypotheses, which will be described shortly. However, even before hypotheses could be formulated, an analysis of the consistency of North Korean policy statements as they appeared in North

Korean mass media was made. This interim study had to be made in order to determine if the *perceived* change in North Korea's stand on concluding a peace agreement, as reflected in its mass media, was real. This shorter, interim research effort will be described briefly because it involved many of the analytical steps described in earlier sections of the text.

In order to determine if the apparent change in North Korean policy toward reunification was real or illusory, it was first necessary to determine how consistent North Korean public statements had been after Kim Il-sung's interview with the Japanese Socialist Party leader had been reported. It should be noted at this point that very often the larger, overall research problem gives rise to smaller, more specific problems. In formal research programs, this "distillation" process is not at all uncommon and is a very important part of limiting the scope of a problem to manageable proportions.

In order to determine consistency in the public announcements by North Korea, all KCNA wire services from January 16 to April 30, 1972, that were received through normal distribution channels were reviewed. The alert reader who recalls the description of sampling in chapter 9 will realize that this "sample" and the whole sampling process left much to be desired. For example, the wire service releases were provided by the Foreign Broadcast Information Service (FBIS). FBIS (at that time) monitored North Korean wire service transmissions on an ad hoc basis, according to an FBIS spokesman. If a transmission seemed important to the monitors, then it was transcribed; if the transmission was unrelated to monitoring guidelines, then it was ignored. Consequently, the researchers had no idea of the number of wire service reports actually transmitted by KCNA, their frequency of transmission, or their periodicity. In short, the researchers had to use what they received. This condition is not unusual in intelligence research and analysis.[1]

Hundreds of wire service releases were examined, of which seventy-eight pertained to peace proposals. This examination, it should be noted, involved both the exploratory and the investigative stage of data collection. The wire service releases were those that were made between January 16 and April 30, 1972. Having examined and identified every wire service release relating to the problem of unification, the researchers classified and coded the releases according to which one of four different peace proposals suggested by North Korea at various times from as early as April 12, 1971, to January 10, 1972, was addressed in the specific release.[2] The steps involved in the coding and classification procedure were similar to the steps described earlier in this book. Categories were established and data (wire service releases in this case) were assigned to the categories based on "fit."

After the data were classified, hypotheses were tested relating to the consistency reflected among the wire service releases. Ignoring the details for the purpose of this brief description, it was concluded that the wire service releases were highly consistent in the manner in which peace proposals were addressed from the period of January 16 to April 30, 1972. Although earlier (and more restrictive) proposals were still mentioned, the more militant proposals were attributed to foreign spokesmen. The most recent proposal—the one that seemed to signal a change in policy—was mentioned most frequently by party cadre members. This conclusion became an input to the larger problem addressed in the project, the problem of determining if, in fact, North Korea had changed its previous policy regarding the conclusion of a truce agreement with the Republic of Korea. This was the primary focus of the study.

HYPOTHESIS FORMULATION

On the basis of the analysis of the consistency of North Korea's public statements pertaining to reunification (as well as other observables), three hypotheses relating to North Korea's "peace offensive" were formulated. The formulation of the hypotheses involved inductive processes as described and reiterated briefly throughout the book. The hypotheses were as follows:

1. North Korea is attempting to reduce the hostile climate that existed on the peninsula for twenty-seven years. (For brevity's sake, this will be referred to as the "peace hypothesis.")
2. North Korea is maintaining the former level of tension. (This will be referred to as the "business-as-usual hypothesis.")
3. North Korea is carrying out a plan of deception by making what purports to be a peace proposal merely as a guise for concealing hostile intentions. (This will be referred to as the "deception hypothesis.")

An examination of these three hypotheses shows that the third hypothesis was not incompatible with the first two hypotheses, even though it was "opposed" to them. Needless to say, these three hypotheses did not exhaust all possible hypotheses.[3]

DATA COLLECTION

For the greater part, the researchers had neither the resources nor the authority to actually collect data. Instead, the researchers had to settle for data received through normal channels. In certain instances, data relating to incidents and conditions along the demilitarized zone were provided to the researchers through intelligence channels. None of these data were in a form that required any detailed statistical analysis.

ANALYSIS AND FINDINGS

Rather than describing all of the data (observables) that were examined, a number of the more significant events examined will be described. Each major observable, or group of observables, was tested against each of the three hypotheses in order to determine under which hypothesis the observable was most plausible. (A Bayesian analysis could also have been employed here.)

1. The lengthy KCNA release on January 15, 1972, described an interview Kim Il-sung had with the editorial committee of the Japanese newspaper *Yomiuri Shim bun* in which Kim answered some "questions" raised by the newsmen on January 10. Discussing the problem of reunification, Kim proposed that "a peace agreement . . . be concluded between the North and the South and the armed forces of North and South Korea be cut drastically under the condition where the U.S. imperialist aggressor troops are withdrawn from South Korea."[4]

    It was not clear to the researchers what sequence of events was being proposed; for example, would a peace agreement be *concluded* after U.S. forces were withdrawn or before? This ambiguity became significant in the further analysis because, as the statement stood, any of the three hypotheses stated above seemed plausible. On the basis of this one input, the analysts hedged by giving equal weight to all three hypotheses.
2. Beginning in the middle of January, KCNA made reference to the January 10 peace proposal almost daily. Some of the initial ambiguity in wording was resolved in subsequent "interviews" with Kim Il-sung and particularly in a meeting that Kim had with a Japan Socialist Party official, Kanji Kawasaki. It became quite clear that what was being said was that a peace agreement

between the North and South could be concluded *before* U.S. forces were withdrawn. The researchers were inclined to consider this observable as supporting the peace hypothesis, although the deception hypothesis was not completely ruled out.

3. As was pointed out earlier, there was some question about the consistency with which North Korea treated the peace proposal issue. As analysis revealed, North Korea was highly consistent in its treatment of peace proposals, reverting only occasionally to a "hard-line" stance and then attributing this stance to foreign spokesmen. This consistency supported the peace hypothesis, but again, the deception hypothesis was not completely discounted.

4. Analysis must consider the total situational context. In August 1971, Red Cross delegates from the North and South began meeting on a fairly regular basis to solve problems of relocating missing members of families and to solve other humanitarian problems. Initially, North Korea's coverage of the talks (by KCNA) was characterized by severe criticism of the tactics of the Korean National Red Cross (KNRC-ROK) and by statements supporting their own position. After January 1972, however, the tone of North Korea's coverage changed. Rarely was any direct criticism made of the KNRC, and the coverage became essentially factual and objective. The changing tone of KCNA's coverage reflected the progress that the delegates were making. After months of disagreements and stalemates, an agenda was finally agreed to by both parties, and full-scale talks were scheduled. Interestingly, a hotline telephone linking the North and South Red Cross delegations was installed—a precursor of things to come, as it turned out. The toning down of vituperative attacks and the progress of the Red Cross meetings could not be separated, and together they strongly supported the peace hypothesis. The deception hypothesis was ranked second.

5. Returning to the "peace proposals" again, by the middle of February, whatever doubt the researchers had that what was being proposed by North Korea was a "new" proposal diminished rapidly as media from the Soviet Union and the People's Republic of China praised the new "epochal" January 10 proposal. Furthermore, the U.S. press reported meetings that *The Washington Post* correspondent Selig Harrison had with North Korean spokesmen in Japan. Although unofficial, the input from Harri-

son was entirely plausible under the peace hypothesis. Again, the researchers opted for the peace hypothesis rather than the business-as-usual or deception hypotheses.

6. Exposure that analysts have to the "other side" is generally vicarious, through media. But others along the demilitarized zone in Korea had more direct contact with the other side. There were two types of contact: one "symbolic" and the other real. The symbolic contacts were in the form of loudspeaker broadcasts, which, until early summer of 1972, rivaled the exchanges between Taiwan and the Chinese mainland for bitterness and abusiveness. The other contacts with the other side were engagements with armed infiltrators and agents. With respect to North Korean loudspeaker broadcasts, their tone changed noticeably in the spring of 1972. According to a statement made by ROK Defense Ministry, "Communist propaganda, usually full of abusive and slanderous words, showed a considerable change in contents as well as in expression." In addition, the statement went on to say that the number of North Korean loudspeaker broadcasts declined from twenty-five a day to about sixteen broadcasts. This observable refuted the business-as-usual hypothesis but supported the peace hypothesis. Naturally, the deception hypothesis still remained viable.

7. North Korean loudspeakers were not the only medium whose output changed. A monitoring of KCNA output revealed that the number of wire service releases containing anti-ROK statements declined from a high of 27.4 percent in January to 10.2 percent in April. This observable, like the preceding one, also ruled out the business-as-usual hypothesis, but supported the peace hypothesis.[5]

8. Credibility of the word increases as the word is consistent with behavior. The researchers reasoned that if North Korea were in fact sincere in its purported peace proposals, aggressive behavior, hostile acts, and the like committed by North Korean personnel should decline. The observables in this case are summarized in a ROK Defense Ministry statement, which is quoted in part below:

> North Korea has infiltrated neither armed guerrillas nor agents into the Republic of Korea during the last seven months. . . . Not a single case of spy infiltration has been detected during the

seven-month period beginning last December. The number of cease fire violations on the part of North Korea was also reduced to 7,308 during the first six months this year. This compares with 7,900 reported during the corresponding period of last year. Since the beginning of this year, the Communists have committed 168 cases of border provocations, which represent a 50 percent decrease from the like period of last year.[6]

The business-as-usual hypothesis was refuted unequivocally by this observable. It was quite apparent that North Korea was not conducting its activities vis-à-vis the ROK in the same manner as it had in the past. The deception hypothesis could not be excluded completely, but the complexity of the events militated against this hypothesis. In short, the hypothesis that was most strongly supported by the observables was the peace hypothesis.

To summarize an analysis that took four months to perform, the researchers concluded that on the basis of extant observables (table 13.1), North Korea was in fact pursuing a "peace offensive" both in word and in deed. The deception hypothesis was not discounted, but it came in a very distant second. The business-as-usual hypothesis was discounted because too many observables directly refuted it.

Table 13.1. Evaluation of Observables in Light of Three Different Hypotheses

OBSERVABLES	HYPOTHESES		
	PEACE	BUSN.-AS-USUAL	DECEPTION
KIM'S INTERVIEW WITH YOMIURI SHIMBUN EDITORS	✓	✓	✓
KIM'S INTERVIEW WITH JSP OFFICIAL KAWASAKI	✓		✓
NO. TIMES PEACE PROPOSALS MENTIONED IN KCNA	✓		✓
CONSISTENCY ON MANNER OF ADDRESSING PROPOSALS	✓		✓
PROGRESS IN NK-RC DISCUSSIONS	✓		
CHANGE IN "TONE" OF NK'S COVERAGE OF RC DISCUSSIONS	✓		
"UNOFFICIAL" INTERVIEW WITH WASH POST REPORTER	✓	✓	✓
DECLINE IN NO. OF AND INTENSITY OF LOUDSPEAKER BROADCASTS	✓		
NO INFILTRATORS CAPTURED SINCE 1 JAN 1972	✓		
DECLINE IN CEASEFIRE VIOLATIONS (50% FROM SAME TIME PERIOD LAST YEAR)	✓		
DECLINE IN NO. ANTI-ROK STATEMENTS (KCNA)	✓		

VALIDATION

A rare instance in which the conclusions of an intelligence re-searcher were corroborated occurred on July 4, 1972, when a seven-point communiqué was issued jointly by North Korea and the Re-public of Korea. It stated, in part, an agreement on three principles of reunification; an agreement to refrain from "slandering and calum-niating" the other side and from committing armed provocations; and, reminiscent of the earlier Red Cross talks, an agreement to in-stall a permanent direct telephone link between Pyongyang and Seoul. In short, the peace hypothesis was dramatically supported by this announcement.

★ ★ ★

Events that have transpired in Vietnam, Laos, and Cambodia since the time this short study was concluded have impacted significantly on both North Korea and the Republic of Korea. That the findings of this study have virtually no significance today epitomizes a notable char-acteristic of much intelligence research: it is highly perishable.

NOTES

1. North Korea had a relatively low priority compared with North Vietnam and the PRC during this period, and it is understandable that, given finite re-sources, government researchers could not respond to a sampling plan on a rel-atively low-priority target. Thus, the sample of data used by the researchers was of very questionable representativeness.

2. North Korea had made a number of different proposals over the years. Most of the proposals were "hard-line" and obviously stood little chance of be-ing accepted by the ROK. The point of the short analysis was to determine if the proposals made after Kim Il-sung's new "epochal" proposal referenced any of the earlier hard-line positions.

3. As a matter of interest, one of the researchers' first tasks was to consider the range of possible hypotheses in order to establish a limited, workable num-ber of plausible hypotheses. The reader will recall that a minimum of three hy-potheses should be postulated, as was the case in this instance.

4. Lest there be any confusion about the dates, Kim Il-sung's latest "peace proposal" was made during an interview purportedly held January 10. Issues raised at this interview were later clarified in another interview, which was carried by KCNA on January 15. This wire service release was received on or about January 16 by the 24th PSYOP Detachment analysts.

5. Determining this percentage reduction, as crude as the analysis may have been, involved some simple statistical techniques, and determining whether the statements were hostile, neutral, or conciliatory involved the processes of coding and classification.

6. *Seoul Haptong*, 0914 GMT, July 5, 1972.

Index

About the Author and Editor

Jerome Clauser is the author of several publications on intelligence education and training pertaining to intelligence methodology. His previous books include *Voice of the United Nations Command: A Description of a Strategic Radio Broadcasting Psychological Operation* (1971) and *An Overview of Collateral Psychological Operations in the Republic of Korea* (1972).

Jan Goldman is the author or editor of numerous articles and books on intelligence including *Ethics of Spying: A Reader for the Intelligence Professional* (Scarecrow, 2005) and *Words of Intelligence: A Dictionary* (Scarecrow, 2006). He is the editor for the Scarecrow Professional Intelligence Education Series.